GLOBAL LATIN/O AMERICAS

Frederick Luis Aldama and Lourdes Torres, Series Editors

Affective Intellectuals and the Space of Catastrophe in the Americas

JUDITH SIERRA-RIVERA

THE OHIO STATE UNIVERSITY PRESS | COLUMBUS

Library of Congress Cataloging-in-Publication Control Number: 2018014530

Cover design by Susan Zucker
Text design by Juliet Williams
Type set in Adobe Minion Pro

For Marco and Tatú

CONTENTS

ACKNOWLEDGMENTS

THIS BOOK was made possible thanks to the funding of the Penfield Research Fellowship (administered by the University of Pennsylvania [Penn]), the Department of Spanish, Italian, and Portuguese at the Pennsylvania State University (Penn State), and the Center for Global Studies at Penn State. Brief versions of my conceptualizations of *social space, space of catastrophe,* and *archi-textures* apperared in "Carlos Mérida's 'Goce Emocional': An Aesthetics Proposal Circumventing the Space of Catastrophe of Mexican Nationalism," published in *The Comparatist* (vol. 41, 2017, pp. 41–59). I also presented early ideas on the relationship between friendship, Puerto Rican soldiers, and U.S. wars in "The Affective Politics of Friendship in Puerto Rican War Stories," which appeared in *Latino Studies* (vol. 13, no. 2, 2015, pp. 207–26). *Latin American Research Review* (vol. 53, no. 2, 2018) published an early version of chapter 5. This book is also the product of a very long journey, filled with many brilliant and generous interlocutors.

My initial reflections developed in close dialogue with Malena Rodríguez Castro and Juan G. Gelpí at the University of Puerto Rico (UPR), where they first introduced me to the literary contexts of Mexico and Chile, to the complexity of cultural studies, and to Carlos Monsiváis's and Pedro Lemebel's urban chronicles. My years at UPR were also marked by continuous conversations with Ángel (Chuco) Quintero Rivera and Carmen Rita Rabell. Both of them contributed to my research training. This academic scenario could not be completely understood without the figure of Arcadio Díaz Quiñones, who, as an invited professor, taught a seminar that changed my focus toward the examination of intellectual discourses in relation to the catastrophe of war.

At Penn, Yolanda Martínez-San Miguel challenged every single one of my ideas, helping me achieve a stronger argument. Thanks to her critical readings, I complicated my analysis by integrating categories related to body politics (race, gender, and sexuality) to my study on the history of ideas and intellectual history. At Penn, too, I learned very much from Sara Nadal-Melsió, Román de la Campa, Michael Solomon, and Jorge Salessi. In particular, Jorge taught me how to trace traditions that operate against the grain, or more precisely, how to read *a contrapelo* what seemed to be a static tradition, to make it talk in a new language. Jorge was also the person who gave me intellectual and emotional support at critical moments during those years. To Ben Sifuentes-Jáuregui, Lawrence La Fountain-Stokes, and Ignacio Sánchez Prado, too, I am eternally thankful for their rigorous readings of my work and for their support throughout my career.

My year at Middlebury College has probably been the most challenging and rewarding one in my career. I learned so much that my brain hurt! I appreciate how I grew as a scholar thanks to what my colleagues there practice on a daily basis: let your teaching guide your research. Patricia Saldarriaga, Fernando Rocha, Marcos Rohena-Madrazo, Enrique García, Luis H. Castañeda, Irina Feldman, Roberto Pareja, and Juana Gamero de Coca taught me how to be a better teacher and researcher. To all of them I am grateful for the long conversations about my work.

At Penn State, I have been fortunate to count with the support of all my colleagues: William R. Blue, Sherry Roush, Paola (Giuli) Dussias, John Lipski, Rena Torres Cacoullos, John Ochoa, Nicolás Fenández Medina, Matthew J. Marr, Maria Truglio, Mary Barnard, Julia Cuervo-Hewitt, Karen Miller, Matthew Carlson, Marianna Nadeu Rota, Krista Brune, and Sarah J. Townsend. I must extend especial gratitude to my Latinoamericanist colleagues—John, Julia, Krista, and Sarah—for their critical readings of different parts of this manuscript. At Penn State, too, Hoda El Shakry and Shaoling Ma were generous enough to read an early version of chapter 4 and provided me with feedback that, thanks to their research on other contexts of war and on emotions, contributed a richer bibliography to my study. To my graduate students, I owe much needed reflection and bibliography; especially to Joshua R. Deckman, who was my research assistant and who has become a key interlocutor for my work in Caribbean and Latinx Studies.

Inside and outside of these and other institutional contexts, I have been engaged in an ongoing conversation with many friends. To Laura Torres-

Rodríguez, I owe key questions that have informed my study, but most significantly, I owe her my sanity at times of saturation. Matthew Goldmark, Ana Sabau, and Daylet Domínguez shifted, in different manners, my way of thinking about specific phenomena analyzed in this book. Sandra Casanova-Vizcaíno, Gerardo Pignatiello, Oscar Montoya, and Selma Feliciano-Arroyo have helped me to navigate the long and complex literary tradition of the Caribbean and Latin America. I am also indebted in many ways to my ongoing conversations with Felipe Cala, Carl Fischer, Enea Zaramella, Laura Gandolfi, Alejandra Josiowicz, and Elena Valdés. This book is also possible thanks to the support I received at Penn from Lidia León-Blázquez, Larissa Brewer-García, Andrea Cote Botero, Nelson Cárdenas, Anna Cox, Raquel Albarrán, and Luis Moreno-Caballud.

I have written this book in a language that has always been foreign to me. Linda Grabner translated from Spanish to English early versions of chapters 1, 3, and 4 (including the quotes from literary and critical texts in Spanish). Robin Myers and Joanna Zuckermann Bernstein copyedited the introduction, chapter 2, and chapter 5. Finally, Marianna Nadeu Rota proofread the whole manuscript after the many changes it went through over the years. Marianna's incommensurable knowledge of language and attention to detail guaranteed the clarity in discourse throughout the book. Also, Marianna's comments and questions helped the development of the argument. Finally, as my friend, our long-distance conversations made me at ease with writing in this foreign language.

At the Ohio State University Press, Kristen A. Elias Rowley has been the light to guide me gently in every step of this difficult process that is publishing the first book. I could not have asked for a more dedicated and passionate editor. I am also thankful to the editors of the Global Latin/o Americas book series, Lourdes Torres and Frederick Luis Aldama, for their confidence in this project. I am excited to be part of this transdisciplinary and transcontinental series. I am grateful to the two anonymous readers for their invaluable feedback, which has made this book's argument stronger.

Finally, words cannot even begin to express all my debt to my intellectual interlocutor, husband, and accomplice, Marco A. Martínez Sánchez, and my late kitty, Tatú. They nourished me with food and love in every step of the way. Our little family resides within this book's pages. I am also grateful to my mother, Cándida Rivera Díaz, and the whole matriarchal clan of the Rivera Díaz family in Puerto Rico and the diaspora. Now more than ever, when we survive a catastrophe that threatens to aniquilate our existence in the island, *seremos siempre montones.*

Emotional Intellectual Interventions and the Politics of Collective Enunciation in the Neoliberal Space of Catastrophe

IN 1956, Nilita Vientós Gastón, a Puerto Rican intellectual who wrote a weekly column in the widely circulated newspaper *El Mundo*,[1] vowed to keep creating *malestar* [discomfort] in her audience with respect to the island's colonial status and urged other Puerto Ricans to cultivate this feeling as well. Her dire call to embrace *malestar*, a Spanish word that expresses physical and emotional pain (malaise, uneasiness, and unrest), sought to challenge an essay by University of Chicago professor Daniel J. Boorstin, published that same year in *The Yale Review*.[2] Boorstin's "Self-Discovery in Puerto Rico" established that the writing of the Constitution and the creation of the Commonwealth of Puerto Rico (*Estado Libre Asociado* or ELA) had ended U.S. colonialism on the island back in 1952; hence, Puerto Rican intellectuals should abandon their public interventions and agitation against the United States. More precisely, Boorstin asserted, Puerto Rican intellectuals should work strictly within academia and focus on advancing theories that truly corresponded to the island's new political reality. For Vientós Gastón, however, "ese malestar tiene un 'objetivo,' sacudir la rutina, mantener el espíritu alerta, no dejar adormecer la conciencia"

---

1. Nilita Vientós Gastón was a Puerto Rican lawyer, university professor, literary critic, founder and editor of two academic journals (*Asomante* and *Sin Nombre*), and the first woman president of the *Ateneo Puertorriqueño*.

2. Daniel J. Boorstin was a professor of American history at the University of Chicago; between 1975 and 1987, he was also the librarian of the United States Congress.

(99) [discomfort has an "objective": to shake up routines, to keep the spirit alert, to prevent conscience from going numb]. Vientós Gastón's advocacy for discomfort thus urges Puerto Rican intellectuals to stay engaged with everyday life in such a way that this uncomfortable spirit and consciousness can be shared and strengthened among as many people as possible. Reading her essay more than sixty years later, I can still feel the anger she masterfully used to launch and spread her convictions.

It is hard to know if Boorstin ever read Vientós Gastón's reply to his essay. We might doubt that a white male professor, teaching at one of the top research universities in the United States and writing for one of the most prestigious academic publications, would read a Puerto Rican woman writing for a mainstream newspaper on the island. Either way, the answer is not essential to the story. She was not writing to him or for him; rather, she was using his ideas to advance her own within her audience, which was probably wider than his. Throughout her rebuttal of Boorstin's article, Vientós Gastón's discourse builds up her anger, directing it toward his ideas and positing them as the enemy. What is more, she stresses, this man, his ideas, and his country are not like "us"; he is one of those scholars in the United States, "un país en que el intelectual . . . es mirado por la masa con recelo; un país cuyas minorías [intelectuales] . . . no intervienen o intervienen con timidez en la cosa pública. Son más bien espectadores" (193) [a country in which intellectuals are regarded by the masses with suspicion; a country whose (intellectual) minorities do not intervene, or intervene shyly, in the public sphere. (U.S. intellectuals) are more like spectators]. This emotional maneuver also serves to characterize "us" as a country where society trusts intellectuals precisely because they feel the need to intervene in everyday politics as well as in theoretical debates.

While the anecdote about Vientós Gastón and Boorstin addresses a perceived cultural rift, it also illustrates two different political imaginations that were engaged in a passionate debate across the Caribbean Sea and in the middle of the Cold War.[3] Rather than accentuating a geographical divide, the debate emphasized a shared political context and an intellectual reflection on their role in society. With a focus on contemporary productions, this book explores present-day manifestations of continuously shared circumstances and ongoing deliberations by examining five different contexts within Latinx

---

3. Jean Franco has extensively studied the position negotiated by the Latin American lettered city in the Cold War context. See *The Decline and Fall of the Lettered City*.

America:[4] Mexico, Central America and the United States, Chile, Puerto Rico, and Cuba. More precisely, each of the five chapters studies a particular need expressed by Carlos Monsiváis, Francisco Goldman, Pedro Lemebel, Josean Ramos, and Sandra Álvarez Ramírez; how each need becomes urgent at different historical crossroads; and how, at these specific times, the authors' interventions inform their subsequent work. By analyzing a diversity of print, radio, and web materials, this study centers on very specific questions related to why, when, how, and to whom these authors speak. Such details guide me in understanding their political positions with respect to the crisis each one addresses and, most importantly, to the broader scenario of neoliberalism that I read as a space of catastrophe in the capitalist social realm. Following Henri Lefebvre's ideas, I will conceptualize "space of catastrophe" not as a particular event but rather as a phenomenon that reveals a transition between what he conceives as space modes of production.

In this scenario, the five studied authors negotiate their political positions with an intended audience—which, I will argue, is imagined as an intimate community of debate, even in the cases of Monsiváis, Goldman, and Lemebel, three widely read intellectuals. This political imagination reinforces its desire for an intimate public sphere by maneuvering emotions to strengthen the concept of an affective "we," which entails the construction of a collective enunciation. As I will elaborate later on, in thinking about the notion of an affective "we," I am mostly indebted to Sara Ahmed's theorization of the relationship between discourses, emotions, and what she termed "objects of feelings;" that is, bodies (material or symbolic) that are impressed with affects to be circulated in order to move imagined collectivities toward or away from them (2015, 11–12). I want to propose, then, that the five intellectuals in question are not trying to emotionally persuade an audience so much as to shift it toward "other" bodies (indigenous peoples, Afro-descendants, immigrants, LGBTQ sexualities, inhabitants of poor neighborhoods, and survivors of militarism and war). In their intellectual discourses, all of these bodies, which are usually impressed with hate and disgust, become protagonist voices that instead impress themselves (their bodies and their stories) with a kind of revolutionary love that I conceptualize as a force that centers on the present and has potential to alter, even though slightly, sociopolitical relations.

---

4. I will be using the name *Latinx America* to refer to the geographical context that includes Latin America, the Caribbean, and the Latinx population in the United States and Canada. I prefer to use *Latinx* (ending with an *x*) to recognize gender and sexual fluidities.

Therefore, throughout its five chapters, this book fills a significant gap in the study of the relationship between materiality (space and bodies) and political imagination in order to propose an alternative to two dominant models in the critical production on Latinx American intellectual history and history of ideas. First, my primary argument is that the porosity of emotions in fact lies *between* what was defined by Ángel Rama as two opposite realms ("the real city" and "the lettered city") in Latin America. The five authors examined in the pages that follow operate within this porosity. Given the mediation of this porosity of emotions, we cannot continue adhering to a divide between mind and body, ideas and feelings, reasons and passions, nor, as I will later argue, can we create new ones between feelings, emotions, and affect.

Second, even though I am using the categories of Latin America, the United States, and Latinx (to refer to the context created by Latinx cultural subjects in the United States) in order to talk about specific events and circumstances, we must keep advancing studies that address the continental and Antillean continuity between what has been called in Spanish *América* and in English *the Hemispheric Americas*. Despite the imperial necessity of constructing a divide between North and South,[5] geographical continuity has always been reinforced by historical processes of colonization, racial anxieties about *mestizaje* and *mulataje*, cultural coincidences and interchanges, population displacements and imagined frontiers, and intellectual and artistic dialogues. The imperial urgency to establish two different continents within a geographical continuity is thus detrimental to any kind of research that claims to be comparative in nature. With this book, I hope to participate in cutting through this geographical conception by highlighting three other continuities: disasters and crises that manifest a space of catastrophe affecting everyone in the world; social and political movements that go beyond national frontiers through a network of allies; and intellectuals who speak in hopes of reaching audiences in different contexts—audiences that, in turn, could become the allies needed by local movements.

---

5. As historicized by Walter Mignolo, "America, as a continent and people, was considered inferior in European narratives . . . [and] the idea was refashioned in the U.S. after the Spanish-American War in 1898, when 'Latin' America took on the inferior role" (2005, xv). It is also important to remember that *América* (the continental concept) was a European invention, too (see O'Gorman, 81–99).

A SPACE OF CATASTROPHE CALLED NEOLIBERALISM

Crisis scenarios tend to direct our interpretations of their outcomes toward tragedy and its effects. We usually use the word *catastrophe* to refer to such circumstances, and this word—from Greek to Latin—exhibits a history of suffering, expectancy, and even hope in the face of these events. If catastrophe is the moment when the world turns upside down and the established order is altered, giving heroes an opportunity to recognize their flaws (Rosenthal, 31), then the arts of destruction have given humanity a gap in space and time to reflect on our vulnerable relationship to the world and the social structures we have built in an attempt to protect ourselves. Bodies come to the forefront in catastrophes, as we speak about numbers of deaths, injuries, losses, disappearances, and survivors. "We" humans become similar to the rest of the living; therefore, the human body takes on the full force of action in its initial struggle for survival. After all, there is no way to know when the extraordinary circumstances of disasters will end, and since the future cannot be foreseen, it becomes even more pressing to experience the whole impact of the present. Nevertheless, what we recognize as catastrophe (moments of intense crisis) usually "resolves," which means "we" (humanity at large) forget about "them" (those affected) and continue living in our familiar state of normalcy.

What if we are living within a systematic catastrophe? What if that which we perceive as catastrophes (natural or sociopolitical) are just critical instances that give us a glimpse of structural dysfunction? I believe that we can read Rama's *La ciudad letrada* though the lens of these questions. In Rama's argument, the lettered city is responsible for producing and reproducing sociopolitical and economic systems that are catastrophic for the real city's inhabitants. Since European colonialism and *criollo* revolutions, the lettered city was able to gain and retain economic, social, and cultural advantages that allowed intellectuals (writers and politicians) to maintain their authority over knowledge and ideology. Withholding that authority was fundamental to the survival of the lettered city—and the constituted definition of a nation—, which always felt threatened by the real city and its transformations (often depicted as barbarism or "the masses"). At the center of this threat lies every racialized and sexualized body: indigenous peoples, blacks, peasants, workers, migrants, women, and queers. Therefore, the real city becomes the potential catastrophe for the lettered city.

This tense relationship between the lettered and the real cities seems to serve as a background for other Latinoamericanist critics who have furthered studies of catastrophe either as a metaphor or as a concrete disaster. For example, Patrick Dove has analyzed how unique characteristics of tragedy are present in Latin American literature at different periods. As stated by Dove, "the idea of catastrophe" in foundational texts, such as Sarmiento's *Facundo,* precedes concrete notions of "nation" and "modernity" and describes the violent process by which the modern national state was built, as well as the utopian discourse of such an endeavor; that is, "political and cultural autonomy and social justice" (11). In his examination, Dove discusses authors who, like Borges, Rulfo, and Vallejo, used the same tragic model as a "counterfoundational perspective," which distrusts foundational narratives, equates modernity with catastrophe, and hopes for a "less violent, less barbaric, more democratic" foundation (15). Another example is Mark D. Anderson's argument on what he identifies as a very specific kind of disaster writing in Latin America. Anderson analyzes how natural disasters are culturally mediated by narratives that seek to retain or achieve "social and political power" in Latin America (7). His study also acknowledges that these narratives cannot be viewed in isolation; they work in conjunction with an established consensus in order to "reauthorize or deauthorize political figures and ideologies" (191). In the end, this kind of writing aims to portray natural disasters as political events, and consequently as a product of human errors. Therefore, human vulnerability is ameliorated in the face of nature.

By focusing on Lefebvre's concept of "social space," I would like us to imagine a more fluid and complicated relationship between what Rama identified as the lettered city and the real city. This complication of his argument will show us that there are connections—beyond mere rhetorical resources—between the materiality of everyday life and intellectuals' political imagination. It will also demonstrate that natural disasters, for example, can only become "catastrophes" when they involve other spheres of the material production of space. Lefebvre's historical and philosophical study helps us understand that, for any economic system to succeed, it must produce a particular kind of space that can adequately move and control things, bodies, and ideas. The capitalist-state mode of production has established an intrinsic relationship between national territory (mapping through the transport, flow, or network of geographical resources), social space (the state: that is, institutions, laws, and values that constitute a space of representation or a way to dictate social relations), and mental space (people's experiences and concepts in representing or thinking about the system they inhabit; 2009, 224–25). This mode of production has also created a kind of space that is fractured (divided into lots and parcels), homogeneous (bought and sold as units of equivalent value), and therefore enables speculation to thrive (space is a commodity; 235). Within these conditions, the body tends to disappear from social space (that is, the body is not represented), everyday life becomes increasingly engulfed by the consumption of commodities, and unless they revolt, common "users" of space are reduced to passivity and silence (235). If we situate Rama's argument within this system as outlined by Lefebvre, we can see that the lettered city corresponds somehow to social space (or to the state and its system of representation). We cannot understand social space, however, without considering how it functions in coordination with the rest of space. Moreover, for Lefebvre, who was writing "Space and State" during the 1970s, a text included in the fourth volume of his *De l'État*, the state was destined to lose many functions of social space to the private sector, retaining only the function of representation (240).

Lefebvre also believed that the capitalist mode of production was already creating the conditions for a "space of catastrophe," that is, a space of systemic destruction and "ruinous tendency" (248). A space of catastrophe yields convulsions that could be capable of destroying the present mode of production and generating a new one. For example, Lefebvre saw colonization as one of the crises that demolished mercantilism and gave way to capitalism (249). Besides the state losing its exclusive domain over social space, Lefebvre identified other characteristics that could indicate a space of catastrophe for the capitalist mode of production. The first feature would be the emergence of transnational conglomerates of capital that control natural resources, flows of energy, and the labor force; second, the existence of supranational or transnational corporations with productive capital that continues to grow while poverty remains a matter of state responsibility; third, the transnationalization of labor, which hinders relations among workers; and finally, protests and struggles that shift their focus toward everyday life and the environment (246–48). For some of Lefebvre's most fervent readers, catastrophe must then be understood as "a space that is at once both a summit of capitalist relations and precisely, therefore, the point at which revolutionary agency might occur" (Beech, 193). The first question for the contemporary moment, however, is whether we still live in a capitalist-space mode of production, in a kind of transitional space of catastrophe, or in a new form of space mode of production.

All five of the crisis scenarios I study in this book can be seen as moments in which we witness capitalism evolving into something else. As Monsiváis relates in his chronicles, the 1985 earthquake in Mexico City revealed structural deficiencies in the construction and maintenance of buildings that evidenced, in turn, a sinuous relationship between the state and private interests. This natural disaster also confirmed that the state and its representations of the nation no longer coincided with mental space, or people's experiences and representations of the system. A decade later in a number of Central American countries, peace agreements and transitions to democracy did not decrease the number of migrants to the United States. Goldman's journalism confirms that these events helped reduce international pressure on local oligarchies, which saw greater monetary opportunities in trafficking drugs and humans, both of which were in demand in the U.S. market. Similarly, the Chilean transition to democracy in 1990 sealed the state's destruction and disrupted its ability to control the influence of private interests on public matters during the Pinochet dictatorship (1973–89). Lemebel's radio program denounced this destruction, as well as the human cost for political dissidents and marginalized communities.

In the Caribbean, the U.S. military's increased recruitment after 9/11 of Puerto Rican public university students on the island not only told "us" that "we" were back at war; it also showed that education for the poor was only possible through military service in an economic conflict camouflaged as patriotism. Ramos's journalism and autobiography connected the scenario of the early 2000s with earlier circumstances (the Korean War and the years after the Vietnam War) in which Puerto Rican soldiers, who shared a background rooted in poverty and an experience of racism within the military, were confronted with very different opportunities after completing their service, depending on the kind of war and the socioeconomic context that awaited them. Since the 1990s, socialism in Cuba has been evolving into something else, too. This process seems to manifest what Lefebvre diagnosed as part of his theory: socialism "must produce its own space, which can no longer be a capitalist space" (2009, 248). If socialism operates within capitalism, a transformation of capitalist space will impact socialism, as well. As Álvarez Ramírez's blog entries document and discuss, Cuba's precariousness has been especially hard for black women—those most gravely affected by poverty, even in socialist societies. Moreover, after the institutionalization of the Cuban Revolution (1959), black women (and black lesbians, in particular) have faced a constant struggle for true inclusion in state representation.

We use the word *neoliberalism* to characterize the system we have experienced since the 1970s, as well as to describe worldwide situations that have much in common with the examples I analyze here. Amid the struggle to advance workers' rights, women's reproductive rights, and civil rights, many nation-states ventured new sociopolitical reforms to help expand the middle class, protect public health, and generate a more inclusive constitutional nation. As David Harvey recounts in *A Brief History of Neoliberalism,* this context provoked a reaction from the corporate capitalist class, which funded think tanks to formulate a political and ideological response that would bend the possible outcomes of such social movements toward strengthening private interests' influence on the political and ideological spheres (9–19). If, according to Lefebvre, the capitalist state had, at some point in time, held control over the majority of its national territory, for Harvey, the state's role under neoliberalism was now mostly to protect "individual entrepreneurial freedoms and skills, . . . strong private property rights, free markets, and free trade" (2). In terms of material production, the main objectives were to empower finance capital (movement of capital) and to accelerate means of transportation and communication (movement of labor and production). Nevertheless, in order to secure power over national resources and networks, the corporate class also needed to control the administration of the state. The only way to access this control was through entering the ideological field. After all, either by the imposition of dictatorships or a heavy influence on electoral outcomes, this transition—from what was initially the capitalist state into something else— needed social consensus or justification without a revolutionary threat (Harvey 39). Therefore, as Harvey has lucidly explained, neoliberalism was not something that came upon us from one moment to the next. It was the product of a detailed, coordinated planning process, a long series of steps taken by the corporate class around the world.

At the very least, then, neoliberalism is the space of catastrophe of capitalism. This means that for decades now we have found ourselves in the middle of a transition. As Harvey describes in an interview with Bjarke Skærlund Risager, many more crises (of all kinds) have transpired since the 1970s than between the period spanning from 1945 to 1973. Going back to Lefebvre, we must see these crises as symptoms or signs of the true catastrophe, which is a dysfunctional system. In order to better understand this phenomenon, however, we must also bear witness to the present and to everyday life. This has been the intellectual objective in each of the works I study here—an objective that has complicated the relationship between the lettered city and the real city in Latinx America.

THE FORCE OF THE PRESENT AND THE POLITICAL ACTION OF INTELLECTUALS IN THE NEOLIBERAL CONTEXT

Neoliberalism brought new challenges to intellectual interventions in the public sphere and in their relationships to other social groups. Focusing on the Chilean and Argentinean postdictatorial contexts (post-1989), Francine Masiello argues that intellectual discourses under neoliberal democracies were distancing themselves from new political movements based on commonalities, alliances, and communities; movements, in other words, that were capable of building a solid collaboration between different sectors in society. Specifically, drawing examples from the works of Beatriz Sarlo and Néstor García Canclini, among others, Masiello explains that intellectuals in the 1980s and 1990s seemed to oscillate between distrust of micropolitical groups (identitarian politics) and pessimism (the market will swallow every counterestablishment action; 2001, 35–37). For Masiello, this intellectual scenario responded to a context immersed in "the art of transition," not only at the macroscopic level (economic and political structures) but also at the microscopic level of everyday life and of cultural and artistic production. That said, some intellectuals were able to transition and maintain deep connections with the rest of society, while others emerged out of the transition.

What Masiello describes for the Southern Cone context coincides with what has been happening in the rest of the world, especially during these first decades of the twenty-first century. New and emerging kinds of political movements, as Harvey has said, have become more and more "autonomous and anarchical" in recent decades (Risager). He also sees what Lefebvre had perceived as early as the 1970s: resistance has been moving toward politics centered on everyday life. This does not mean that workers' fights for labor justice (production) are over. It means that new struggles also focus on the value or cost of life (consumption) as well as on politics of the body, all of which points to the relationship between bodies and the produced space they inhabit. This new kind of politics usually avoids the figure of a leader and does not call for a cultural mediator. For people like Boorstin, who had thought that those were intellectual roles by definition (leadership and mediation), the function of the intellectual would be unnecessary: they would no longer be required because society itself would have changed. Of course, this argument would not agree with Antonio Gramsci's study on how intellectual work is intrinsically related to all the other spheres of production. According to Gramsci, every new social group "creates together with itself, organically" a set of intellectuals who give "awareness" to the group of its economic, social, and political functions within society (113). Therefore, intellectuals respond to the social group from which they emerge.

If neoliberalism has relied on a more decentralized, more flexible mode of production than those of the past, it has also generated social groups that depend heavily on networking (faster, bigger, and more heterogeneous webs). At the same time, networking has become one of the most-used tools for organizing political resistance against neoliberalism, which is why recent events (such as the Arab Spring or the Chilean Winter) exhibit anarchical forms. Just like Gramsci said, these new social groups have also created a new kind of intellectual. Nonetheless, as I examine each of the cases here, we will see how some intellectuals are products of past movements (for example, Monsiváis's writing is indebted to the 1968 movement), while others have more recently emerged (like Álvarez Ramírez, who has been part of the Cuban blogosphere and the LGBTQ movement on the island since the 1990s). What they all have in common is a profound understanding of the present and a willingness to stay connected with politics focused on everyday life. This understanding, and this connection, is what in turn gives their writings an in-depth insight into specific crises and into the neoliberal space of catastrophe.

In *After Fukushima: The Equivalence of Catastrophes,* Jean-Luc Nancy meticulously reflects on critical junctions, like Fukushima, that urge us to think, write, and philosophize about the boundaries we share with time and space. Fukushima—an earthquake and a tsunami that exacerbated the deficiencies of a nuclear plant—is an example of a systemic catastrophe. For Nancy, this catastrophe is the general equivalence, or the "general interconnection," between nature, energy systems, institutions, technology, the war industry, and finances, by which capitalism assigns values to all kinds of products, lays down the ground rules for all exchanges, defines conditions of life, profits, and creates wealth that is injected into the same system: capitalism (5). The Fukushima nuclear plant evokes a technology that was developed for the massive annihilation of enemies; in this sense, this disaster is reminiscent of Hiroshima and of an intimate fear of our own destruction. In other words, it triggers a moment that questions our capacity to make sense of our human condition and to engage with the outside world. This subject—our ability to connect with others and to find meaning in such a connection—has been a constant in Nancy's work. Writing in the context of the 1990s and against the backdrop of the Balkan Wars, he was already reflecting about what he called *la brèche,* translated into English as "the opening" (2000, xiii). In Nancy's view, the opening appears when the progressive line of history, moving us toward "the horizon of *the whole,*" is broached to reveal the wholeness of our present world (xii). For Nancy, the wholeness of the present pushes us from both inside and outside, leaving us naked at the center of such opening. He exhorts us to "remain exposed" to the unknown; that is, to "what is happening to us" (*ce qui nous arrive,* in French), which we still cannot name or define (2015, 8). It is in our exposure to the full force of the present experience that Nancy sees an opportunity to puncture the capitalist system of general equivalence, because we develop "an esteem in the most intense sense of the word. . . . [We recognize] something more precious than any price" (38–39). As I will also argue for each of the cases I study, this residence in the uncertainty of the present generates other kinds of thinking, including those represented by forms of experience and knowledge that have been marginalized by the Western/modern paradigm of progress: those of popular culture, indigenous peoples, black feminisms, and what is constructed as the "Third World."

Monsiváis, Goldman, Lemebel, Ramos, and Álvarez Ramírez are practitioners of "border theory," and they operate from a "dichotomous locus of enunciation" (Mignolo 2012, 85); that is, they inhabit "the frontiers between local non-Western and nonmodern memories and the intrusions of modern Western local history and knowledge" (xiv). Border theory marks the limits of Western knowledge (coloniality and modernity) and works from/within difference (geographical, racial, gendered, and/or sexual) to create and disseminate the kinds of knowledge that have been excluded from the Western matrix. While Nancy posits that our total nakedness before the immensity of the present and the uncertainty of *ce qui nous arrive* can cut through general equivalence, Walter Mignolo proposes that border thinking reshapes the interior and exterior borders of Western knowledge/geographical imperialism, thus decolonizing other local histories and conceptions of the world. W. E. B. Du Bois, Gloria Anzaldúa, Frantz Fanon, and Édouard Glissant are some of the key intellectual influences in Mignolo's approach to the potentiality of border thinking. To this list, I would like to add the five authors I analyze here in order to examine how border thinking also inhabits emotions that emphasize the limits of what we have understood as rationality—that is, as Western knowledge. Moreover, as I will argue, specific emotional loci of enunciation operate from and for the racialized and/or sexualized body in order to potentially gain ground within social space.

BODY POLITICS AND EMOTIONAL IMPRESSIONS

In 2012, Mabel Moraña and Ignacio Sánchez Prado edited an anthology of essays, *El lenguaje de las emociones: Afecto y cultura en América Latina,* following the conference "Reading Emotions in Latin America" (Washington University in Saint Louis, 2011), which reflected on what has been called the *affective turn* (Clough and Halley) and *affect theory* (Gregg and Seigworth) in Latin American criticism and cultural studies. Sánchez Prado's "Presentación" and Moraña's "Postscríptum" identified three lines of study that analyzed affect in Latin American criticism. The first works on the causes and effects of sentimentality or forms of any given emotional character in music, literature, film, among others. The second line inquired into consumers, their practices, and the repercussions of those practices on fixed identities. Finally, the third line pertained to postdictatorial contexts and the affective politics of memory.

Nonetheless, as Sánchez Prado correctly recognized, no critical work existed with the primary goal of studying, in the contemporary Latin American context, what Ahmed called "the cultural politics of emotion" (2015, 11). This remains a void in the field of affect studies in the region. My argument rests, then, on Ahmed's analysis of emotions as "social and cultural practices" that "shape" individual and social bodies into "objects of feeling," compelling, for example, grief, love, hate, fear, or shame (9–11). As these objects of feeling circulate, or "move, stick, and slide . . . we move, stick, and slide with them" (14), which means they generate emotional effects and actions. Following Ahmed, emotions are not only attached to the materiality of the body and the world; just like ideas, they are actually constitutive of such materiality. Therefore, our representations of social space—and our willingness to move toward or away from someone or something—are sculpted by emotions, too. Moreover, language (as with any other system of representation) can become a "form of power in which emotions align some bodies with others, as well as stick different figures together, by the way they move us" (195). In this analysis, emotions themselves use language as a resource to delineate social space through objects of feelings; hence, the dichotomies between body and mind, as well as between emotion and thought, are sterile.

A tendency in critical studies on affect that consider the Latin American context has been to view emotions as a sociopolitical phenomenon that has only recently emerged. For example, in *Coming to Our Senses*, Dierdra Reber propounds her theory of a "headless capitalism" by tracing a narrative in which, following the triumph of capitalism and most notably after 1989, an epistemological shift toward "the nonrational" has occurred; through this shift, "feelings and togetherness become the new basis of forming knowledge and political action" (xiv). For Reber, "I feel, therefore I am" replaces what she identifies as the Cartesian binary (body vs. mind), "I think, therefore I am" (xiv). Reber defines the capitalist and free-market epistemology as a "feeling soma," which advocates for being "heterogeneous and unified" and for going without a "leader or authority," because, as a model, it "self-regulates intuitively and nonrationally, at the level of 'wanting' a supremely ethical and egalitarian human experience" (xiii). However, these feelings and ideas are not the only ones associated with, or promoted by, the narrative of capitalism and the free market. As Sianne Ngai has discussed, "Capitalism's classic affects of disaffection [disgust, envy, and paranoia, for example] (and thus of potential social conflict and political antagonism) are neatly reabsorbed by the wage system and reconfigured into professional ideals" (4). Moreover, we must remember that other kinds of epistemologies have always existed, operating outside of and in the borderland with Western (capitalist) knowledge, which have used and expressed themselves through emotions in a way similar to what Reber describes as a "feeling soma." The twentieth century, for example, as Jean Franco explains, was marked by a "tradition of catholic anticapitalism wedded to a notion of 'good' use value against evil exchange" that can be found in the writings of Ernesto "Che" Guevara and Ernesto Cardenal (2002, 3). Returning to Ahmed, we must remember that ideas and emotions build ideologies that, in turn, construct objects of feelings often capable of moving people away from such objects.

This intrinsic relationship between ideas and emotions is hardly new, nor is it a product of capitalism or neoliberalism alone; indeed, research on the Latin American colonial period, for example, has demonstrated its prevalence in eras prior. Specifically, in his beautiful historical analysis of "worldly wonder" in Latin America, Jerónimo Arellano has shown that a particular kind of affect can emerge and evolve over time in relation to different social contexts, knowledges, and material productions (xiv–xv). Arellano's research on European chronicles of conquest and colonization in the Americas gives way to an in-depth analysis of the emotions that gather around the effect/affect of wonder. Although ambitious in terms of the long period he sets out to examine, Arellano teaches us that emotions need to be carefully conceptualized and historicized as an integral part of cultural formations.

Nevertheless, the dissociation between ideology and affect dominates even the argument of Jon Beasley-Murray's *Posthegemony,* one of the most frequently quoted books on the study of affects in Latin American political theory. In its very first pages, Beasley-Murray establishes that "social order was never in fact secured through ideology. . . . Social order is secured through habit and affect" (ix). Proceeding from this statement, Beasley-Murray argues that we have never experienced hegemony; in reality, consent has always been gained through "immanent processes" of "habit, affect, and the multitude" that "incarnate a logic from below that requires neither representation nor direction from above" and that, as such, "undo the spatial metaphor of 'above' and 'below'" (xi). In a brief and powerful position paper, Bruno Bosteels responds to Beasley-Murray's interpretation of Gramsci's political ideas on hegemony by noting that Gramsci was "foremost a philosopher of the integral state, and not of hegemony" (5). As Bosteels points out, Latin American readers and practitioners of Gramsci's ideas throughout the twentieth century were mostly interested in how to create a fluid connection between intellectuals and "the people" as they defined them (urban workers and the *campesinado*).[6] Therefore, in Latin America, Gramsci's notions on "passive revolution, transformism, or the integrated State" were more important in informing political movements across the region than hegemony ever was (Bosteels, 11). Finally, Bosteels also identifies a series of binaries established by Beasley-Murray: "coercion and consent, direct domination and hegemony, . . . emotion and affect, transcendence and immanence, discourse and habit, people and multitude, constituted and constituent power" (Bosteels, 10). I want to further explore Beasley-Murray's dichotomy between affect and emotions, which follows Brian Massumi's framework.

In *Parables for the Virtual,* Massumi outlines a genealogy of the concepts of affect, movement, and potentiality, tracing them through the ideas of Bergson, Spinoza, Deleuze, and Simondon. For Massumi, affect is impersonal, while emotion is personal (28). This is what allows him to investigate affect as a force that moves and creates potentialities that do not have a clear start or endpoint (8–9). In his analysis of Latin American politics, Beasley-Murray asserts that historic narratives translate affective forces and their unpredictable movement into static, manageable emotions related to specific events: "The affective . . . is represented [in history] as reactive, secondary, the essence of passivity. . . . Affect's primacy and excess is translated into the secondary residue that is emotion" (131). Emotions are, then, negatively described as "the essence of passivity" or as a "residue." I agree with Ahmed that this kind of "affective turn" has worked hard to create a false distinction between affect and emotion, one in which the former seems to be above the latter (2015, 206–7). Moreover, as such studies define affect as the "active" (movement) and emotion as the "passive" (residue), we find ourselves once again in the presence of a binary that much resembles the dichotomies between mind and body, ideas and emotions, and masculine and feminine. Therefore, Ahmed raises the following concern: "When the affective turn becomes a turn to affect, feminist and queer work are no longer positioned as part of that turn" (206). Since my work focuses on bodies that have been subjected to processes of racialization and sexualization, as well as on intellectual discourses that have (auto)inscribed these bodies with emotions capable of gaining momentum and opening up the space of state representation, I share Ahmed's suspicion and have decided to propose an analysis of emotions in Latinx America that is anchored in feminist and queer studies.

---

6. For a complete study on Gramsci's influence on Latin American intellectuals and their politics, see José M. Aricó's book.

In this sense, my study of emotional intellectual discourses resonates with Masiello's insistence on examining "the power of the margin," which "resituates intellectuals in relationship to distant subjects and urges, however problematically, a linkage between worlds commonly divided by indifference" (2001, 3). More specifically, Masiello explores intellectual and artistic "gendered readings" of Chilean and Argentinean neoliberal democracies in order to work through this (usually constructed) division between the two worlds (40). Besides the shift from dictatorship to neoliberal democracy, then, Masiello also recognizes the transition from "focus on social class alone to matters of sexuality and gender" (3). Moreover, Masiello views gender and sexuality as two axes that inform "project identities," which work within a social structure to challenge the system that sustains forms of oppression while also creating a space for innovative action and possible transformation (38). I would argue that, within the five contexts I study in this book, further complications arise when we consider ethnicity and race.

NEGOTIATING COMMUNITIES

National and other identitarian (homogenizing) discourses have relied on "the promise of happiness," as Ahmed has denominated the set of associations (choices and relations) that promise to guarantee a path of success (belonging to a determined nationality, social class, race, sexuality, etc.), and, therefore, of future happiness (2010, 2). Promising happiness in exchange for disciplined bodies reinforces social norms as if they were "social goods" or commodities that add value to a person (2). Within political and economic discourses of happiness, then, objects of feeling determine the "flow" of bodies in space. Unhappy bodies do not flow; that is, they are not welcomed into a social space molded by the promise of happiness, because they do not choose actions and relations that reinforce social norms: unhappy bodies "feel alienated from the world as they experience the world as alien" (11–12). Ahmed traces the etymology of *unhappy* and discovers that it has been associated with misfortune, trouble, wretchedness (characterizing a stranger, exiled, or banished person), and a state of being miserable, vile, or despicable (17). Hence, to be unhappy is to refuse alignment with the norms that would guide us onto the path of happiness, and so, we become "troublemakers, dissenters, killers of joy" (17). While the pursuers of happiness try to fit within a definition of a national and/ or neoliberal "we," I will argue that, in the intellectual discourses I study here, unhappy bodies stick together and seek to form another kind of "we," gathering together around spaces and body politics that seek to alter the neoliberal space of catastrophe.

In considering the multiplicity of "we" forms that emerge in the 1990s, after the collapse of the Cold War model and its rigid two-"we" configuration, Nancy's *Being Singular Plural* analyzed what was felt as an imperative to define the world itself: our world, the world that matters to us, the immediate. New alignments needed to be established in the global sphere; at the same time, local oligarchies were trying to seize and/or protect particular territories. "We" became a powerful and immediate word to justify war as a defense against possible dangers. Survival became imperative—a need that, even when expressed in individualistic terms, is always achieved within the herd or the clan. Understanding that the call for survival had to be conceived beyond an "autistic multiplicity" of identities, Nancy asks: "What if [the autistic multiplicity] lets us know that it is itself the first laying bare [*mise à nu*] of a world . . . with no meaning beyond this very Being of the world: singularly plural and plurally singular?" (2000, xiv). This question, which at first seems to direct us toward the notions of "unity," "togetherness," and "harmony" that have been used in the discourse of neoliberal multiculturalism and envisioned as a Band-Aid solution for violent socioeconomic and political conflicts, was actually a radical proposition at the time. At the core, the implications of this question were pointing us toward a bigger "we" that needed to fight for "our" world. But fight against what or whom?

When she published the provocativly titled *The Politics of Everybody* in 2016, Holly Lewis called us back to examine the possibility of an inclusive "we." Yet, in the book's very first lines, she urged us to understand that, whenever there is a "we" demanding inclusion, there is also a "they" feeling threatened (1). For Lewis, then, the idea of "everybody" can move us "to demand 'our' inclusion in 'their' world; [everybody] reminds us that 'we' are the ones who make 'their' world possible—which of course means the world was always 'all of ours' all along" (1). On the question of how solidarity is achieved, Lewis criticizes the ways in which the strategy of "liberal pluralism" acknowledges and even celebrates difference only insofar as this profusion of solidarity does not alter power relationships (9). While solidarity is necessary, as Nancy also pointed out, in the sense of "a political recognition that our futures are tied together" (Lewis, 257), Lewis returns us once again to the imperative of defining who is included in the "our." Therefore, solidarity "implies antagonism, the taking of sides" (259). Every political position departs from experience, and experience is something we share with others. Solidarity begins in this sharing and continues to expand as our experiences accumulate; it can also be achieved through negotiations that may anchor or modify our political positions. For Lewis, there are solidarities to be forged among the Fanonian "wretched of the earth," which in Lewis's work means everyone who shares experiences of class, gender, racial, and/or sexual struggle, hence the subtitle of her book: *Feminism, Queer Theory, and Marxism at the Intersection*. I find this proposal provocative in its own right and deeply helpful for my own study.

Through their emotional discourses, Monsiváis, Goldman, Lemebel, Ramos, and Álvarez Ramírez generate readings from the perspectives of unhappy genders, sexualities, ethnicities, and races, and proceed to work toward the formation of affective communities. These communities negotiate their positions among themselves and with the rest of the social space through debate of ideas and feelings. My key questions will aim to understand who is the "we" that speaks in each case and, more fundamentally, how this "we" stresses the relationship that each intellectual seeks to establish with a determined community. In terms of content, how does each author define the enunciating "we"? Which bodies are included in this collectivity? Which kinds of emotions does the intellectual discourse press upon those bodies so that they will stick together? What is the relationship of this particular "we" with a larger sphere (for example, the nation or neoliberalism)? Furthermore, what is the medium (or combination of mediums) employed by each of the authors? What are the means by which their productions come into circulation? Which platforms and languages do they use? Who interacts with these materials, and how does their interaction expand and/or modify the enunciating "we"?

DESCRIPTION OF CHAPTERS

The first chapter analyzes a series of Monsiváis's essays and *crónicas urbanas* published in journals, newspapers, and books between 1985 and 2005. These texts focus on the decisive events of the 1985 earthquake in Mexico City and the 1994 Zapatista insurgency, as well as on the aftermath of both events. In this twenty-year span, Monsiváis develops the idea of a racial, social, and sexual emergence that diversifies the Mexican social space. Specifically, Monsiváis's texts provide a critical analysis of those moments in which a national homogeneous "we" becomes, even if momentarily, a diverse set of voices screaming "not without us." At the center of his writings, the racialized and sexualized bodies of rural immigrants to the city, indigenous peoples, feminists, and sexual minorities cut through their systemic marginalization. As I will argue, Monsiváis examines the national "promise of happiness" through the perspective of these unhappy bodies. Moreover, I will demonstrate that what I conceptualize as his "cruel optimism" becomes intertwined with the movement (flow/commotion) that each unhappy emergence initiates to intervene in the neoliberal space of catastrophe.

In the second chapter, which studies a series of Goldman's journalistic pieces (1980s and 1990s) as well as his book *The Art of Political Murder* (2008), I continue to think about the relationship between unhappy bodies and the promise of happiness. For more than two decades, Goldman's writing—published in Spanish and English in the United States and in various Latin American countries—has discussed civil wars, U.S. military interventions, and political corruption in several Central American countries, as well as the neoliberal exacerbation of trafficking (guns, drugs, and humans) between the region and the United States. As I will explain, Goldman's heritage, life experiences, and travels have given him a unique opportunity to easily move back and forth between the Central American and U.S. contexts. I will argue that this movement, both geographical and cultural in nature, creates a "borderland" locus of enunciation from which he mediates and translates between the histories, politics, and cultures of the U.S. and Central American peoples. In discussing Goldman's interventions, which have taken advantage of every possible outlet in mainstream and alternative media, I will demonstrate that his political/intellectual imaginary is a transcontinental emotional community of readers that grasps the complexity of Central America, its problematic political relationship with the United States, and the importance of the isthmus to the idea of a continental continuity between the Hemispheric Americas.

In the subsequent three chapters, I will examine the relationship between intellectuals and unhappy bodies, too, but I will also emphasize the use of angry and loving (erotic) discourses. In the third chapter, I analyze the radio program *Cancionero* and the book *De perlas y cicatrices*, which Lemebel broadcasted and published, respectively, during the 1990s in the context of the democratic transition in Chile. By examining the structure and efficacy of *Cancionero* as a repertoire of political action and of *De perlas y cicatrices* as an archive of intellectual thought, I inquire into the politics of performance as contrasted with monolithic gestures of official silence in regard to Pinochet's military dictatorship and its victims. I argue that the performance of the melancholic and angry voice of *la loca*, a queer character who embodies Lemebel's intellectual discourse, manages to invoke an affective and dissident community that rejects the democratic-neoliberal consensus in Chile. *La loca*'s queer desire radicalizes collective affects by interrupting the supposed politico-identitarian assent to the "whitewashing" of Chile during the transition to democracy. The chronicler's voice in *Cancionero,* as well as his writing in *De perlas y cicatrices,* conveys an urge to communicate an experience that gathers shared angry and loving feelings—which re-create, in turn, haunting memories about disappeared young bodies. In this sense, the spectral voice broadcasted through the radio evokes a missing body. Both the voice and the body it conjures leave their mark on the written archive, too. Within this acoustic/written impact, listeners and readers can share feelings of an angry and loving melancholy as well as of queer desire. Collective angry melancholic love for the corporeal thus demands active queer desire that keeps memory alive in the present.

The last two chapters develop a study on the Caribbean, specifically on Puerto Rico and Cuba. The fourth chapter studies a series of articles and the autobiography *Antes de la guerra,* published post-9/11 by Ramos, an intellectual who speaks to college students about his and other Puerto Ricans' experiences in the U.S. military and wars. I examine how his intellectual discourse deploys male friendship as an affective politics full of angry love and how these politics mediate such experiences. I propose that the emotive intellectual voice calls to the community of Puerto Rican students, who will perhaps listen to and share the feelings conveyed by his memories, which also evoke the contemporary context of military recruitment and war. In my analysis, I argue that the angry love of this male friendship resists the logic of militarism and war—a logic based solely on national love. By focusing on these affective dynamics and their potential political effects, my argument departs from the 1898 paradigm of criticism, which has tended to read cultural representations of militarism and war almost exclusively in terms of their association with the U.S. invasion of the island. This chapter also examines how students responded to Ramos's writings and studies. In my analysis, Ramos's writings and students' reactions address a history of military colonialism in order to highlight the contemporary connections between neoliberalism and war. At the center of this phenomenon lie the bodies of the young and poor, a vulnerable population that views the military as their chance to access higher education. Ramos's writings are marked with the presence of this vulnerable body, and its absence—death or illness—becomes a collective locus of enunciation.

The final chapter studies Sandra Álvarez Ramírez's blog, *Negra cubana tenía que ser,* also known as *Negracubana* (2006–), where the author writes about the sociopolitical implications of being black and lesbian both in Cuba and elsewhere in Latin America. My analysis considers Álvarez Ramírez's blog entries, the comments she receives, and the online network of black LGBTQ activism that the blog builds with other individuals and organizations. I place

Álvarez Ramírez's blogging in dialogue with a tradition of black feminism in the Americas, as well as with cyberfeminist thought and activism. I propose that this complex dialogue serves, both theoretically and practically, the primary purpose of her blog: fostering a physical and virtual love and sexual revolution that can resignify the Afro-Cuban woman's body. I will thus consider the potentiality that digital networking offers for the expression of this "other" body. My main argument is that Álvarez Ramírez's enunciation of her body politics (black lesbian feminist), through the vast virtual network she has constructed, disrupts the Cuban official discourse that still proclaims the utopia of Ernesto "Che" Guevara's *hombre nuevo*. By contrast, *Negracubana*'s revolutionary love is sexual, occurs in the present moment, and is centered on black women's bodies, experiences, actions, agencies, and legacy.

CHAPTER 1

No sin nosotros

Monsiváis's Emergent, Moving, and Cruel Optimism

IN 2015, at a restaurant in Mexico City, I overheard a group of young men in their early twenties sitting close to our table talking about the disastrous earthquakes that happened on September 19 and 20, 1985. One of them was telling the others about how his father had helped rescue some people who were trapped in an elevator. His friends were listening intently while also intervening to provide other facts they had learned about those days when the city was paralyzed by the natural disaster. Just like that, other family and friends' stories emerged, and the four storytellers continued talking about other victims and spontaneous heroes. Once in a while, brief silences interrupted their animated conversation, moments that were left empty for them and their listeners to wonder in amazement.

This ordinary eventuality should not amount to much if it were not for what in reality made it extraordinary: thirty years had gone by since the earthquakes; none of the storytellers had even been born at the time. Somehow, though, those young men were able to talk about those stories with a kind of familiarity that can only be felt when we have experienced the events told. And this is why this eventuality is, for me, the best way to explain what Walter Benjamin beautifully said in "The Storyteller" about the relationship between experience and narration: "Experience which is passed on from mouth to mouth is the source from which all storytellers have drawn. And among those who have written down the tales, it is the great ones whose written version differs least from the speech of the many nameless storytellers" (84). Fragments of experiences lived in 1985 have become stories that have been passed on between families and friends for decades now. In (re)telling the stories and adding others to the ones they knew, those four storytellers and their listeners were apprehending something unknown, something that cannot be "learned" like other kinds of knowledge can; and we were engaging with this something through experiences never lived, and yet, still revived as if we were there, too.

The earthquakes of 1985 demonstrated what many inhabitants of the most affected neighborhoods had been denouncing for a long time: lack of maintenance in some cases and serious flaws in building structures in others, all of which amounted to "charges of corruption against companies" and state agencies (Brewster, 102). The natural disaster also evidenced the state's bureaucratic inefficiency to respond accurately to the emergency, as different agencies clashed over responsibilities and jurisdictions (Krauze, 67). In terms of the ideological sphere, while the publication of the report from the Comisión Nacional de Reconstrucción, entitled *México está de pie,* announced that the city and the country were ready to move on (15) just a month after the earthquakes, the most impoverished and affected sectors of the city had to struggle for years to come against a governmental reticence to acknowledge and address their struggles (Moreno and Ruiz Durán, 155). This disparity showed the disconnection between the state's political imagination, urban geography, and the inhabitants' necessities.

Meanwhile, as the young storytellers were recounting, many city dwellers took to the streets and began to organize and take over the management of the emergency. When looking at the different collections of testimonies that 1985 has generated throughout the decades, for every time someone tells us about the debris mountains, there is also a declaration detailing how the inhabitants of the city participated in rescues and built shelters for the victims (Aguilar Zínser, 13). It seems that the testimonies are as eager to talk about the trauma as about a sense of community that was experienced in the midst of the disaster.

The amount of documentation and testimonies, as well as the many monuments, memorials, and even the inclusion of the event within the school narrative of the official national history,[1] could make us think that 1985 is one of those traumatic events that trigger, as Andreas Huyssen has critically noted, a "fear of forgetting" that comes hand in hand with an "overload . . . [of] the memory system" (17). After neoliberalism, some critics, like Idelber Avelar,

---

1. For example, at the junior high level, textbooks approved by the secretary of public education talk about the earthquakes and the work of volunteers (see Rico Galindo et al., 240–47).

have been anxious about how the politics of consumerism has turned the past obsolete: "The market operates according to a substitutive, metaphorical logic in which . . . the past is to be forgotten because the market demands that the new replace the old without leaving a remainder" (2). This perspective tends to lead us toward a tireless search into the past, looking for some kind of lost perfection that succumbed violently. The 1985 earthquake and the political aftermath, however, do not adapt to this kind of interpretation. Contrary to similar disasters in other places, the memory of 1985 that has survived is more related to something discovered or gained than to loss.

Going back to the young men telling stories in the restuarant, endearment, rather than dread, punctuated the four narrators' stories, too. And, yet, we may still ask: Were those young men feeling nostalgia, or even mourning, for something they have not experienced? I never asked, but they did not seem sad or angry when telling the stories; to me, they looked amazed, and also hopeful and optimistic, as if knowing that that something had shifted "structures of feeling," our perception of, and interaction with, "our simultaneously expanding and shrinking present" (Huyssen, 24). Something emerged in 1985, and it was still felt in 2015.

MONSIVÁIS'S INTELLECTUAL SHIFT AND *LA ÉPICA A LA VUELTA DE LA ESQUINA*

What kind of intellectual discourse could problematize the emotions of hope and optimism without robbing the experience of 1985 of the possibilities it opened into the future? How would this discourse attend to the specificity of the event's present circumstances while also putting it into a historical perspective? What would be its political imagination and its effects?

In this chapter, I will study how Carlos Monsiváis's writing, in the span of twenty years (1985–2005), interacts with the opening of possibilities that emerged in 1985. The analyzed texts—*Entrada libre: Crónicas de la sociedad que se organiza* (1987), some of his chronicles and essays about the Zapatista movement, and *"No sin nosotros": Los días del terremoto 1985–2005* (2006)— construct a temporality that exhibits both a literary gaze focused on the experience of the present and a narrative voice resorting to the examination of other moments in history in search for continuities and disruptions of sociocultural and political tendencies. I propose that there are tones of hope and optimism in these texts, but that these emotions are politically engaged with the past and the present in such a way that they work against the promise of happiness of the neoliberal state. My main objective will be, then, to understand the alternative political imagination that arises from Monsiváis's texts during this twenty-year period.

As I will document, much has been said about Monsiváis's work and, especially, about *Entrada libre,* one of the most studied books by critics. In this chapter, I want to insert my ideas into the ongoing critical debate on the author's use of emotions and how particular ones help him in the articulation of an intellectual vision for the social space in Mexico. For this purpose, first, I will begin with an exposition of what Raymond Williams's concept of "emergence" adds to our understanding of how Monsiváis's narrative voice and gaze transit between past and present, while also envisioning a future. This is an analysis that Jean Franco and Mabel Moraña have already started; thus, I will complicate it by considering how the idea of *movement* acquires different senses in the author's work and radicalizes the notion of emergence and of temporality in the examined texts. For now, I will say that *movement* has both a very concrete reference—the Movimientos Urbanos Populares (MUPs) that become primal agents of change in Monsiváis's texts—and abstract implications: the constant evolution of what are presumed to be fixed categories, specifically, nation and identity.

Second, I will examine Monsiváis's use and expression of optimism by following the ideas of Lauren Berlant and qualifying the emotion as a "cruel optimism," that is, as a kind of feeling that attaches us to objects in a way that impulses us to be and take action in the world. When considering how temporality and optimism build a specific political imagination in Monsiváis's work, I identify a number of critics who have already studied long periods of the author's writing and defined his vision in relation to social phenomena, historical processes, and writing itself. I believe that my focus on a specific twenty-year period, in relation to 1985, adds to the analysis of how Monsiváis's writing is always thinking about the relationship between what he studies and how he studies it, that is, his art of representation. Also, my interpretation seeks to push the impact of emotions on political imaginations further.

In this sense, the main question that guides my critical reading is: How does optimism become an emergent and moving force that keeps transforming Monsiváis's writing and his vision for social space in Mexico? By bringing together the qualifying words *emergent* and *moving,* of course, I am considering the potential of optimism both as a force behind concrete movements and as an emotion that moves (commotion).

Since his first anthology of chronicles, *Días de guardar* (1971), Monsiváis's discourse engaged with three fundamental motifs: the discovery of new and old images by wandering through the city, a critical gaze formed from the knowledge gained from that wandering, and the exploration of that critical gaze by using literary language, especially irony. At the same time, the "I" begins to play with its identity, which sometimes becomes a third person, a character that is an object of (auto)criticism through irony (Gelpí in Corona and Jörgensen, 2002, 214; Faber, 79). According to Moraña and Sánchez Prado, the art of irony in Monsiváis operates as a critique that reveals national mythologies and ideologies as phenomena and narratives produced by the state nationalism; that is, Monsiváis's irony reveals that there are no essential truths (2007, 10–11). Not only has the intellectual used irony against the state and its imagined nation but also against illusions of authenticity regarding traditions, popular culture, and mass culture (11).

All of these characteristics speak of a genre that Monsiváis practiced and, in addition, thought about: the *crónica urbana*, that hybrid genre between literature and journalism that has produced some of the best writing in Latin America.[2] When talking about the development of the genre in Mexico, Ignacio Corona and Beth E. Jörgensen affirm that thinking about this kind of hybrid form is also "an inquiry into the role played by the chronicle and the chronicler in Mexico's public culture and cultural history" (4). Monsiváis's role as a *cronista* is best described by Jörgensen: "Part expert witness, part critic, part ironist, and part professional skeptic, the narrator portrays what other participants do and say from a distance, always minimizing the degree of his own active engagement" (2004, 91). This fluidity in the construction of a narrative identity also adjusts very well to the different processes of sociocultural and political transformation his voice addresses (Del Sarto, 187–88)—and not just through the chronicle. We also need to consider Monsiváis's use of the essay as the genre where he pauses to try out his ideas. As José Ramón Ruisánchez eloquently argues, in his essays, Monsiváis opts to take a step back and to offer all possible solutions, without certainty (244–45). After all, the essay and the urban chronicle are literary genres that go hand in hand with the history of modernity in Latin America (Sánchez Prado, 2007, 303–5).

In fact, it has been through the essay that Monsiváis has talked about the practice of the chronicle. For example, in "De la Santa Doctrina al Espíritu Público. (Sobre las funciones de la crónica en México)" (1987), Monsiváis examines the practice of the genre, concentrating on the main Mexican chroniclers of the nineteenth and twentieth centuries, among them Guillermo Prieto, Manuel Gutiérrez Nájera, Salvador Novo, and Elena Poniatowska. In speaking of Poniatowska, it seems to me that Monsiváis also speaks of his own style and purpose: "la espontaneidad que se compensa con arrojo, la ideología

---

2. For a study of the genre of the chronicle or the *crónica urbana* and its development in Latin America, see studies by Julio Ramos, Aníbal González, and Susana Rotker.

visceral y la épica a la vuelta de la esquina" (771) [spontaneity that is balanced out by courage, visceral ideology, and the epic just around the corner]. Moreover, for me, it is no accident that the publication of this reflection on the chronicle coincides with that of *Entrada libre*. If, as others have said, *Entrada libre* is the anthology of chronicles where Monsiváis witnesses the debut of Mexican civil society (Gutiérrez Mouat, 235–36), a "mature sphere of action" (Egan, 2001, 210), a "spontaneous generation of democratic life" (Tyler, 91), and the beginning of the future of democracy in Mexico (Jörgensen in Corona and Jörgensen, 2002, 86), I would like to add that, while this book marked the beginning of an intellectual project (in terms of the literary work and the political imagination), something continued to move (evolve/emote) throughout the decades. In the collection of chronicles and essays I study here—all of which somehow share 1985 as an epicenter—, I believe there is a constant intellectual shift between action (chronicle) and thought (essay) needed to best understand the phenomenon of *la épica a la vuelta de la esquina*.

EMERGENT, MOVING, AND CRUEL OPTIMISM

When approaching intellectual production as an active process in constant change, Williams confesses: "Once the central body of thinking was itself seen as active, developing, unfinished, and persistently contentious, many of the questions were open again, and, as a matter of fact, my respect for the body of thinking as a whole . . . significantly and decisively increased" (3–4). Williams, of course, is talking about the long Marxist tradition; nevertheless, I believe that Monsiváis's body of work merits the same question Williams asks about Marxism: how to approach it creatively, while also respecting the long critical dialogue that has already been going on and which, in turn, has changed our way of thinking about the same work at different times in history (4–5). Therefore, while Monsiváis's intellectual thought was always interested in social processes that were in progress, I also see Monsiváis's writing as a social process itself: "active, developing, unfinished, and persistently contentious"; that is, constantly emerging, in movement.

Williams's way of renovating Marxism was through a study of sociocultural productions as material phenomena (space and bodies interacting). For him, "no mode of production and therefore no dominant social order and therefore no dominant culture ever in reality includes or exhausts all human practice, human energy, and human intention" (125). In general, whatever dwells on the margins of the dominant or off its radar is expressed in everyday life, the personal, the private, the natural, and the metaphysical. Residual tendencies, says Williams, have been formed in the past and act effectively in the present through the expression of phenomena that cannot be adequately contained within the dominant. The example he offers is that of the agrarian society, which has been incorporated, idealized, and fantasized by industrial capitalism. On the other hand, emergent tendencies refer to new forms of experiences, relationships, and social and cultural practices. Williams notes that it is very difficult to distinguish between the emergent as an alternative or oppositional phenomenon to the dominant, and one that is simply a new phase of the dominant (novelty). Although the dominant will always try to incorporate the tendencies, there is still movement between the dominant, the residual, and the emergent. The problem will be how to take into account the perceptions and practices of the emergent before they can be incorporated into and made invisible by the dominant. In that prior moment, they appear as "pre-emergent" (132) and, according to Williams, are barely perceptible.

Because the preemergent operates in the interstices of what we have conceived of as dichotomies (subjective/objective, experience/belief, feelings/thoughts, and personal/social), Williams proposes that we need to approach this type of phenomena as "a kind of feeling and thinking which is indeed social and material, but each in an embryonic phase before it can become a fully articulate and defined exchange" (131). Lived experience of the preemergent, for Williams, expresses itself and, therefore, can only be dealt with through

> meanings and values as they are actively lived and felt, and the relations between these and formal or systematic beliefs, . . . elements of impulse, restraint, and tone; . . . affective elements of consciousness and relationships: not feeling against thought, but thought as felt and feeling as thought: practical consciousness of a present kind, in a living and interrelating continuity. We are then defining these elements as a "structure": as a set, with specific internal relations, at once interlocking and in tension. (132)

According to Williams, at times of preemergence, art and literature will be what may reflect the precise structures of feeling of the moment, since it is in these fields of thought that we find rhythms and figures that let us sense the experiences that begin to emerge. For me, then, the concept of "structures of feeling" (132) is what lets me probe the relationship established between intellectual thought, emotions, and social processes in Monsiváis's work.

In using Williams's ideas to examine Monsiváis's work, I join the voices of other critics who have already begun such study. For example, focusing mostly on his essay *Aires de familia* (2000), Franco establishes that the greatest anxiety in Monsiváis's work is the way the dominant has processed and continues to process the past in service to the present, such that it acts as mythology (2007, 194). Toward the end of her essay, Franco presents one of the questions that I take as a starting point to analyze the mirroring effect between Monsiváis's set of texts that I examine here: How can a multiplicity of emergences be mobilized without some concept of universality? (202). As if he were answering the question that Franco had left open, Héctor Domínguez Ruvalcaba says that the only effort to establish a kind of universalism in Monsiváis would be his pursuit of a desire for differences (2012, 205). This idea turns into a critical proposal that inquires further into the intellectual political imagination in relation to national constructs when Sánchez Prado argues that, in Monsiváis's discourse, the nation begins to be transformed by a diversity that requires a redefinition of what it means to be immersed in the circuit of relations that shape what we still call Mexico (Sánchez Prado, 2003, 20).

I believe that we do not need to be anxious about leaving behind or embracing concepts that refer us to universal categories, such as *nation*; rather, when studying a work of literature such as Monsiváis's, we should interrogate how those categories evolve. And, as I will detail in my textual analysis, the use of "we" in Monsiváis's texts resignifies the homogeneous meaning that state nationalism attempted to give to *nation* and to a *national* "we." As I see it, the "we" in Monsiváis's writing is simultaneously inclusive and explosive to the extent that it relates to the emergent movement of diversity in Mexico. Indeed, *diversity* is a concept to which I will return later in order to further push our understanding of how it is conceived and used in Monsiváis's texts; but, for now, I will say that the diverse "we" is integrated by unsuspected links that emerge between different kinds of unhappy bodies, a concept I explained in the introduction, and that in this chapter will take the form of marginalized urban subjects, rural migrants, indigenous peoples, women, and sexual minorities.

Going back to the critical emphasis on the structures of feeling, Moraña has specifically studied how these function in Monsiváis's cultural criticism. She establishes that, for Monsiváis, cultural criticism becomes a chronicling of "social drives" that run through the collective imaginary (2007, 51). My analysis works very closely with Moraña's interpretation. Nevertheless, while Moraña focuses more on sociocultural aspects, I want to center my attention on how Monsiváis's texts relate to the materiality of geographies and bodies, and to how everyday life (re)makes public space. This change in focus, which might seem minor, becomes paramount when considering Moraña's interpretation of the concept of *catastrophe* in her study of *Entrada libre*. I agree with her on the final effect caused by the 1985 earthquake, which she describes as "a time of enlightenment" (37). However, the questions that orient my reading of *Entrada libre*, and which run through this chapter, seek to exceed the dichotomy that seems to be present in Moraña's statement: ideological sphere/ material sphere.

In this sense, as I explained in the introduction, my analysis is guided by the thinking of Lefebvre and proposes these questions: How does a particular disaster (the 1985 earthquake) speak about a space of catastrophe (neoliberalism)? Therefore, how does the 1985 earthquake account for both material (geography and state) and ideological (representations) levels? How does Monsiváis manage to wield an intellectual discourse that takes into account both levels and explains their interconnection? As I will explain, *Entrada libre* becomes, for me, the intellectual moment when Monsiváis's discourse is not afraid to locate its gaze and voice within the affective realm, which, in turn, will construct a perspective able to understand the complexity of social space after the 1985 disaster.

When talking about the affective character of Monsiváis's texts, critics have put forward different interpretations. For some, there is a constant resorting to sentimentalism, especially in the author's cultural critique (Estrada, 31). For others, the analysis of his essays in particular reveals doubt and ambiguity that amount to hopelessness (Ruisánchez, 254). Yet others have recognized that his writing admits both irony and empathy, humor and serious analysis, radical critique and optimism (Mahieux, 491). Still, others go on to characterize his body of work within a cluster of emotions that include optimism, hope, and utopianism. For example, Linda Egan has argued that Monsiváis proposes a kind of "utopianism," which she defines as a desire for action that is tempered by patience and reason (2001, 233–35). More specifically, utopianism in his texts is "a fleeting quality that [the intellectual gaze] glimpses . . . when civil society mobilizes" (233). Egan has gone on to talk about how, in some instances (such as in "Los milenarismos"), there is characterization of men and women who are invested in transformation processes as heroes (2012, 240–41). However, when taking into consideration Monsiváis's writing style, the load of words like *optimism* and *utopianism* should be moderated. For instance, Sara Potter has already shown us in her analysis of the essay *Aires de familia* that Monsiváis's act of writing denies resolutions and prefers to dwell in the contradiction of the present: "'El gozo de Monsiváis' is . . . found in the crossroads" (28). In another example, Sánchez Prado prefers to qualify the emotion as a kind of strategic optimism (2007, 317). In this sense, Sánchez Prado relates Monsiváis's work to other authors who, throughout the development of modernity, in Latin America and elsewhere, have had to have faith in order to imagine an emancipatory project (323). What all of these interpretations have in common is that the expressed emotion in Monsiváis's texts is irrevocably linked to an acute sense of temporality: what was, what is, and what could be. And, as I have explained, that sense goes hand in hand with the structures of feeling that allow the intellectual discourse to grasp emergences and their movements.

I want to continue to develop this discussion of the affective locus of enunciation in Monsiváis's discourse by conceptualizing the emotions of hope and optimism and, later on, by analyzing specifically how this cluster works in the texts in relation to the addressed phenomena and to the intellectual's political imagination. As I discussed in the introduction, neoliberalism, as well as national and other identitarian (homogenizing) discourses, have relied on the promise of happiness. Related to this promise, we will find the emotion of hope, which, as Ahmed tells us, reaffirms bodies in their openness and motivates them to reach "towards what is possible" (2015, 185). When thinking about hope, we often think about the future: What possibilities exist in the future? Nevertheless, as Ahmed reminds us, "hope without politics is a reification of possibility (and becomes merely religious)" (184). Hope for the future cannot be isolated from the need to take action in the present. I believe that, in Monsiváis's discourse, to hope is to be involved in restless action to the point of anxiety, because "we" know that what "we" are doing in the present may translate into effective change—not yet, but soon. All past and future depends on "us" here and now. The present moment of hope witnesses a difference, an emergence in the structures of feeling, as Williams would say. It is also a gap or a *brèche,* as Nancy defined it, that leaves "us" vulnerable and open to the present experience and to action. This is the moment to do "the work of teaching, protesting, naming, feeling, and connecting with others" (Ahmed, 2015, 188). After all, an interstitial future requires hope that is "mine" as much as "yours"; it is "our" willingness to be a fearless part of this world.

Berlant defines optimism in a way that is close to what Ahmed tells us about hope: optimism is an emotion that works in the present and projects itself into the future (Berlant, 1–4). What Berlant adds to the cluster of hope/optimism is the notion of attachment: "All attachment is optimistic, if we describe optimism as the force that moves you out of yourself and into the world in order to bring closer the satisfying something that you cannot generate on your own but sense in the wake of a person, a way of life, an object, project, concept, or scene" (1–2). Optimism/hope moves us toward something that is beyond us and, therefore, needs us to work in relation to that something. Going back to the anecdote with which I opened this chapter, that something could keep us attached for decades, moving with it. And that something is, I argue, what Monsiváis's structure of feeling is able to see in its preemergent state and, furthermore, to continue tracing into its unsuspected (re)emergences.

Berlant also explains that optimistic attachments may provoke other emotions that may not feel "optimistic," because the movement into which optimism/hope throws us might take us through a process that seems to never end; that is, we may not reach what we hope for (1–2). This is what leads Berlant to talk about "cruel optimism": "Optimism is cruel when the object/ scene that ignites a sense of possibility actually makes it impossible to attain the expansive transformation for which a person or a people risks striving" (2). As I will discuss, in Monsiváis's discourse, the nation as a project to be imagined is what lies at the center of the twenty-year discussion of the social emergence of 1985. And the nation as a project becomes an attachment that sometimes generates a hopeful kind of optimism and, at times, a cruel one. I concur, then, with Sánchez Prado when he states that Carlos Monsiváis's work can be located somewhere between the constant necessity to establish and sustain a nation and the critique of the discriminatory mechanisms that such impulse entails (2007, 300). For me, an additional point to consider when talking about this kind of tense relationship between the intellectual discourse and the nation as an imagined project is: What does it mean to be moved by cruel optimism?

In my critical reading of Monsiváis's texts, I argue that to be moved is to become part of a nation that, as imagined in this intellectual discourse, has been made by movement and is in movement, always emerging in diversity. To move the nation, to diversify it, is to open it up for the unhappy bodies by the unhappy bodies. Furthermore, I believe that, at the textual points when the intellectual voice acknowledges being emotionally moved, the writer reaches a wider and more heterogeneous audience. Being publicly moved is something that, as I suggest, some readers have not been able to forgive Monsiváis for. To understand this conflict better, I want to first explain the complicated relationship between intellectuals, state, and the concept of *nation* in the Mexican context.

INTELLECTUAL POLITICAL IMAGINATIONS IN MEXICO

The relationship between the Mexican state—imagined and institutionalized by the Partido Revolucionario Institucional (PRI) during the 1920s[3]—and intellectuals has been one of collaboration at times, antagonism in many other

3. The Mexican Revolution (1910–17; these years vary according to different interpretations of the revolutionary process) was institutionalized into a state during the 1920s and,

instances, and always challenging to navigate. It is very difficult to understand, then, why by 1991 the following statement was establishing a rather simplistic division when thinking about Mexican intellectuals: "those serving the State and those independent of it" (Camp et al., 12). After all, the imagination of the nation is always linked with material and ideological aspects of social space, many of which are intervened by the state and through which any proposition needs to interact at some point or another.

For Roger Bartra, there have been a number of intellectual productions that have contributed to the mythology by which the imaginary networks of state power have been able to persist. Specifically, essays searching into a definition of *lo mexicano* were an expression of the dominant political culture (14). More than a division between serving the state or being independent of it, for Bartra, the complexity of this mythology and its networks of power created a national culture that established which subjects are inside the nation and which ones are kept outside. Within this same kind of interpretation, Claudio Lomnitz-Adler proposed that Mexican intellectuals' obsession has been the definition of a national culture in relation to the state's project of modernity. In particular, essayists, for Lomnitz-Adler, have developed a "psychodrama"—that is, history seen as a family drama (1–14). Returning to Octavio Paz's *El laberinto de la soledad,* Lomnitz-Adler proposes that this kind of intellectual psychodrama behaves as "a vicious cycle that is built on the tensions that occur between the maze of social relations that exist within the national space and the ideologies regarding a common identity, a shared sense of the past, and a unified gaze towards the future" (3). Both Bartra and Lomnitz-Adler are thus interested in the complex ways by which political imaginations construct a diversity of narratives that explain material phenomena, including processes of institutionalization.

Regarding the relationship between intellectual imaginations and the state, Sánchez Prado has identified a number of authors who, without being outcasts of the state or its dominant national culture, have known how to propose alternative national projects (2009, 1). Since the beginnings of the revolutionary state, "intellectual nations" have presented a fundamental characteristic: a desire to build an autonomous space for literature (7). While for Robert T. Conn the idea of an "aesthetic state," that is, "an intellectual and artistic community . . . as a utopian Mexican and Latin American Republic of Letters" (4), ambitioned to function outside of the influence of the institutional state—the government—and even disassociated from the *ciudad real,* Sánchez

---

by 1929, into a sole party, the Partido Nacional Revolucionario, which eventually became the PRI. For an in-depth historical analysis, see Enrique Florescano's book.

Prado's intellectual nation is still very much immersed into the *ciudad real*'s affairs as well as the state's. The autonomy of the intellectual nation did not mean a complete rupture in order to conceive a world only for intellectuals, an "aesthetic state." This is why, for Sánchez Prado, Mexico becomes a social space where writers continue to occupy an active role in the public sphere, and at the same time these intellectuals can articulate an antiestablishment discourse (2009, 11). Therefore, Mexican intellectuals did not have to choose between "serving the State" or "being independent of it." Rather, they could collaborate with state institutions or projects and also write an autonomous narrative to imagine other kinds of nation.

Mexican intellectuals' active role in the public sphere has been particularly notorious after 1968, and, according to Roderic A. Camp, they have "contributed strongly to the grassroots democratic landscape, writing numerous editorials and columns on the necessity for expanded political space and electoral integrity" (16). Of course, the increase of open intellectual animosity against the government came as a reaction to the 1968 massacre at the Plaza de las Tres Culturas, Tlatelolco, in Mexico City, at the hands of President Gustavo Díaz Ordaz's government, which moved against students and other supporters of a student strike that had been going on for months and that threatened to disrupt the programmed Olympic Games in the city. Examples of the rift that followed the massacre included Paz's resignation as the ambassador in India in 1968 and Carlos Fuentes's resignation as ambassador in France in 1977, when President José López Portillo named Díaz Ordaz as ambassador to Spain. For some time after 1968, the government fought against discourses that associated the concept of the intellectual with any kind of "public prestige" and instead promoted one in which intellectuals were part of a "sinister conspiration," in collaboration with foreigners and communists, against Mexican national culture (Volpi, 360). This kind of official discourse was followed into action when, for example, President Luis Echevarría Álvarez (1970–76) pressured the newspaper *Excélsior* to oust then editor Julio Scherer García due to his critical pieces (Brewster, 88–92). Nevertheless, at the same time, the government understood very well that intellectuals were fundamental for the state. Therefore, a (re)formulation of the intellectual's function was published by the PRI's Órgano Teórico del Comité Ejecutivo Nacional, which established that intellectuals should guide "the masses" down a road toward liberation, that is, a road that contributes to the country's economic, social, and cultural development, while respecting Mexico's "national personality" (21–22). This tense relationship will continue until another breaking point: 1985.

The intellectuals' reactions to the earthquakes of 1985, however, cannot be compared to the ones toward 1968. In 1985, many of them offered their thoughts and solidarity, but only a few wrote intensely about the disaster, its causes, and its consequences. Some examples, besides Monsiváis, are Elena Poniatowska's *Nada, nadie: Las voces del temblor,* Cristina Pacheco's *Zona de desastre,* and Carlos Fuentes's *Cristóbal Nonato.* Even if both events were disastrous (albeit in different ways) and even if the government played a role both in 1968 and 1985, given that 1968 meant an attack on what was understood as the epicenter of the *ciudad letrada,* most intellectuals felt compelled to react. In contrast, I believe that, because 1985 was especially violent toward many of the most dispossessed sectors in society, the event showed which intellectuals were interested in talking to this audience and which were not. Monsiváis was, of course; and he was also interested in tracing a narrative that could relate both tragedies.

ENTRADA LIBRE, DISTANT VOICES BURST UPON THE CITY

Entrada libre describes the economic and political scene of the 1980s in Mexico through a narration of two urban disasters: that of the earthquakes (a natural disaster) and that of Pemex in San Juanico, State of Mexico (an industrial one). The urban context is clearly seen as a fragment (Salazar, 69–76) and as a grotesque body, dying and being born at the same time (159–68). Throughout the texts, a series of popular actors will carry out political actions, independent of leftist parties and organizations, among them the urban poor, rural, and working-class movements, and independent unionism. It is also important to notice the geographical and temporal shifts in the book: the chronicler starts in 1985 in the middle of the city; he then reaches back toward earlier events that occurred between 1981 and 1984 on the margins of the city and in the country; and he finally moves toward the future, between 1986 and 1987, in a city swollen with a contemporaneity forged by those voices from without and within. In this anthology of chronicles, then, Monsiváis announces a centralism in ruins (Klahn, 177) and highlights a permeability—thanks to migrations (Klahn, 189; Egan, 2001, 197) and popular movements—between the outside and the inside of the city.

From the title of the book, *Entrada libre: Crónicas de la sociedad que se organiza,* and that of the prologue, "Lo marginal en el centro," Monsiváis emphasizes democracy as a practice or an exercise: "Quienes ejercen la democracia desde abajo y sin pedir permiso, amplían sus derechos ejerciéndolos" (11) [Those who exercise democracy from below without asking permission increase their rights by exercising them]. The verb *ejercer* stands out in this quote because it points as much toward taking power as it does toward a constant practice that does not have a smooth movement: "Los métodos de rehabilitación democrática cansan y recuperan, desgastan y liberan a sus practicantes que explican sin cesar la índole justa de este movimiento, sometido al ritmo de una manifestación tras otra, una reunión tras otra, repartir volantes y redactar desplegados" (11) [The methods of democratic rehabilitation tire and reenergize, wear down and liberate their practitioners who explain unceasingly the just nature of this movement, subjected to the pace of one demonstration after another, one meeting after another, handing out flyers and composing (magazine and newspaper) inserts]. This movement to the tune of meetings and demonstrations exercises not only democracy but also a collective work that forms communities, "una fuerza desconocida (por inesperada)" (13) [an unknown force (because it is unexpected)]. Democracy is, therefore, the emergence of the communal, which in turn, materializes in communities' everyday life, that is, it is bodies working with other bodies on the (re)design of public space.

To speak of the everyday domain, Monsiváis turns to Lefebvre, whom he quotes in his prologue: "La crítica de la vida cotidiana implica concepciones y apreciaciones sobre la escala de la estructura social" (Lefebvre, qtd. in Monsiváis, 2001, 14) [The critique of daily life implies conceptions and appreciations of the scale of social structure]. For Lefebvre, daily life moves between the three components of social space—geography, institutions, and imaginary order—and its material and symbolic practice has particular influence on the meanings in play in the imaginary order. For Monsiváis, however, the emergence of the everyday practices in the city is the potentiality that feeds the urban movements: "Lo cotidiano . . . es ahora con frecuencia el marco de la disidencia o la configuración de la alternativa, el terreno propicio donde el sujeto individual y los pequeños grupos ven con más claridad las funciones de la democracia en la sociedad global" (14) [Everyday life . . . is now frequently the frame of dissidence or the configuration of the alternative, the favorable territory where the individual subject and small groups see more clearly the workings of democracy in global society]. Democracy is, then, exercise and daily materiality as well as a connection to a global imaginary.

Although the term *civil society* appears in this prologue, it is not to discuss its definition, but to auscultate the possibilities this word can create. Monsiváis's interpretation of the communal, however, is not related to the supposedly new appearance of civil society in Mexico. Rather, for the intellectual voice in *Entrada libre*, the purpose of the book is to keep debating the meanings of the 1985 earthquakes, beyond fixed concepts or definitions: "Me propuse acercarme a movimientos sociales, no para registrar toda la historia sino algunos fragmentos significativos de entrada libre a la historia o al presente, instantes de auge y tensión dramática" (15) [I set out to study social movements not to document the whole history but, rather, some significant fragments of free entry to history or to the present, peak moments of dramatic tension]. It is a theoretical purpose that, in turn, becomes a kind of intellectual action, an engagement, with regard to the emergence of the communal in the everyday doings of the present and, thus, of the doings of history. For this discourse, then, temporality will move back and forth, as the borders of the present and the past collide at points where the intellectual gaze detects instances that can connect to the experience of 1985.

F. Scott Fitzgerald's quote at the end of the prologue—"Admitir por ejemplo que las cosas no tienen remedio y mantenerse sin embargo decidido a cambiarlas" (qtd. in Monsiváis, 2001, 15) [Admitting, for example, that things have no solution and remaining, nevertheless, determined to change them]— leads readers to see, since the very beginning of the text, the recognition of a cruel optimism that will guide the intellectual voice into the study of a structure of feeling that, precisely, deals with the same maxim. "Las cosas" refers to both the material and the ideological realms (*cosas* as concrete objects and *cosas* as indefinite ideas). In this sense, "we" want to change *las cosas*, but since *las cosas* can be so many and so ungraspable at once, "we" work immersed in them without really seeing them. That is the blindness of everyday life; and, yet, that blindness is what guides "us" otherwise, as we create "our" structure of feeling, which seems to be this contradictory cruel optimism; "we" need to change *las cosas* even while knowing that it is an impossible task. Throughout this book, that stubborn blindness will set the pace of a guarded optimism.

I want to first spend some time exploring these initial ideas in the text entitled "Viñetas del movimiento urbano popular," published a year after the 1985 earthquakes, since it offers the opportunity to analyze how the chronicler's gaze in *Entrada libre* pursues and narrates the processes of awareness-raising among the most marginalized urban populations. "Viñetas" focuses on one of the main characters in Monsiváis's work: a woman—and specifically, how a woman recently arrived in the city, where she "descubre la potencia de su voz" (240) [finds the potential of her voice]. But before discovering the potential of her voice, her uniqueness, this woman belongs to the sphere of the residual, as Williams would call it:

> La "desesperación urbana" y su imagen arquetípica: la pareja desciende del camión, con bultos que incluyen 6 niños, y se lanza a conquistar el Edén subvertido. En su pueblo no hay trabajo ni agua, los latifundistas le imponen precios de hambre a sus productos, un hijo se les murió por falta de atención

médica . . . A la gran ciudad llegan en busca de parientes, de amigos, de la suerte que da Dios.

¿En dónde se instala la Pareja Legendaria? En barracas, pedregales, cerros, zonas minadas, viviendas semiderruidas. Alguien les dijo que por allí podrían quedarse, y no tienen nada que perder, ésa es su característica, nada que perder. (237)

"Urban desperation" and its archetypical image: the couple gets off the bus, with bundles that include 6 children, and set themselves to conquer the subverted Eden. In their village there is neither work nor water, the landowners set starvation prices on their products, one child died for lack of medical attention . . . They come to the big city looking for relatives, friends, God's blessing.

Where does the Legendary Couple lodge? In shacks, rocky fields, hills, minefields, tumbledown housing. Someone told them that they could stay there, and they have nothing to lose, that's their characteristic, nothing to lose.

The vignette offers us an image of the day-to-day reality of the mass migration from the country to the urban centers. This phenomenon reached its peak between the 1970s and 1980s, and, as we shall see in Monsiváis's descriptive vignette, it will be that peak that gets shaken so violently in 1985 and afterward keeps supporting a now ineluctable outcry. Both in the chronicles in *Entrada libre* and in later texts, this will be an urban emergence in continual motion until 2005.

Although the character that opens the text is collective, *la Pareja* [the Couple], as the narration proceeds, we witness a process of independence on the part of the woman, who receives a first name, Eva, in the section entitled "Eva toma la palabra." This mythic name, which indicates a rebellion in the face of the patriarchal order, becomes in Monsiváis's text a discovery of the potential of Eva's voice:

Una tarde se discute lo del agua, y ella ya no aguanta, y como no dando crédito a lo que oye, pide la palabra y dice que ya está hasta la madre, . . . tiene ganas de llorar pero prefiere decir que ya no aguanta, se enoja todavía más y grita que no es justo. . . . Al callarse, un frío inmenso la sacude. *Habló en público.* Ella, tan atemorizada ante la perspectiva de siquiera quejarse. (239–40)

One afternoon they are arguing about water, and she cannot take it any more, and as if she cannot believe what she's hearing, she asks permission to speak and says that she's had it up to here, . . . she feels like crying but she chooses to say she cannot take it any more, she gets even angrier and yells that it's not fair. . . . When she stops talking, she is shaken by a huge shiver. *She spoke in public.* She, who is so scared by the thought of even complaining.

What is more, Eva will become *doña* and *señora,* an activist and leader who inspires other neighbor women with courage: "La Eva eterna de paso rápido y humildito desaparece, y la remplaza Doña María o Doña Lupe o Señora Araceli" (239) [The eternal Eve of quick and humble steps disappears, to be replaced by Ms. Mary or Ms. Lupe or Ms. Araceli]. Therefore, that woman who was invisible within the confines of the Couple manages to form a new collective with the neighboring women, that multiplicity of *doñas* and *señoras* among which many Evas discover the potentiality of a feminine movement: "Más vehementes o menos vehementes, más informadas o menos informadas, pero seguras de algo: su participación en los asuntos de la colonia las ha hecho distintas, ya no se dejan tan fácilmente, ya no quieren dejarse" (240) [More or less vehement, more or less informed, but sure of something: their participation in the matters of the neighborhood has changed them, they are no longer so easily led, they no longer want to be led]. Thus, it will be the neighbor women who set the constant pace of the urban poor movements, which will face bureaucracy:

> Contra la dilación infinita, la constancia en los plantones. . . .
>
> En el duelo entre el tiempo de la burocracia . . . y el tiempo de los peticionarios, algo han adelantado estos últimos. . . . Y es ya político el uso de su paciencia." (244–45)

> Against the infinite delay, persistence in the protests. . . .
>
> In the duel between the time of bureaucracy . . . and the time of the petitioners, the latter have made some progress. . . . And the use of their patience is now political.

That tenacious, patient rhythm of potential voices that open new possibilities is the one that bursts out in visible networks in 1985, taking the authorities by surprise.

In this sense, we can also see in that pace a preemergence that surfaced emphatically in movements in the face of the earthquake's space of catastrophe. It is also a pace that Monsiváis's work locates as being from the outer fringes of the city and in constant movement against and from that city, like the mark in the title that superimposes two photographs included in the photo-essay that appears in the very middle of *Entrada libre*: "El movimiento urbano-popular: La lucha contra la ciudad y desde la ciudad, la militancia femenina" (n. pag. in photo-essay) [The urban-poor movement: the struggle against the city, from the city, feminine militancy]. If the continual migration from the country to the city shows us a preemergence, *la militancia femenina* generates and maintains the pace of the emergent *movimiento urbano popular* and captivates the chronicler's gaze in those years and later, in the years of the Zapatista mobilization during the 1990s and 2000s, as I will discuss later on.

In *Entrada libre,* the chronicle "Los días del terremoto" records the outbreak of voices from the city that, like the collective of women in "Viñetas," discover that their contributions in the urban space generate a potential movement that opens previously unsuspected possibilities. Centered around the earthquakes of 1985, the chronicle "Los días del terremoto" identifies this natural disaster as a kind of catalytic agent that manages to magnify the emergence of this movement of urban voices. Consisting of all of Monsiváis's chronicles published in the magazine *Proceso* during the days of the earthquakes (2001, 15), this text is presented unedited; that is, the articles are unchanged from their first appearances throughout 1985 until their inclusion in *Entrada libre* in 1987. This detail highlights a contrast between "Los días del terremoto" and Monsiváis's normal writing method, in which he shapes his articles through editions and reeditions, from newspapers and magazines to anthologies. It is worth asking, then, why alter his method in "Los días del terremoto"?

I suspect that this text escaped his usual writing method because of a sense of immediacy and urgency that the author wanted to preserve. These feelings will survive in a chronicle that moves between a description replete with details and aphasia to account for the thorough analysis of everyday life, death, survivors, and the misery of the life that remains. These techniques also serve to allow the intellectual gaze to take into account the emergence of *la épica a la vuelta de la esquina,* which in "Los días del terremoto" begins like this:

> Día 19. Hora 7:19. El miedo. La realidad cotidiana se desmenuza en oscilaciones, ruidos categóricos o minúsculos, estallidos de cristales, desplome de objetos o de revestimientos, gritos, llantos, el intenso crujido que anuncia la siguiente impredecible metamorfosis de la habitación, del departamento, de la casa, del edificio. . . . El miedo, la fascinación inevitable del abismo contenida y nulificada por la preocupación de la familia, por el vigor del instinto de sobrevivencia. Los segundos premiosos, plenos de energía que azora, corroe, intimida, se convierte en la debilidad de quien sufre. (17)

Day 19. Time 7:19. Fear. Daily reality is scrutinized in waves, categorical or minuscule noises, breaking glass, the collapse of objects or facings, shouting, crying, the intense crunch announcing the next unpredictable metamorphosis of the room, the apartment, the house, the building. . . . Fear, the inevitable fascination with the abyss contained and nullified by worry about the family, by the strength of the survival instinct. The urgent seconds, full of energy that frightens, corrodes, intimidates, becomes the weakness of those who suffer.

The narration places itself within a present demarcated by verbs and indicators of day and time, right down to hours and minutes, while the meticulous observation of the moment turns the chronicler into a survivor and a witness. The story is, then, the result of an experience shared by everyone, *el miedo* unleashed by the earthquakes. If, for Benjamin, a story worth telling was one based on experience, whether the storyteller's or that of others; for Giorgio Agamben, a witness is someone who speaks on behalf of the real witness, the one who faced horror (had the experience) and cannot speak (33–34). This is why serving as a witness is also admitting "the impossibility of bearing witness" (Agamben, 34). Going back to Benjamin, in the story, only fragments of experience survive; and, in "Los días del terremoto," the chronicler is the bearer of a fragmented experience that he attempts to narrate from his perspective and that of other survivors (all witnesses for those who can no longer speak).

In "Los días del terremoto," *el miedo* has a precise start in the scrutiny of everyday life, because this natural disaster has altered the relationship between body and space, and with it, daily experience:

Me di cuenta de todo a fondo, como que el pavor lo hace a uno consciente de cada movimiento, y al mismo tiempo, como que el pavor es una inercia autónoma. . . . Me afligía y me serenaba, pero sin dejar de hacer las cosas, de gritar, de apresurar, de tranquilizar, de planear la salida, todo tan acelerado que no oía, sólo veía espectáculos. (17–18)

I became deeply aware of everything, like how fear makes one aware of every movement, and at the same time, how fear is an independent inertia. . . . I got upset and I calmed down, but all while still doing things, screaming, worrying, calming down, planning my escape, all so fast that I didn't hear, I only saw spectacles.

How, then, does this self-aware subject reconstruct himself in the face of this experience? And, further, how can he deal with it? Although the chronicler is aware, from the same starting point, of the fact that the recounting of events will remain incomplete due to the absence of other fragments, he begins to restructure the *logos* from that same absence that causes aphasia.

From the Centro Histórico to Tlatelolco, the description of each scene begins with a review of out-of-place and useless objects: "En medio de la danza de varilla, cemento y hierros retorcidos, se esparcen las ruinas domésticas: colchones, televisores, zapatos, ropa, papeles, fotografías, sillas, máquinas de escribir, máquinas de coser, muebles, automóviles convertidos en chatarra" (53) [In the middle of the dance of rebar, cement, and twisted iron are scattered the ruins of households: mattresses, televisions, shoes, clothes, papers, photographs, chairs, typewriters, sewing machines, furniture, cars twisted into scrap metal]. This list of broken and dislocated objects offers, first, a synecdochic description of the disaster. Seen out of their usual places and uses, they give evidence, like silent witnesses, of a broken daily routine and of the loss of human life. Their disproportionate and illogical accumulation, paradoxically, makes us think of the emptiness of meaning. It is from these objects, second, that the literary language of the chronicle articulates metaphors that, in turn, direct the intellectual gaze toward the identification of an even deeper break, that of the Mexican nation, as a project imagined throughout the decades as a synonym for the PRI:

> De la conmoción surge una ciudad distinta (o contemplada de modo distinto), con ruinas que alguna vez fueron promesas de modernidad victoriosa: el Hotel Regis, la SCOP con sus extraordinarios murales de Juan O'Gorman, el Multifamiliar Juárez, la Unidad Nonoalco-Tlatelolco, Televisa, el Centro Médico, el Hospital General, la Secretaría de Comercio. (24)

> From the commotion arises a different city (or considered differently), with ruins that once promised a victorious modernity: the Hotel Regis, the SCOP with its extraordinary murals by Juan O'Gorman, the Juárez Apartments, the Nonoalco-Tlatelolco Unit, Televisa, the Medical Center, the General Hospital, the Ministry of Commerce.

Through his gaze, from press reports and from survivors' testimonies, Monsiváis presents, for example, the situation in Tlatelolco: ruins, destruction, refugee camps in the Plaza de las Tres Culturas, all circumstances in which, again, the PRI has a starring role. Through a detailed chronology of events and a presentation of official statistics, in addition to references to documents and expert analyses of the topic, he reconstructs a case history of the disaster that is filled with irregularities, corruption, property speculation, and

violations of basic public health regulations (54–56). This recounting is sum-
marized in a single sentence: "Fue breve el sueño de la unidad habitacional
integrada y autosuficiente" (55) [It was a brief dream of an integrated, self-
sufficient *unidad habitacional*."[4] Thus the remains of the earthquake's horror
lead, metonymically, to the ruins of the Mexican project of modernity, eroded
over the intervening decades and, according to Monsiváis's narrative and the
analysis of others, lacking in planning and administrative ethics for a long
time.

Moreover, Monsiváis's writing dwells uncomfortably in the place of the
1985 loss and, from there, it reminds us of other previous losses, linked phe-
nomenologically to the name of the same place: Tlatelolco. Through the testimony of Laura, a survivor and neighbor in the *unidad habitacional,* our
chronicler establishes a connection between the tragedy of 1985 and that of
1968: "Lo del 68 fue un crimen por soberbia; lo de ahora es un crimen por
negligencia, y esas muertes deben contribuir a que el pueblo viva mejor" (59)
[What happened in 1968 was a crime of pride; what happened now is a crime
due to negligence, and those deaths should contribute to making life better for
the living]. In this declaration, there is a dual mourning in joining the remembrance of the victims of the two catastrophes. In addition, disaster and crime
have remained linked through a place. Tlatelolco now becomes an immediate
referent for both dates.

Rubén Gallo has offered a provocative interpretation of Tlatelolco, defining the place as a *lieu de mémoire* (111–12), a concept by Pierre Nora: "There
are sites, *lieux de mémoire,* in which a residual sense of continuity remains.
Lieux de mémoire, settings in which memory is a real part of everyday experience" (Nora, 1). Nevertheless, I would like to go beyond the sense of eternal
loss carried by that concept, because I am more interested in focusing on the
political actions that intervene in Tlatelolco (1968, 1985). For me, the idea of
emergence opens up possibilities for thinking about the past and the future
from a standpoint of our present influence on public space. This, above all, is
also what guides me best in reading a text like Monsiváis's, in which the gaze
is fixed on Tlatelolco, not to long for what it was, but to identify what it is and
imagine what it could be.

Anderson has judged that *Entrada libre,* like other texts reacting to the
1985 earthquake, was in reality responding to an electoral event, the 1988
presidential elections, and, therefore, developing a narrative of emerging
democracy (147–66). Nonetheless, this interpretation negates the profound

---

4. *Unidades habitacionales* were housing projects developed by the Mexican state for
working-class families, especially those who worked for the government.

understanding that Monsiváis had of historical processes. More accurately, *Entrada libre* becomes a representation of a struggle between popular manifestations and traditional discourses' intention to coopt these emergences (Sánchez Prado, 2007, 313). In this sense, for Monsiváis, what 1968 and 1985 have in common is a tragedy that has been treated with disregard, oblivion, and impunity by resorting to sport spectacles—the 1968 Olympic Games and the 1985 World Cup of Football, both hosted in Mexico City right after each violent event (Sánchez Prado, 2007, 313).

Moreover, it is the structures of feeling that allow Monsiváis's intellectual writing to identify the Tlatelolco of 1985 as a new emergence of that other movement, apparently struck down and in a residual state, the Tlatelolco of 1968:

> A diario, en el auditorio Antonio Caso de la Unidad, las asambleas modifican las demandas económicas. . . . La organización crece, en medio de los campamentos de damnificados, del rescate de cadáveres, de los escollos jurídicos y administrativos y de la penuria de la mayoría. En las asambleas es arduo el aprendizaje de la nueva cultura urbana. Junto al presídium (que apenas lo es, nadie permanece en su sitio más de 20 minutos), un compañero explica el intríngulis inmobiliario, las sutilezas jurídicas, el alud de requisitos. Y la palabra *vecino* sustituye a *compañero*. (57)

> Daily, in the Antonio Caso auditorium of the complex, the assemblies modify economic demands. . . . Organization grows, in the midst of the refugee camps, the rescue efforts for the bodies of the dead, the legal and administrative hurdles, and the poverty of the majority. In the assemblies it is an arduous task to learn the new urban culture. Next to the presidium (which it hardly is, nobody stays in their place for more than 20 minutes), a comrade explains the mysteries of real estate, the legal subtleties, the deluge of requirements. And the word *neighbor* replaces *comrade*.

There is a recuperation of an understanding apparently forgotten, that of social and political organization, but it comes through another understanding: that of the precariousness of everyday life in the city. It can be said, then, that the potentiality of 1968 (*compañero* as affiliation within an organized political movement) is recovered, but in a very different way in 1985 (*vecino* as material and emotional attachment). In both, urgency causes the call for a public space.

If neighbors are ready to transform the urban space, so is Monsiváis's reporting to follow them in the process. As happened with the women in

"Viñetas," what was only thought of as solidarity keeps evolving into a "toma de poderes" [seizure of power]:

> No se examinará seriamente el sentido de la *acción épica* del jueves 19, mientras se le confine exclusivamente en el concepto de *solidaridad*. La hubo y de muy hermosa manera, pero como punto de partida de una actitud que, así sea efímera ahora y por fuerza, pretende apropiarse de la parte del gobierno que a los ciudadanos legítimamente les corresponde. El 19, y en respuesta ante las víctimas, la ciudad de México conoció una *toma de poderes*, de las más nobles de su historia, que trascendió con mucho los límites de la mera solidaridad, fue la conversión de un pueblo en gobierno y del desorden oficial en orden civil. Democracia puede ser también la importancia súbita de cada persona. (20)

> The sense of the *epic action* of Thursday the 19th will not be seriously examined as long as it is confined exclusively to the concept of *solidarity*. There was [solidarity], and very nicely [implemented], but as a starting point for an attitude that, even if ephemeral now and necessarily so, tries to appropriate the part of the government that legitimately belongs to the citizens. On the 19th, and in response to the victims, Mexico City experienced a *seizure of power*, one of the noblest in its history, that transcended by far the limits of mere solidarity. It was the conversion of a people into a government and of official disorder into civil order. Democracy can also be the sudden importance of each person.

In the first place, he emphasizes the phrase *acción épica* [epic action], an adjective that is repeated on the same page to refer to the work of the neighbors and other volunteers, and which Monsiváis will use again in his essay "De la Santa Doctrina al Espíritu Público" to describe the scenes that occupy the genre of chronicle. In the sense of his description, these actions are worthy of epic because they are heroic, and, therefore, they become protagonists of history. Interestingly, Monsiváis's chronicle is constituted as historical narration, an epic without poetry, of the material and emotional movement of the neighbors. But this intellectual narration, in contrast to an epic or history, is done in the present. Thanks to structures of feeling associated with the cluster of optimism/hope, Monsiváis's text captures an emergence of a movement that has opened a *brèche*—as Nancy would say—where the wholeness of the present has left city dwellers vulnerable and where most of the *vecinos* are willing to embrace such vulnerability, which is life itself.

Second, the passage begins to direct us through a political discussion that will revolve around the terms for naming this kind of *acción épica*. In exchanging *solidaridad* for *toma de poderes,* Monsiváis argues in favor of a phenomenon that begins to transcend the immediacy of the seismic disaster. The *toma de poderes* becomes a reordering of space and bodies, according to which a different kind of democracy is inaugurated via the collective action that is taken in the public space. The *desorden oficial,* then, cedes before the *acción épica.* "Los días del terremoto" is thus the story in the present progressive of the restitution of the public space as a place for discussion.

In the midst of this epic action in the terrain of the ordinary, the term *sociedad civil* appears, appraised thus by Monsiváis: "La sociedad civil existe como gran necesidad latente en quienes desconocen incluso el término, y su primera y más insistente demanda es la redistribución de poderes" (20) [Civil society exists as a great latent necessity in those who do not even know the term, and its first and most insistent demand is the redistribution of powers]. For him, so-called *sociedad civil* is not so much a fixed relation between signifier and signified, but rather acquires meaning through action. To explain the relations of power that are produced around the phenomenon, Monsiváis resorts to a brief historical overview:

> Durante mucho tiempo, [sociedad civil] sólo significaba la ficción que el Estado tolera, la inexistente o siempre insuficiente autonomía de los gobernados. Luego, reintroducida por teóricos gramscianos, la expresión se restringe al debate académico. Al PRI no le hace falta: tiene ya al pueblo registrado a su nombre. Luego de una etapa de recelo, los empresarios y el Partido Acción Nacional adoptan alborozados a la sociedad civil en su versión de "sectores decentes que representan al país," y la Iglesia ve en ella a otro instrumento para promulgar sus "derechos educativos," la negación frenética del Estado. A la izquierda política el término le parece, por su heterodoxia ideológica, . . . creíble y sospechoso. (78–79)

> For a long time, [civil society] only meant the fiction that the State tolerates, the nonexistent or always insufficient autonomy of the governed population. Later, reintroduced by Gramscian theorists, the expression is limited to academic debate. The PRI does not miss it: it already has the people registered in its name. After an initial period of mistrust, the businessmen and the National Action Party enthusiastically adopt civil society in their version of "decent sectors that represent the country," and the Church sees in it another instrument for promoting their "educational rights," the frantic denial of the

State. For the political left, the term seems . . . [both] credible and suspicious because of its ideological heterodoxy.

For Monsiváis it will be fundamental, then, to sever the phenomenon from any possible co-optation by traditional social actors. To do this, he begins his definition from the negative: *sociedad civil* is not any of the previous assumptions. Following his reading of an *acción épica,* which operates its affective movement within the everyday sphere and transforms the public space, the first thing that his gaze highlights is the heterogeneity of the *sociedad civil* now, in the aftermath of the earthquakes:

La sucesión de catástrofes deja oír las voces populares, un acontecimiento inusitado. Estamos frente a colectividades cuyo repertorio magnífico de hablas y experiencias, se ha ido construyendo en los intersticios de la industria cultural, al margen de los poderes y, desdichadamente, al margen casi siempre de la lectura. Detrás de una sociedad inerte y convencional, ni tradicionalista ni moderna, se descubrió la dinámica de grupos y sectores, combinados desigualmente, la mayoría de ellos suspendidos en sus manifestaciones críticas y creativas por las censuras del autoritarismo. (80)

The succession of catastrophes allows popular voices to be heard, an unusual occurrence. We find ourselves before collectivities whose magnificent repertoire of words and experiences has been being formed in the interstices of the culture industry, away from the powers, and, unfortunately, almost always left out of the reading. Behind a conventional and inert society, neither traditionalist nor modern, was found the dynamics of groups and sectors, combined unequally, most of whose critical, creative manifestations were squelched by the censorship of authoritarianism.

In this sense, I do not believe that Monsiváis thought that Mexican *sociedad civil* was born out of 1985, but, rather, that it was transformed. This was a context in which a myriad of different voices took the public space. This diversity becomes unmanageable for conventional models of representation because they do not respond to the assumptions made about a "people" or a "mass." Added to the unrepresentability, the factor of surprise disarms possible strategies of contention by traditional actors. It is in the unrepresentable and sudden aspects of the phenomenon that Monsiváis locates the potentiality for social change created by this emergent movement; that is, a restructuring of the social space based on diverse inclusions and no longer on exclusions in the name of the homogeneity of the fictitious national "we." It is the start of a heterogeneous, optimistic/hopeful "we."

VOICES IN MOVEMENT FROM THE SOUTH AND THE COMMOTION OF THE "I"

Between 1994 and 2003, Monsiváis contributed chronicles and essays to all five of the volumes published under the title *EZLN: Documentos y comunicados*. In the last volume, when talking about the specificities of the EZLN (Ejército Zapatista de Liberación Nacional) as a *movimiento*, he also delves into *movimiento* as a phenomenon that needs to lie at the center of any political imagination proposing a revolutionized social space:

> La estrategia ética del movimiento . . . quizás admita esta descripción: se reivindican la potencia y la razón de ser de *las causas perdidas,* la primera de ellas los derechos indígenas. . . . No sólo se libra la batalla política sino también, y básicamente, se afirma la acreditación moral de los movimientos al margen de sus derrotas o victorias parciales. . . . Por primera vez en muchísimo tiempo, se fomenta la mentalidad a mediano y largo plazo de que carece históricamente la izquierda latinoamericana. (*EZLN* V, 20)

> The ethical strategy of the movement . . . could perhaps be described thus: The potential and the purpose of *lost causes*—the main one being indigenous rights—are vindicated. . . . Not only is the political battle joined, but also, basically, the moral standing of the movements is asserted as distinct from their losses or partial victories. . . . For the first time in a very long time, a medium-term and long-term mentality, which the Latin American left has historically been lacking, is promoted.

A *movimiento* is, above all, an ethical proposal that embraces a commitment in the present with what has not been achieved yet. Partial victories or defeats are also embraced as part of a present that, while in movement, keeps opening possibilities that could perhaps continue the same or begin another *movimiento* in the future.

For Monsiváis in 1994, what the EZLN propels toward national and international visibility is the emergence of indigenous subjectivities, declaring independence from indigenist paternalism: "El avance [del EZLN] desbarata el sentido tradicional del indigenismo: proteger a esos 'menores de edad' ciudadanos, los 'seres frágiles' por antonomasia" (*EZLN* III, 462) [The advance (of the EZLN) confuses the traditional meaning of indigenism: to protect those "minor" citizens, the "fragile beings" par excellence]. By the fifth volume, the emergence continues to move: "Por vez primera, una mujer indígena le habla al Congreso de la Unión" (*EZLN* V, 16) [For the first time, an indigenous woman speaks to the Congress of the Union]. Therefore, throughout those years, Monsiváis's intellectual gaze identified a movement that goes beyond the indigenous denominator to underline a much more complex diversity.

For the political imagination in Monsiváis's writing, then, the potentiality of the 1985 civil society has come to be an "osadía inconcebible" [inconceivable audacity]:

> A principios de año [1994], cuando el EZ le dio sitio principalísimo en su discurso a la sociedad civil, ésta, en el campo de la izquierda y el centro izquierda, era un amasijo de buenas intenciones y grandes recuerdos (los días del terremoto, el 88, las pequeñas y grandes conquistas). . . .
> Al delirio totalizador se opone, mayoritariamente, el deseo genuino de paz y democracia, y la novedad: ya se filtran los planteamientos de las minorías culturales y sexuales, las perspectivas feministas y homosexuales, hace todavía diez años una osadía inconcebible. (*EZLN* I, 315–16)

> At the beginning of the year [1994], when the Zapatistas gave absolute priority to civil society in their discourse, this civil society was, on the left and the center left, a hodgepodge of good intentions and great memories (the days of the earthquake, 1988, the small and large conquests). . . .
> The majority of the opposition to the totalizing delusion is the genuine desire for peace and democracy, and novelty: the ideas of the cultural and sexual minorities, feminist and homosexual perspectives, spread an inconceivable audacity just ten years ago.

The concept of *sociedad civil,* although it continues to appear constantly throughout these five volumes, is again diluted in Monsiváis's conceptualization. When all is said and done, the *osadía inconcebible* feeds on "fervor comunitario" [community fervor] which can overcome the hopelessness that electoral results continue to instill (*EZLN* II, 469). Throughout his descriptions, Monsiváis refers to this fervor as something "emotivo" [emotional] and "inclusivo" [inclusive], "en la medida en que el deseo afirmativo es parte de un esfuerzo individual y colectivo de participar en los asuntos de todos" (472) [to the extent that affirmative desire is part of an individual and collective effort to participate in the affairs of everyone]. It is, in short, the courage to appropriate the public space to reconfigure it based on debates that include the unhappy bodies that were never on board with the neoliberal nation's promise of happiness.

This is why an important detail to note in Monsiváis's work, at the turn of the century, is how his intellectual discourse begins to set aside the term *sociedad civil* to experiment more with the term *diversidad* [diversity], which is how he denominates the collective agent of the *osadía inconcebible*. And I believe that we cannot understand Monsiváis's notion of diversity without taking into account his approach to the topics of gender and sexuality, which are the focus of the posthumous anthology of essays *Que se abra esa puerta: Crónicas y ensayos sobre la diversidad sexual* (2010). This is how he conceptualizes diversity in relation to Latin America:

> En América Latina la diversidad, término que es ya un muy vasto espacio social, convoca muchísimas causas antes incompatibles. Si *lo gay* se describe en lo básico como la emergencia de la minoría más relegada, y si *lo queer* es un término aún desconocido, la diversidad permite movilizaciones más vigorosas y persuasivas, lo que también sucede con las minorías indígenas, las religiones no católicas, y las tesis y luchas legales y sociales del feminismo. (290)

> In Latin America, diversity, a term that is already a very vast social space, covers so many causes that were previously incompatible. While *gay* is described at its most basic level as the emergence of the most marginalized, and *queer* is still an unknown term, diversity allows more vigorous, persuasive mobilizations, which also occurs with the indigenous minorities, the non-Catholic religions, and feminism's legal and social theories and struggles.

It seems to me that, in speaking of *diversidad,* Monsiváis manages to better conceptualize an emergent movement that in the long run breaks down the presumed homogeneity of the nation, since it is linked to identities that have fought to become visible within the national imaginary. Moreover, these decades of Monsiváis's writing about movements anchored on class, racial, gender, and sexuality demands brings about a diverse "we" that in turn pushes against what is understood by the national "we."

For example, returning to the five volumes of *EZLN: Documentos y comunicados,* in talking about the 2001 Zapatista march, his intellectual gaze focuses on how that diversity has opened the way, how it has appropriated the sacrosanct symbols of the nation and given them a new meaning:

El manejo y la reapropiación de los símbolos [nacionales] se oponen al gran ghetto de la marginalidad étnica, y los indígenas, como nunca antes, se apropian como por vez primera, o con emoción inaugural, de la Bandera, el Himno Nacional, los bastones de mando, las ceremonias que ahora no resultan "folclóricas" sino expresión orgánica de las comunidades. (*EZLN* V, 24)

The management and the reappropriation of [national] symbols stand in opposition to the great ghetto of ethnic marginality, and the indigenous people, like never before, for the first time, or with an initial emotion, appropriate the Flag, the National Anthem, the scepters, the ceremonies that are no longer seen as "folkloric" but rather as an organic expression of the communities.

The meaning of *nation* is broadened, and, thus, for Monsiváis, the cry of this emergent and in-movement diversity, "¡Ya basta!" [Enough already!], serves to take away the signifier *nation* from the very few who have wanted to keep it through exclusions: "No dejarse es incluirse [en la nación]" (*EZLN* V, 37) [To not give up is to be included (in the nation)]. Considered from the emergence of the cry *¡Ya basta!*, then, the "national we" should be read and learned a different way.

It is quite interesting to note how in Monsiváis's production during the first decade of the twenty-first century, irony provides him with an initial opening to become emotional and allows him to open his discourse into other possibilities. It is an emotional state that varies in its comfort level with irony; and, in this sense, the intellectual voice is "highly skeptical and yet also hopeful" about the Zapatistas (Jörgensen, 2004, 90). For example, when he begins to report his experience with the EZLN in 1994, he says, "La ironía no se acomoda aquí en Aguascalientes" (*EZLN* I, 322) [Irony does not fit here in Aguascalientes]. But later, in the same text, he tries again to fit it in, and this time he achieves it through an indirect route, through an analysis of the intellectual discourse of *Subcomandante* Marcos that would also seem to be addressing his own. In the following quote, there is also a profound reflection on what it means to be a media intellectual who tries to build affective ties with a malleable diversity even as he feels the need to maintain the always-critical gaze of irony:

El militante de hierro necesita flexibilizarse, el redactor ocasional se vuelve escritor, el dirigente poblado de opiniones aisladas se ve obligado el día entero a integrar panoramas, el sarcástico por naturaleza profesionaliza su modo de abordar la realidad. . . . Al estilo de Marcos lo marca no la cursilería

. . . sino el afán de conciliar la diversidad de intereses profundos . . . busca remediar con ironía su falta de cinismo. (455–57)

The iron-willed activist needs to become flexible, the temporary editor becomes a writer, the manager full of isolated opinions is obliged to spend the whole day integrating viewpoints, the natural sarcastic person turns their approach to the world into a career. . . . Marcos's style is not marked by flamboyance . . . but by the desire to reconcile the diversity of deep interests . . . he seeks to remedy his lack of cynicism through irony.

The year 1985 had opened in Monsiváis's work the dual belief, in line with that quote from Fitzgerald, that there is no fixing things, but that we must insist on changing them. I think that over the course of a decade of writing about racial and sexual diversity, his cruel optimism becomes radically focused on what the potential of an emergence in constant movement has done to his intellectual gaze and writing. He has been moved, and he is not afraid to express it and to even formulate it as part of his analysis of the phenomenon he is witnessing. For example, he sometimes wonders, "¿Por qué conmueve o, para ser más específicos, por qué me conmueve la marcha del EZLN?" (*EZLN* III, 468) [Why is the Zapatista march so moving, or to be more specific, why does it move me?]. At other times, he gives himself over to emotion without trying to subdue it with reasons, although he might attribute it to a protagonist impulse he always shies away from in his chronicles: "Me conmuevo sin poder evitarlo, y no intento razonar mi emoción porque me enfrascaría en un simposio unipersonal" (*EZLN* V, 30) [I am moved without being able to help myself, and I do not try to rationalize my emotion, because I would bury myself in a one-man symposium]. But there is a moment in his narration of the Zapatista march of 1997 when he gives himself over to a reflection that enlightens us as to the meaning of emotion in his intellectual discourse:

Si vale el testimonio personal, en pocas ocasiones me ha importado tanto una marcha. . . . Lo de hoy es singular porque mundos por entero distintos se descubren y se integran. Luego sabré del azoro y el desbordamiento de los zapatistas, incrédulos ante la recepción y el Zócalo colmado; por lo pronto certifico lo inigualable de la vivencia utópica. . . . Admito el pasmo ante esta aparición de pobreza rural, indescifrable según mis códigos. . . . Es en verdad insólito atestiguar lo que en nosotros casi siempre repercute como expresión en el vacío: la *verdad nacional*. Esta marcha es genuina y en tiempos de globalización expresa en un país globalizado y postnacionalista, cuánto, inesperadamente, sobrevive de la lucha social y el repudio al racismo. (*EZLN* III, 469)

If personal testimony is worth anything, very seldom has a march been so important to me. . . . Today's is unique because completely different worlds have discovered each other and become integrated. Later I will learn of the excitement and frenzy of the incredulous Zapatistas in the face of their reception and the overflowing Zócalo; for now I can verify the incomparability of the utopic experience. . . . I admit to astonishment before this appearance of rural poverty, unfathomable by my codes. . . . It is truly incredible to witness what almost always strikes us as an empty expression: *national truth.* This march is genuine and in [these] times of globalization it expresses how much of the social struggle and the repudiation of racism unexpectedly survives in this globalized, postnationalist country.

The urban diversity, protagonist of his chronicles, matches the march of another diversity, that of the indigenous south. What this discourse decodes between emotion and shock is the commotion of the enunciating "I." And this commotion is unforgivable for critics like José Aguilar Rivera, who in 2001 reacted to Monsiváis's texts about the EZLN by denouncing his sentimentalism, which was impairing his rational judgement (9–13). By then, though, Monsiváis was already comfortable in the uncomfortable affective locus of cruel optimism. From this locus, he imagined a national "we" integrated by a diversity of unhappy bodies.

THE POLITICAL IMAGINATION OF A DIVERSE AND UNHAPPY "WE"

Around the years when he finished publishing his collaboration on the volumes about the Zapatistas, Monsiváis's book *"No sin nosotros": Los días del terremoto 1985–2005* appeared. This new project begins with the essay "Después del terremoto: de algunas transformaciones en la vida nacional" and follows with the reproduction of the chronicle "Los días del terremoto." I consider that the reproduction of this chronicle seeks to maintain a sense of immediacy and urgency, as it was felt and represented in 1985. By 2005, however, the editorial gesture would seem to point us not only toward the social space with which the literary discourse interacts but also to the materiality of the work itself. It could be said that there is an intention to bear the memory of these events and, furthermore, of the representation that took charge of announcing them—the chronicle as such. In this sense, I feel that the chronicle "Los días del terremoto" also becomes a starting point for this line of production in Monsiváis's work. It would seem to indicate that the writing of this text in 1985 signified for him a different understanding in his intellectual-literary vision.

In this section, I analyze in detail the part of the essay called "Después del terremoto" to show how Monsiváis utilizes his two preferred genres (essay and urban chronicle) and how he explicitly links the social phenomena that have occupied him for twenty years: the popular movements of the 1980s, the Zapatistas' advance during the 1990s, and the explosion of sexual diversity in the public sphere. I believe this link that he established becomes even more emphatic towards the end of the essay, where he repeats something he had already said in the last volume of *EZLN: Documentos y comunicados*: "La retórica de inspiración indígena, ese *nosotros* que tantos textos y discursos impregna, pocas veces con buenos resultados, acude a la circularidad de las frases que van y vienen, se fijan, se apartan por instantes del ritmo elegido y retornan" (58) [The rhetoric of indigenous inspiration, that *we* that permeates so many texts and discourses, seldom with good results, resorts to the circularity of phrases that come and go, that are set, that are excluded for a while from the chosen pace and return]. I would like to propose, then, that this essay is not only a summary or a repetition of this intellectual's thinking, but, even more compellingly, it traces and embraces the structures of feeling encompassed by the movements that have guided Monsiváis's political imagination.

In remembering the events of 1985 and pondering what survives from that experience, the essayist highlights the actions that redefined public space in close relation to everyday materiality:

> Invocados, los cientos de miles de voluntarios integran simultáneamente una visión premonitoria de la sociedad equitativa y su primera configuración práctica. Sin andamiaje teórico, lo que surge en los días del terremoto desprende su concepción ideológica de lo ya conocido, de lo que no sabía que se sabía, de las intuiciones como formas de resistencia, del agotamiento de las asambleas, de las vivencias del dolor y, muy especialmente, de lo inconfiable que resulta el depender de las autoridades. (11)

> Invoked, the hundreds of thousands of volunteers constitute a portentous vision of an equitable society, and, simultaneously, its first practical configuration. Without a theoretical framework, what arises in the days of the earthquake separates the ideological conception of what is already known

from what they didn't know they knew, about feelings as forms of resistance, about the exhaustion of the assemblies, about the experiences of pain, and, most especially, about the lack of trust that results from depending on the authorities.

It is in this crisis of the everyday domain that the knowledge of experience—what was *ya conocido* or *lo que no sabía que se sabía*—is sharpened. This puts us, then, in the territory of structures of feeling, particularly when Monsiváis talks about *intuiciones como formas de resistencia* and of *vivencias*. Going back to the anecdote that opened this chapter, this is the something that emerged in 1985.

As Williams says, experience is "meanings and values as they are actively lived and felt, and the relations between these and formal or systematic beliefs" (132). In the quote in Monsiváis's essay, the precariousness of the materiality of daily life generates meanings and values that are lived and felt actively in such a way as to create a widespread break with the systematized belief that the state—that is, the PRI, which controls the state—will be responsible for its constituents. But, above all, for Monsiváis the *intuiciones* and *vivencias* of the urban bodies will mark a political reconfiguration that finally recognizes the diversity of the city: "Su credo es sencillo: la vanguardia del cambio no es ya el proletariado, el fantasma que en vano recorre los manuales marxistas, sino los movimientos" (12) [Their creed is simple: the vanguard of the change is no longer the proletariat, that phantom that runs in vain through Marxist manuals, but the movements]. MUPs will multiply in beginnings and endings, as well as in organizing and reorganizing, which will both evoke and continue a constant movement, and, again, diversity becomes what sustains that continuity.

In this essay, he returns to 1968, too; and, as with the events of 1985, he dedicated a book of chronicles and a commemorative essay to it: *El 68: La tradición de la resistencia* (2008). Nevertheless, it is worth taking the time to analyze the relationship he established between 1968 and 1985, because it also guides us toward a distinction between the two events. This distinction is essential for understanding not only the historical reporting in this essay, but also the logic of constant movement in his thinking:

En 1968 se reinicia la batalla por el espacio público, y una consecuencia es la matanza del 2 de octubre. En 1985, por cortesía de la Naturaleza, luego del terremoto del 19 de septiembre, se trastorna por unas semanas el uso del espacio público. De manera espontánea, cientos de miles de capitalinos ejercen funciones (entre ellas el tráfico) en los ámbitos antes sólo a disposición del régimen. A lo largo de unos días, se construye algo semejante al gobierno paralelo o, mejor, similar al de una comunidad imaginaria (la Nación, la Ciudad), antes no concretada por carecer de presencia en los medios electrónicos. (30)

In 1968 the battle for public space begins anew, and one consequence is the massacre of October 2. In 1985, after the September 19 earthquake, the use of public space is disrupted for several weeks, courtesy of Mother Nature. Spontaneously, hundreds of thousands of people living in the capital perform functions (including directing traffic) that had previously been exclusively in the hands of the regime. For several days, something similar to a parallel government—or better yet, something similar to an imaginary community (the Nation, the City)—is constructed, something never before achieved for lack of a presence in electronic media.

A social history of almost twenty years stretches between those two tragedies, 1968–85. Monsiváis refers to it through a synthesis of social movements that take place simultaneously or follow one another closely. Included among these are the MUPs, feminist movements, ecclesiastical communities, and rural and working-class urban environmentalism (16–29). Taking into account the historical narrative that Monsiváis offers about these social movements throughout the decade of the 1970s, it could be said that, in his discourse, while 1968 emerged in intellectual memory because it was centered on the students' protagonism in the university context, the expanded, inclusive protagonism of 1985 was made possible by a continual action in the public space on the part of the sectors most marginalized in terms of social opportunities. That is, 1968 dynamized an action based on the knowledge of other possibilities in the social sphere. Later, in the proliferation of constant, democratizing movements, and thanks to the catalytic agent of the 1985 earthquakes, a greater quantity and diversity of people could take charge of the public space from the 1980s onward.

In his story about the decade of the 1990s and the early years of the twenty-first century, Monsiváis again focuses on the movements and their actions in the public space; in particular, on those that have to do with identities that diversify and transform what is understood as the nation. More radically than in prior decades, in the 1990s, that diversity explodes and proliferates. As in previous publications, in this essay not only do the differences between minorities diversify a society but they guarantee the democratization of the public sphere:

Una sociedad democrática propicia la diferencia, no simplemente la tolera. Más allá de su calidad de opinión divergente en la serie de prácticas y puntos de vista muy compartidos, la diferencia debe representar una opinión sistemática. Una minoría articulada, opuesta a los puntos de vista consensados, no sólo ayuda a evaluar el estado de los derechos humanos en cualquier comunidad, sino también determina las posibilidades de cambio de una sociedad. (48)

A democratic society fosters difference, it does not merely tolerate it. Beyond its quality of diverging opinions in the series of practices and very commonly shared points of view, difference should represent a systematic opinion. An articulate minority opposed to consensual viewpoints not only helps to evaluate the state of human rights in any community, but also determines the possibilities for change in a society.

Thus, I think it is also less than a coincidence that in 2000 Monsiváis's study of Salvador Novo's work takes as its subtitle "Lo marginal en el centro," the same phrase used as the title for the prologue of *Entrada libre*. There is a very significant repetition in this intellectual work to auscultate the moments in which unhappy bodies open the doors of national social space.

If diversity is the potentiality that opens possibilities for democratizing social space and transforming the nation, Monsiváis once again finds in the Zapatista armies the conglomeration of points needed to strengthen the projection of power that social, racial, and sexual difference has. Above all, in this new essay in 2005—two years after the publication of the last volume of *EZLN: Documentos y comunicados*—Monsiváis sees the Zapatista movement as the potentiality of a diversified left that delights in its diversification. This is shown mostly in his intellectual discourse, after commenting on the Zapatistas' support for the Gay and Lesbian Pride March in 1999, when he says: "Por vez primera un sector de la izquierda mexicana adopta una actitud . . . de inclusión orgánica de la diferencia a nombre del más excluido de los sectores: el indígena" (47) [For the first time a sector of the Mexican left adopts an attitude . . . of organic inclusion of difference in the name of the most excluded sector: the indigenous people]. In addition, the appearance of the Zapatistas in this essay denotes some structures of feeling that are nourished by and expand the experiences in activism forged around daily life, the same activism that burst upon the scene in 1985: "Este giro de lo político [el causado por el EZLN] se acentúa en la vida cotidiana. . . . Grupos de vecinos . . . desean proteger la naturaleza, la armonía urbana, la economía de los desprotegidos, los derechos de las mujeres y de las minorías. Chiapas es un incentivo de primer orden" (40) [This turn toward the political (caused by the Zapatistas) is accentuated in daily life. . . . Groups of neighbors . . . want to protect nature, urban harmony, the economy of unprotected people, the rights of women and minorities. Chiapas is a first-class incentive]. From Chiapas, a left integrated by diverse minorities collectively demands *No sin nosotros* [Not without us], a motto that gives the title to the book in which Monsiváis establishes a historical report about various movements; each one different, and yet at the same time similar in the continuity of one after the other: "'No sin nosotros' podría ser la consigna generalizada, en la nación que, en lo relativo a la equidad, siempre se ha caracterizado por incluir a casi todos en la exclusión" (50) ["Not without us" could be the widespread slogan for a nation that, with respect to equity, has always been characterized by including almost everyone in being excluded]. Thus, this reappropriation of the inclusive pronoun names the continual emergence of excluded unhappy bodies. "We" now becomes the pronoun that puts *lo marginal en el centro.*

I return now to one of those quotes that move from publication to publication in Monsiváis's work: "La retórica de inspiración indígena, ese *nosotros* que tantos textos y discursos impregna, pocas veces con buenos resultados, acude a la circularidad de las frases que van y vienen, se fijan, se apartan por instantes del ritmo elegido y retornan" (58) [The rhetoric of indigenous inspiration, that *we* that permeates so many texts and discourses, seldom with good results, resorts to the circularity of phrases that come and go, that are set, that are excluded for a while from the chosen pace and return]. It seems to me that, besides a claim for public space, the rhythm that returns to the intellectual's discourse is the demand made for a fully representative national state, whose collectivities are not affiliated through a fixed identity but rather intersubjectively and, moreover, through ideologies that are not afraid of the affective realm.

This is how the final event with which Monsiváis closes his essay should be understood. He tells of the Marcha del Silencio, organized by the movement against stripping the Partido de la Revolución Democrática candidate, Manuel López Obrador, of his immunity from prosecution. Although he recognizes the candidate's limitations with regard to his run for presidency and takes a critical view of organizing around a political leader, for Monsiváis this is one more example of an emerging "we" that is affective, inclusive, and diverse in subjectivities:

La multitud se aloja en cada persona y en la certeza de *lo histórico* del encuentro, y *lo histórico* se localiza con celeridad: nunca se habían reunido tantos en un acto político, nunca tantos habían querido imprimirle un contenido ético a su presencia, nunca antes tantos habían sido tantísimos, con lo reiterativo de la expresión. (60)

The multitudes are housed in each person and in the certainty of the *historicity* of the encounter, and the *historicity* is rapidly located: never had so many wanted to imprint an ethical content on their presence, never before had so many been so very many, with the reiterative power of the expression.

The certainty of historicity in Monsiváis is shown through the presence of that *tantos tantísimos*. Studying this work, it becomes clear that it is a "we" linked by resistance and the desire to have an impact on the social space and to make it inclusive of multitudes; that is, to make it "ours." It is, furthermore, the eternal return of a public intellectual to his work, as he had defined it, of capturing the *emergence*, the something, *la épica a la vuelta de la esquina*.

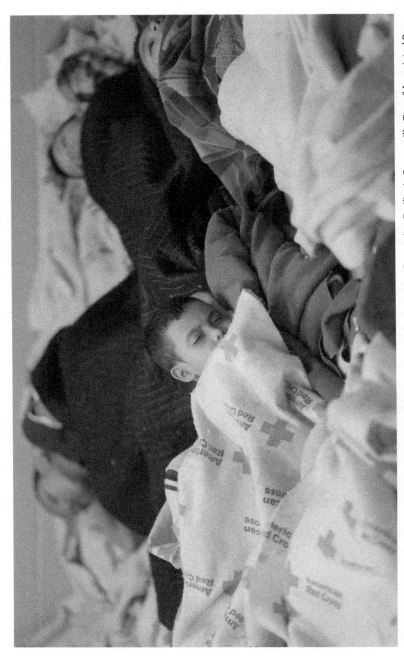

FIGURE 1. "Detainees Sleep in a Holding Cell at a U.S. Customs and Border Protection Procession Facility in Brownsville, Texas." Associated Press photo/Eric Gay.

CHAPTER 2

For the Believers

Francisco Goldman's Moro Hybrid Place as a Bridge for the Agents of Hope

IN JUNE 2014, a photograph of Central American children sleeping on the floor of a detention center in Brownsville, Texas, covered by American Red Cross blankets, appeared in several major news outlets in the United States and abroad. The photograph, taken by Eric Gay, soon gained traction on social media, as well.[1] For a brief moment, this image generated an intense focus on displaced Central Americans crossing the border to the United States from Mexico, interrupting a public debate on then-President Barack Obama's comprehensive immigration reform, which had been stuck in the House of Representatives and which mostly advocated for tougher measures against undocumented immigration.[2] Even though undocumented immigration had been discussed repeatedly by government officials and the mainstream media during the Obama administration, the actual people who were at the heart of the discussion—displaced people—had been mostly invisible. "We" only knew about "them" as an unidentifiable, homogeneous mass of drug traffickers, cartel or gang members, and all sort of other kinds of criminals that

---

1. Among the news outlets that published the photo were *PBS NewsHour* (Tobia), *The Washington Post* (Kollipara), *Al Jazeera America* ("Photos: Inside a Detention Center for Migrant Children"), and *The Telegraph* (Allen and Sherwell), which reported that the photo was shared one thousand times across different social media platforms.

2. For details on the reform, the debate, and the president's executive order, see "Comprehensive Immigration Reform."

"we" needed to fear and hate. Even "sympathetic" media told us that various gangs exploited migrants and extended their influence into "our" territory.[3] It becomes easier to talk about people, and to create legislation concerning those people, when they are scary, hateful, faceless, and nameless: "them."

As Ahmed explains, while fear "opens up past histories of association," which in turn dictates relationships between bodies in the present (2015, 63), hate "generates its object as a defence against [future] injury" (42). Because "we" cannot identify just one body to fear and hate, these emotions "circulate in an economic sense, working to differentiate some others from other others, a differentiation that is never 'over,' as it awaits others who have not yet arrived" (47). The free circulation of fear and hate increases the value of such emotions to the point where violence against any of these suspicious bodies becomes a patriotic act. As violence, in turn, serves to further amplify fear and hate, bodies withdraw from social space and from each other, and, more specifically, these emotions work "to restrict some bodies through the movement or expansion of others" (69). Writing about this topic in February 2017, I am witnessing an escalation of these two forces. As white supremacist discourses are on the rise in all forms of government, even documented travel becomes a peril for brown and black faces or people with thickly accented English. Fearful and hateful bodies are now immersed in, and shrunken by, "our" and "their" fear.

Nevertheless, Gay's photo put an unexpectedly innocent face on the ones "we" did not care to see, and all of the sudden, "we" were forced to take a look. Hate and fear dissipated for a brief moment, and compassion led to a different kind of discourse. After all, these were small, vulnerable children forced to sleep on the floor, protected in a very limited way by the Red Cross. Emma Lazarus's poem "The New Colossus," engraved on a plaque mounted inside the Statue of Liberty's pedestal, began once again to be quoted everywhere, and "we" had to remember that "we" are possessors and gatekeepers of the land of the free. The narrative of the American dream was repeated by some Central American immigrants when interviewed by mainstream media. "Coming here [to the United States] was like having hope that you will come out alive," a mother who was traveling with her child told reporters (Reuters). Most of the children migrated alone—unaccompanied by family members. "We" were moved by "their" hope and wanted to see and know more in order to hope with "them." And so, "we" took action.

---

3. ABC News's "In El Salvador, the Murder Capital of the World, Gang Violence Becomes a Way of Life" is a 2016 example of a sensational look into the operations of Salvadoran gangs throughout the region, in Mexico, and even the United States.

Other photos by Gay precisely showed "us" doing more. U.S. Customs and Border Protection (CBP) officials appeared smiling gently while distributing food and water among the children. The scenes in Gay's photos are reminiscent of natural disasters, where entire families ("real" American families) are often photographed sleeping together in overcrowded shelters or receiving aid from government officials. The debate then turned toward the cause of this presumably unique kind of migration, and it was apparently easy to identify. Criminal organizations and incompetent governments were responsible for this displacement of children. "They" were causing this crisis, and according to nongovernmental organizations: "This is becoming less like an immigrant issue and more like a refugee issue. This really is a forced migration. This is not kids choosing voluntarily to leave" (Wendy Young, Executive Director of the nonprofit organization Kids in Need of Defense, qtd. in Gordon). And yet, how many will be too many? How many more immigrants should "we" offer to hope for? Who else should "we" present with "our" promise of happiness? "We" must keep vigilant; and, under "our" watchful eye, "they" will become hypervisible.

Soon enough, "we" began to read and repeat words associated with natural disasters in describing thousands of Central American children reaching the U.S. border: *flood, tide,* and *surge* are a few examples. It is no wonder, then, that the media coined the phrase *child migrant surge* to name the massive displacement of unaccompanied children that started to attract attention in 2012. The term is even mentioned in a *Wikipedia* article about the phenomenon ("2014 American Immigration Crisis"). Meanwhile, the White House insisted to the American public that the federal government was doing everything possible to "stem the tide" (Simendinger). Therefore, what "we" had perceived at the beginning as a scenario where displaced children were the victims of a natural disaster became one in which a clearer "they" (the children) were the true catastrophe. After all, these children seemed to have come out of nowhere and without a clear explanation. They were, thus, unpredictable, untraceable, indomitable, and therefore scary and deserving of hate. These children looked innocent, but they reminded "us" of teenage or adult migrants, who are constantly associated with dangerous gangs and welfare programs. Just like that, the unaccompanied minors lost any visible trace of childhood.

The arrival of the unaccompanied Central American children at the U.S.-Mexico border was a key moment in an ongoing discussion about migration, its causes and consequences, and its representation within a nationalist discourse in geographies, such as the United States, that still operate like empires, politically and economically (Grandin, 196–222). When examining today's inflammatory, anti-immigration discourse, Thomas Nail compares it with the historical narrative about the Goths, who, seeking refuge from the Huns, invaded the Roman Empire. In both instances, the figure of the migrant was viewed as the promise of a catastrophe, and thus, migrants were barbarians, that is, unable "to speak the *language* . . . [and] to use the *reason* of the political center" while exhibiting "an excessive geographic *mobility* in relation to the political center" (Nail, 2015, 192). In his comparison, Nail focuses more on the causes and effects that create migrants than on the significance of describing the United States as an empire. Migration is one of the consequences of economic, political, and military imperialism, and the Central American history of civil war, poverty, and corruption are "bound to U.S. imperial history" (Arias and Milian, 136). Even though Nail cites economic imperialism as one of the causes of migration, he mostly focuses on the dynamics of transnational capital and on internal (national) struggles between the center and the periphery in the migrants' countries of origin. The United States as a political entity (a national state with a history of military interventions and invasions) seems to be a passive agent that, for Nail, has to only focus on the consequences of migration and how to accurately incorporate migrants into the political center (of the empire). If not, there could be repercussions: "The Goths destroyed Rome because of its imperialism and exploitation. If the U.S. is not careful, history may repeat itself," Nail writes (2014). In his article, Nail concludes by warning of a possible catastrophe at the hands of mistreated migrants, but, in his book, the author seems to celebrate migration as "the true motive force of social history" (2015, 7). Migration is thus seen as the catalyst for either the destruction or the regeneration of the empire, and once again "we" are in charge of policing, protecting, and integrating the "other" into "our" safe center.

In the case of unaccompanied minors, they were even further "othered": called Other Than Mexicans (OTMs) by U.S. federal agencies because they were not from Mexico and, therefore, possessed unidentifiable migrant identities (Arias, 2013, 11). This invisibility corresponds with a lack of knowledge in the United States about the geography that lies south of the Rio Grande and, specifically, about that isthmus that joins the Hemispheric Americas, forming one continuous continent. Under U.S. imperialism, this land was marked as *terra nostra* during the first half of the twentieth century, and it was also necessary to imagine Central America "as non-existent as a culture" (Arias, 2013, 12). It is from this emptiness of meaning that the United States imagines its relationship with the region, its culture, and its people. It is also from this emptiness that the U.S. imagination forges what is thought to be the ideal rhetoric to dissuade other possible OTMs from initiating their movement toward the North. "We" can hope with "you" for a future that will not entail any change or action in "our" present.

The CBP's Danger Awareness Campaign, for example, presents a two-faced narrative, preserving an imagination that defines the United States as both compassionate and belligerent, a combination that pleases the empire's political center. According to the Obama administration's *The White House* blog, this CBP campaign was "an aggressive Spanish language outreach effort and an urgent call to action to community groups . . . to save and protect the lives of migrant children attempting to cross the southwest border" (Kerlikowske). *Aggressive, save,* and *protect* are words that usually go hand in hand with CBP's policing of the border; and, yet, here these words are mixed in with others like *outreach* and *community.* Suddenly, CBP seemed to be saving and protecting immigrant communities and their children. The campaign served as a warning against the dangers of the migration route. Is this trip, however, more dangerous than the political and economic situation in the three countries where most of the migrant children come from: Honduras, Guatemala, and El Salvador? While nonprofit organizations and mainstream media repeatedly say that poverty, government corruption, and criminal activity are the main factors driving the displacement of thousands of Central American people, CBP's television, radio, and print media campaign tells potential migrants to stay put and to work hard to obtain a better future at home. For example, in the video ads, entitled "Sombras" and "La carta," young men talk about their dreams of earning higher salaries in the United States (U.S. CBP, *Defense Video and Imagery Distribution System*). In the first ad, the shadow of a *coyote* [migrant smuggler] talking to a prospective migrant morphs into a wolf; in the second one, one of the young men is shown dead in the desert in the final scene. Both ads conclude by explaining that it is false that immigrants can easily obtain legal status, and they urge parents to protect "our children" from the dangers of the journey and to encourage them to study and work hard in their home countries. While fear is tainting "our" hope, "we" funnel the American dream into the emptiness that is Central America.

GOLDMAN'S MORO HYBRID PLACE FOR A TRANSCONTINENTAL COMMUNITY

What kind of discourse could break through the empire's political center? Who would be its audience? How could this discourse bring visibility to displaced people while also taking into account the complex differences between their communities of origin and their identities? Moreover, how would this discourse have to change throughout decades of Central American displacement? What other emotions could be embedded in this rhetoric to compete with fear and hate?

I want to focus on Francisco Goldman's intellectual discourse and its ability to move back and forth across space and time, addressing, alternately, Central American and U.S. audiences. When talking about Goldman's literature, critics have defined it as transnational (Rodríguez, 2013, 243–44; Irizarry, 1–3; Templeton, 271), transamerican (Vigil, 190–93), and diasporic (Rodríguez, 2013, 27). Some critics have read his literary production within the Latinx tradition (Vigil, 190–93; Caminero-Santangelo, 173–74), while others have put it into dialogue with the Guatemalan canon (Yanes Gómez, 637–41; Zimmerman, 652). Speaking of one of Goldman's novels, *The Long Night of White Chickens* (1992), Arturo Arias has incisively argued that the most remarkable characteristic in this literature is its biculturalism and, specifically, the ability to move between two different histories and sensibilities (Guatemala and the United States) and toward a conflictive political relation (1997, 633–35). For her part, Ana Patricia Rodríguez has examined the chronicle *The Art of Political Murder: Who Killed the Bishop?* (2008) as the product of a transnational migrant imaginary (2013, 41). It can be said that Goldman's agility in writing for readers across the region is due both to his physical mobility—he has traveled extensively—and to his cultural identity, as Goldman is of Jewish-American and Guatemalan heritage. Born in the United States, he grew up between Guatemala and the United States.

In my analysis of his essays and investigative journalism, I want to push further Arias's and Rodríguez's arguments by explaining in detail how Goldman's intellectual movement (between geographies and identities) entails a mobile locus of enunciation that deftly navigates both U.S. and Central American history, politics, and culture. More specifically, I argue that, throughout more than three decades, Goldman has functioned as a kind of cultural translator between U.S. and Central American readerships of the left and center as well as alternative and mainstream media. Much like Monsiváis in Mexico, Goldman is an intellectual who has taken advantage of every possible opportunity to ask hard questions and document even harder realities in the U.S. imperialist relationship with Central America. As my analysis demonstrates, the goal of his narrative movement, mediation, and translation is to forge an actively hopeful community of readers who can understand the nuances of everyday life in Central America, the complex lives of its migrants, the region's problematic political relationship with the United States, and the importance of the isthmus for the political imagination of one single *América*.

Recalling his time spent living and writing in Madrid, Spain, in an autobiographical essay, "*Moro* Like Me," Goldman reflects on how he was constantly discriminated against because he was mistaken for a Moro, a pejorative word used in Spain for Moorish people, Arabs, and Muslims. While Central Americans in the United States have been branded as OTMs and have become the "other" of the "other," in Spain, all Moros—that is, subjects who deviate from a standardized conception of the Western European—are lumped together in the European imagination of a Moroccan identity, which is elusive and broad. In Goldman's reflection on inhabiting two similar positions of "otherness"—Moro and OTM—, he articulates a resistance that dwells precisely on the possibility of a constant displacement between identities (American, Jewish, Guatemalan, and Moro). After all, there is no better survival tactic than to become "a shifting target," which "makes it easier to evade direct hits" (54). Constant displacement between identities also impacts Goldman's writing, which envisions a powerful heaven that he calls a "hybrid place":

In American letters it is something of an old truism that a writer needs his *place*—a postage stamp on earth—that he can call his own. And I used to joke that if that was so, the place most naturally my own was Miami International Airport: Jews flying down from the north, Latin Americans up from the south, and there intermingling. . . . Central America [has] become a part of me . . . joining it to *my* history, as I'd lived there and here in the United States, and in that hybrid of both places at once that can only exist in [the] imagination [I created] *a place.* And maybe that purely literary "place" is my one true place; my imagination's permanent address, where my true progenitors would be novels from the two separate though not unrelated literary traditions [from Latin America and the United States] that have most shaped my particular tastes and ambitions. (66)

From his imagined hybrid place, Goldman's writing intimately addresses two separate, though intrinsically connected, traditions and their readerships, in the United States and in Latin America. As he has conceived of it, Goldman's hybrid place operates within Mignolo's border thinking (discussed in the introduction). Goldman's work strives to tell stories that collect and commemorate fragments of experiences from a region that has lived under war and violence for centuries. His writing style aims to make these stories, their languages, and their wisdom resonate in the U.S. imaginary. Specifically, his use of Spanish words in English-language texts are not mere stylistic ornaments; they present unique concepts that the writer explains at length. Even in his shortest pieces, Goldman makes sure that his U.S. audience can see and

hear Central America through his descriptions of everyday life as he tours cities and talks to their inhabitants. At times, it seems that his voice serves as a
guide or a teacher for those who are venturing for the first time into Central
American topics, as he works to build a bridge between unknown references
and more familiar allusions for U.S. readers. To this end, Goldman often refers
to and quotes U.S. writers, politicians, or journalists who have traveled to, or
lived in, Central America. In his detailed descriptions of the historical context, he includes examinations of key moments and figures that may be more
recognizable to his U.S. readers.

Therefore, Goldman's discourse performs "cultural translation," that is, a
constant negotiation between contexts and identities. Much in keeping with
Mignolo's ideas, Homi Bhabha has argued that cultural translation facilitates
"opening out, remaking the boundaries" (313). For Bhabha, reshaping boundaries impacts temporality, too, because "an interstitial future . . . emerges
in-between the claims of the past and the needs of the present" (313). In my
analysis of three decades of Goldman's journalism and essays, I find that his
imagination of a future is not only interstitial but also contingent on past and
present. Goldman's hybrid place does not imagine a final resolution; and in
this sense, I coincide with Kirsten Silva Gruesz, when she explains that the
kind of historicism that we find in the author's literary discourse is prophetic
or messianic, that is, always looking into a future that is yet to come (79–80).
However, I believe that it is important to notice that the imagined future is
malleable (constantly changing) and depends on a hopeful transcontinental
community. This means that *hope* here, like in Monsiváis's case, acquires a
very different meaning than the religious kind of hope without politics. After
all, a text that moves between languages, readers, and contexts is one that
works in the present to serve an engaged, heterogeneous community. As in
Monsiváis's, in Goldman's discourse, too, to hope is to be involved in restless
action in the opening that the present offers "us," to alter "our" relations with
others and to social space. It is precisely at that opening where Goldman's
writing resides, and this is why his voice is able to connect—through translation—to a transcontinental audience. Specifically, Goldman's imagined audience actively debates Central America's sociopolitical situation and the key
role played by the United States.

Therefore, I want to further examine Goldman's work through the lens of
Bhabha's ideas on translation as blasphemy. In his analysis of Salman Rushdie's *The Satanic Verses* and the controversy that it roused in some sectors of
Islamism, Bhabha detects the act of blasphemy in the performance and not
in the content of Rushdie's text. At the same time, this kind of blasphemy
is an act of cultural translation, "repeating and reinscribing [the Koran] in

the locale of the novel of postwar cultural migrations and diasporas" (324). If "to blaspheme is to dream" a dream "of translation as 'survival,'" that is, "the migrant's dream of survival" (324), we can read Goldman's texts as multiple blasphemies. His texts are cultural translations of the Central American reality, performed by a hybrid intellectual for a foreign (U.S.) audience. Moreover, some of Goldman's cultural translations become reenacted by Central American agents, who read, translate, and distribute the texts in the region, in Spanish. At the end of this process, those who read the texts in Spanish seem to be reading through a double blasphemy about their own circumstances.

In the following sections, I read a selection of Goldman's journalism from the 1980s and 1990s as a way to understand the making of this particular intellectual locus of enunciation. My analysis of these short pieces will guide me, then, into examining *The Art of Political Murder*, which has not been studied in relation to the author's previous journalist publications. The book continues to practice a kind of discourse that disarticulates a persisting narrative in the U.S. mainstream media and government discourse, which stresses an artificial distance between "their" conflicts and "our" exceptional land. Goldman's narratives about very particular local experiences identify the intrinsic socioeconomic relationship between the U.S. and the Central American oligarchies, at the center of which lies the vulnerable body of the politically persecuted, assassinated, and exiled. In Goldman's writing, this vulnerable group takes on a variety of names, faces, stories, and languages, as well as a complexity of emotions that aim to break through the invisibility-hypervisibility combination that engenders hate and fear.

READERS OF RESISTANCE IN EVERYDAY LIFE

Against the backdrop of the 1980s Cold War, Central America became a focus of international media. Although times had changed, the triumph of the Sandinista Revolution in Nicaragua (1979) drew the same kind of frantic attention to Central America that the Cuban Revolution (1959) had attracted to the Caribbean twenty years earlier (Chomsky, 59–116). Nevertheless, Central America had played a key role in U.S. international politics since the nineteenth century, even if at times it had been a quiet one (Grandin, 11–51). The Panama Canal alone required various U.S. military interventions, first, during the construction of the railroad that preceded the canal, and later, during Panama's struggle for independence from Colombia, in order to maintain complete control over canal infrastructure (Maurer and Yu, 1–12). By the 1950s, the whole region was controlled by U.S.-backed dictatorships or pseudodemocratic regimes, and by the 1980s, Central America was undergoing another decade of civil wars in which the CIA played a leading role (Chomsky, viii–xii; Scott and Marshall, 1–50). As Goldman often wrote in his essays, the U.S. media did not pay attention to this long and complex history and its inherent relationship with the U.S. political and economic interests in the region. Often in the U.S. media discourse, it seemed as if violence and war were caused by some sort of spontaneous outburst or cultural forces unique to Central America (James, 5–9).

In contrast to U.S. mainstream media, during the 1980s, Goldman's journalism presented a perspective on the region's conflicts that was developed through his ongoing conversations with Central American journalists and other "insiders" (friends, people he met at restaurants and bars, hosts that invited him to coffee or lunch at their homes, among others). At this point, Goldman was mostly writing for *Harper's Magazine,* a journal that, since its founding (1850), has relied on commissioned and in-depth journalism about national and international political issues, in addition to publishing many of the most recognizable literary voices in the United States (Manning). *Harper's* has been recognized as a journal that includes perspectives that go against the consensus, and this has caused some public controversies for the publication, such as when it published Seymour Hersh's coverage and analysis of the My Lai Massacre by U.S. forces in Vietnam (1970), or more recently, editor Lewis H. Lapham's reporting on the 2004 Republican National Convention. One of the oldest journals in the United States, *Harper's* has survived thanks to its highly educated subscribers, who tend to identify politically with the center-left and the left ("Demographic Highlights"). Although it has never been a widely circulated journal and its audience has been limited to a mostly privileged circle, *Harper's* many awards have granted its contributors visibility in literary and political circles. Therefore, Goldman's articles in the 1980s were addressing *Harper's* readers, among them prominent literary figures, journalists, and politicians who could potentially influence public opinion in the United States. Goldman wanted to present them with a deeply knowledgeable perspective on Central America, stories of how its conflicts transformed everyday life, narrated by local journalists and residents. It seems that the fundamental question that drove Goldman's journalism during this violent decade was: How do people in Central American countries—especially Honduras, El Salvador, and Nicaragua—make sense of (think, discuss, debate) their lives within this context of civil war?

In "The Children's Hour: Sandinista Kids Fight Contras and Boredom" (1984), Goldman focuses on the depiction of Nicaraguan youth during the Sandinista-Contra war. It was young people who ensured the triumph of the

Sandinista revolution, and it was even younger people (seventy-five percent of the Nicaraguan population at the time) who were either keeping it alive or criticizing it (69). Reporting from the base of the Sandinista Popular Army's Battalion of the Reserves 77-95 (the *Bon,* as it was known to its five hundred soldiers), Goldman's journalism conveys the Sandinistas' idealism, youthfulness, and joy—which grounded the "revolution of *chavales*"—through its portrait of young military men[4] having fun:

> Even relatively solemn state ceremonies would begin with Sandinista *coman-dantes,* ex-guerrilla fighters, most of them still in their thirties, sitting on a podium doing a strange patty-cake movement, clapping their hands and slapping their thighs faster and faster, ending in goofy smiles. (69)

Nevertheless, fun had to coexist with waiting: waiting to be called into action, waiting for the next battle, and waiting for war. It was during this waiting that boredom gave way to anxiety, provoked by the knowledge or the ignorance of what that battle might imply for them. Goldman depicts the waiting and the feelings it entailed through his conversations and tours of the city of Managua with Aldo, a battalion leader of twenty-three years of age, who has had some experience in the battlefield. The young leader remembers "not without nostalgia" the beginnings of the Popular Army, when many wanted to keep fighting the guerrilla war, with long hair, beards, and without military hierarchies (71). "Chaos," however, yielded to order in an army where nervousness reigned, either because of the memory of war ("A plane would fly over and the *compas* would be jumping out of the windows") or the men's inexperience ("A few of these people will probably run away . . . the first time we come under fire"; 71). Aldo's testimony about young military men's feelings punctuates Goldman's narration of his time in Managua, where civilian young people share similar emotions, even if they have different political opinions about the revolution.

Goldman's readers learn that Managua's youth are separated into two camps, the *chicos plásticos* and the *vagos,* according to the insults each group hurls at the other. While the *chicos plásticos* watch soap operas, read romance novels, and spend their time at the mall and American fast-food restaurants, the *vagos* participate in the Sandinista militias or, at least, openly support the revolution. But even if Aldo and other soldiers refused to enter a McDonald's because it was filled with *chicos plásticos* who will surely exclude and insult them for wearing military uniforms, Goldman's interview with a seventeen-

---

4. Although the Sandinistas' Army included women among its ranks, this battalion comprised men, exclusively.

year-old *chica plástica* reveals that she and her group of friends are trying to cope with fear and boredom, too: "People are afraid that tomorrow there will be an invasion, and who knows if they will die? So we live the day. Everybody goes to the beaches and the discos" or they die of boredom in front of the television (72). Through Goldman's article, readers can understand how war has influenced and is still affecting young people's daily lives, and yet, readers also learn that life goes on in Nicaragua, with social conflicts that express themselves as they do in the United States, through consumer preferences. This is a perspective that no other U.S. journalist offered at the time, and in fact, toward the end of the article, Goldman critiques the mainstream media through the voice of Aldo, whose comments are reported in indirect speech:

> Aldo said his brother had told him that Nicaragua was portrayed in the U.S. press as a place synonymous with war and violence. Aldo complained about the capitalist press, about its unwillingness to accept Nicaragua's contradictions and the revolution's widespread support. He argued that to do so would go against the press's own interests. (74)

This ventriloquism underscores Goldman's desire for *Harper's* readers to think of Nicaragua as a complex environment, where the United States and its media also play a role. Moreover, it is a call for his readers to openly engage in criticism of U.S. international policy during the Ronald Reagan era.

This ventriloquism is also the beginning of a long reflection about the ethics of journalism that Goldman will sustain through decades of writing. A few years after this article about Nicaragua, he published "Lost in Another Honduras: Of Bordellos and Bad Scenes," a piece on the role of Honduras in the Sandinista-Contra armed conflict, where he expressly distinguishes himself from the rest of the U.S. journalists working in the country. International reporters in Honduras swing between hotel restaurants and bars to talk to high-level officials, both domestic and foreign—strategically positioned sources who can give journalists tips so they can publish the next breakthrough story about the Sandinista-Contra war. Even if officially they may refer to Tegucigalpa as "the Saigon of Central America" (50), Goldman writes about the nickname they have picked for the city: "'Tegoosy,' [the American reporters] like to call it, as if naming a cartoon character. Tegoosy, the poor little goose that just got dragged along" (52). Tegucigalpa, and the rest of Honduras, only becomes important for the U.S. press because of its geographical position in Central America, a region that, in turn, owes its significance to its geopolitical value for the U.S. international agenda during the Cold War. In this sense, instead of offering an independent perspective to the U.S. public, these reporters' journalism seemed to evoke U.S. Assistant Secretary of State Elliott Abrams's words, quoted at the beginning of Goldman's article: "It ends with creating not another Cuba [in Central America] but another Costa Rica, El Salvador, or Guatemala, or Honduras" (49). All of the Central American countries are mere repetitions of a model implemented by the United States. Honduras, at the end of the list, seems to be a vacuum to be filled with military occupations or interventions by the Contras' army, right-wing Cubans and Israelis, U.S. military forces and the CIA, the Salvadoran military forces and the Salvadoran guerrillas, and the Sandinistas, as Goldman reports.

For Goldman, ethical journalism should take an interest in the place where the news is happening: "Whenever I've written about Central America, I've tried to describe how the lives of ordinary people intersect with, and are affected by, the larger political issues that people get so worked up over in Washington" (52). It is then that he becomes a cultural translator, someone who operates between two different kinds of knowledge: "The Honduras that matters in Washington seemed to have very little to do with the Honduras that I was seeing" (52). His border thinking articulates an informed discourse that can work against the U.S. imperial view of Honduras, thanks to the intimate contact Goldman establishes with Hondurans who document what the U.S. mainstream media has no interest in showing to their audience. Goldman finds the Marbella, "a hangout for Honduran reporters" where he also encounters "politicians, government clerks, lawyers," a series of organic intellectuals who discuss openly and loudly "the Honduras that matters to *them*" (53). While foreign journalists have all the privileged information from the Honduran military (the real power in the country), local reporters navigate *their* Honduras to find stories that erode the credibility of those powerful and inaccessible sources.

Goldman professes his admiration for Honduras's strong and independent press, something that cannot be found in other Central American countries, or as it seemed in the 1980s, in the United States, either. He navigates the city with a journalist who is investigating a murder that had been reported as a common criminal act, but that appeared to be related to national and international politics. Goldman discovers that the bordellos near U.S. military bases are where the Honduras that matters to Washington meets the one that matters to the journalists writing for regular Hondurans. Local sex workers who share beds with powerful foreigners hold the secrets to how the Honduran military forces manipulate international politics to gain more power. Although he interviews one of the sex workers and collaborates with his friend on the story about the suspected political murder, Goldman admits, "How the two Honduras[es] were connected was beyond my reach, and would remain there"

(56). While other U.S. journalists may have discarded Tegucigalpa and the rest of Honduras as an unimportant vacuum, Goldman underlines their rich complexity and shares with his readers the little that he was, indeed, able to grasp.

What is then the model for writing and reading about international politics from the United States? Goldman explores this question in "Sad Tales of *la libertad de prensa*: Reading the Newspapers of Central America" (1988), an article that highlights the experience of Central American exiles. Sitting in a Salvadoran restaurant in Brooklyn, New York, Goldman performs and narrates the ritual of many Central American exiles who come to the restaurant to read old issues of their countries' newspapers, "the exile's nostalgia-distended sense of time: a month of Monday newspapers read today as if they are all todays" (57). The urgency to know what is happening in Central America cannot be mitigated by distance or time; as Goldman describes it, political exile is the experience of a continuum that collapses the here and there as well as the past and present. Yet why is the experience of Central American exiles relevant to *Harper's* readers? How can this experience serve as an example for writing and reading about "other" contexts?

In explaining this experience, Goldman plays the role of a teacher who is introducing the reader to the history of Central America and its exiles: "It is here, from my table in the [Salvadoran] restaurant that I will provide for you an introduction to the newspapers of Central America" (57). But in order to read from exile, he offers first a description of the ritual of reading through the detailed observation of someone leafing through a newspaper in the restaurant:

> Our objective isn't to argue or proselytize. We are simply going to read these newspapers in something of the spirit of that splurging Central American exile sitting at the table over there: poring over every page, reading even more attentively than he would at home, collapsing distance in this way and finding his surest footing, without a doubt, "between the lines." He drinks his café con leche, smokes, grimaces, rolls his eyes, looks up in astonishment, and even laughs out loud—a range of laughs, from bitter to hilarious, for it takes many kinds to fully appreciate a Central American newspaper. (57)

The performance of the teacher gives way to another narrative technique: "we" become a community of learners. "We" are reading collectively with "him," the unknown "other," and in doing so, "we" are seeing/reading through his eyes, feeling his astonishment, bitterness, and enjoyment. "We" become a community that shares the experience of reading critically ("between the lines") the articles in Central American newspapers. It is through this communal empathy that "we" can start to understand what is happening to Central Americans in Central America.

As Goldman explains, what "we" encounter in the majority of the Central American newspapers is a simple discourse that echoes the binary propositions of U.S. newspapers: "a voice used by the powerful elite that controls the press to create the illusion that everyone else in the country is in agreement with them . . . except the people who aren't, who are always the enemy and who would be beneath contempt" (61). In these newspapers, the world is divided between a hegemonic "we" and a "they" who is the enemy that wants to destroy "us." In Goldman's discourse, however, there seems to be another kind of coalition or affiliation: if "we"—community of affective learners—read together with this Central American exile, "we" can begin to think about the possibility of other kinds of communal experiences that revolve around open and critical debates, without falling into "ideological obedience or dogmatism . . . or hypocrisy or fear" (62). This is how "we" may appreciate the kind of journalism that goes beyond fear, focusing on people's everyday lives. Alongside Goldman's subjects, "we" are trying to keep our hopes anchored into a present action, which in this case is teaching and learning together.

In the article, Goldman focuses "our" attention on a beautiful piece of journalism about a man in Nicaragua who begins to offer free cars for funeral services, because he has seen how many women and old people are carrying and burying their deceased loved ones, mostly young men who are dying in the Sandinista-Contra war. This story does not exhibit any political inclination (pro- or anti-Sandinista). Rather, it centers on everyday life, which in turn, reminds us of the horror of war and its impact on regular people. Just like in Goldman's journalism, these kinds of local stories about daily life enable readers to grasp a clear sense of macropolitics. Even if there is always something impossible to understand, an untranslatable part of the experience, "we" can learn to read with the "other," inhabit their political exile and their emotions, albeit ephemerally, and form a critically engaged community of readers. "We" can demand more intimate stories like these, more of this kind of journalism.

RELATING TO AGENTS OF HOPE

The 1990s brought another set of challenges for Goldman's discourse. In the context of neoliberalism, which emerged in full force after the end of the Cold War (1989), U.S. international politics experienced a readjustment, and the country's economic interests became key factors driving military interventions. Wars like Desert Storm (1991) and military invasions like the one in

Panama (1989) were prompted by economic interests in the targeted areas (Grandin, 190–95). At the same time, Central American countries that had experienced long civil wars (Nicaragua, El Salvador, and Guatemala) initiated and concluded peace talks. Although there was an official celebration of the return of democracy to the region, national armies still possessed great power and could influence politics (Robinson, 134–73). As the recent military coup in Honduras (2009) showed, civil government is not truly in charge of national affairs in some Central American countries. As I will discuss in the next section's analysis of Goldman's *The Art of Political Murder,* this period was also marked by democratic transitions that provided amnesty to national armies, especially to top commanding officers, and did not call for prosecution of those responsible for crimes against humanity. Nevertheless, Goldman's reporting has continued to denounce past and present political persecutions and crimes. Ever since the 1980s, as Peter Dale Scott and Jonathan Marshall have documented and analyzed, political violence has been mixed up and confused with violence connected to organized crime, at the hands of drug, arms, and human traffickers. In a region where civil wars and political conflicts have lasted more than half a century, it should not come as a surprise that a large part of the population has received some kind of military training and is armed. Several important investigations and court cases have resulted in the exposure of top commanding officers who have been involved in the criminal activities that are currently jeopardizing the region and prompting the massive exile to the United States. The last section of this chapter will address Goldman's coverage of the case of former Guatemalan President Otto Pérez Molina, who served as the director of Military Intelligence during the 1990s and who has been in prison since 2015 for charges related to import and export fraud in Guatemala.

In this section, however, I want to start by analyzing a piece that I believe marks the conclusion of Goldman's period of critiquing the discourse prevalent in mainstream, international media. His journalism would move in a new direction throughout the 1990s. In this article, "What Price Panama?," Goldman questions the sudden absence of Panama and Central America in the U.S. mainstream media at the beginning of the decade. Appearing in *Harper's* in 1990, this piece was published nine months after the United States invaded Panama (December 1989–January 1990) to remove Manuel Noriega from power, in a mission known as Operation Just Cause. As was his style during the 1980s, Goldman focuses on how the political conflict has impacted everyday life, in this case, in the barrio El Chorrillo in Panama City, an impoverished black neighborhood, founded by workers brought from different parts of the Caribbean archipelago to build the Panama Canal (1881–1914). Since the Panama Defense Forces' central headquarters were located in this neighborhood, El Chorrillo was a target of much of the U.S. bombing during the 1989–90 invasion. In the first few paragraphs of his text, Goldman recalls what El Chorrillo looked like on a previous visit, "a teeming, densely populated slum of decaying wooden tenements, their baroquely carved, sagging balconies running in long rows over the narrow streets" (71), and then describes what he finds on this trip: "rubble and ash" (71). A place with a long history of migration, poverty, and violence disappeared in just one night (December 19, 1989), and for Goldman, this physical disappearance at the hands of the U.S. military forces is symptomatic of the discursive one perpetrated by U.S. media against Panama and the whole region:

> Who today in the United States speaks of Panama in the present tense? The country has all but vanished from our major media. Only the wire services maintain bureaus in Panama City, and the stories they produce . . . seldom make the papers. Television news, that world of unmodulated assumptions and fleeting images, no longer focuses its gaze south, toward Central America. All that seems to matter is that the U.S. government has Noriega in a Miami jail cell. (71)

The silence about Panama in U.S. media, in the midst of "the largest American military operation since the Vietnam War" (71), marks a change in the politics of the region as well as in the role that the United States will play. Nevertheless, in Goldman's article, Panama's absence and the change in geopolitics are meticulously analyzed through the particularities of El Chorrillo's history and everyday life in the neighborhood. This is a "vanished neighborhood" that presents itself as a "large emptiness, bulldozed and unpeopled," a kind of phantasmagoria that not only tells us about the recent bombardment but also about a history of poverty, forced labor, militarism, war, and most recently, neoliberalism (72). Goldman notices that El Chorrillo is at the base of the Pacific peninsula that was once called the U.S. Canal Zone, and that some of the old American military installations now function as warehouses for contraband (72). The name of the main avenue crossing El Chorrillo, Avenida de los Mártires, "originally named Fourth of July Avenue by the Americans," expresses at once the history of, resistance to, and violent repercussions of colonialism (72). El Chorrillo, as well as the rest of the Pacific peninsula's neighborhoods, was the base for U.S. military and commercial operations in the Americas; and it was precisely there that in 1964 anti-American riots erupted and were met by a military backlash that left so many dead that the avenue was given a new name, Avenida de los Mártires. As the taxi driver who brings Goldman to the area explains, El Chorrillo had been transformed into an area where violence and poverty were part of everyday life for its inhabitants (72). Goldman's narrative, however, examines the neighborhood through the lens of colonialism and militarism. Even though fifteen thousand of El Chorrillo's former residents are homeless after the bombing, we learn that the reconstruction process is led by "private speculators" who "were planning to turn the land into an oceanfront *barrio de lujo,* a rich person's neighborhood" (73). From military to economic colonialism, the war is just a symptom of the neoliberal space of catastrophe that emerges in El Chorrillo by the late 1980s. Within this space of catastrophe, the disappearance of such an important yet poor neighborhood due to U.S. military and colonial advances in the Hemispheric Americas is a metaphor for U.S. media silence about Panama and Central America since 1989. The Pacific peninsula and the Panama Canal Zone would eventually fade away from a geopolitical landscape that increasingly turned its attention to the Middle East.

By focusing on the survivors, however, Goldman brings their mourning to the attention of *Harper's* readers. As he walks through El Chorrillo, people come and show him empty lots where buildings used to be, where their families and friends used to live, and where many have lost their lives (75–78). Goldman's writing tries to reproduce their frantic voices, how they speak over each other, shouting names, describing horrific sounds of war, and telling stories of war crimes: "The people who ran [from U.S. soldiers] were shot down! Shot down as they ran!" (75). As they mourn the demise of El Chorrillo and its people, Goldman mourns the damage inflicted on Panama and Central America: Operation Just Cause becomes "Operación Injusta Causa" in his writing (73). He condemns U.S. intervention in the area by quoting data about casualties from independent organizations, such as the Catholic Church and Americas Watch, and pointing out violations of the Geneva Convention (72).

"What Price Panama?" is the last piece in which Goldman's discourse would focus primarily on correcting, contradicting, and providing an alternative to the traditional U.S. media coverage of Central America. In the following years, he will go on to write for other outlets—with wider circulation than *Harper's*—and he will pursue new ways to continue fostering empathy and communion between U.S. readers and Central Americans. Specifically, by the mid-1990s, the *New York Times* (*NYT*) started publishing some of Goldman's pieces about Guatemala, just when the country and much of the Central American region were undergoing problematic democratic transitions and launching new electoral systems under the close watch of international entities. With its prestige and wide circulation (Winter and Eyal, 379), the *NYT* offered Goldman a platform where he could reach a bigger audience than at

Harper's. Nevertheless, because it is part of an elite press, the *NYT* reinforces the prevalent political ideology and even influences political and economic outcomes (Islam, 1–13). Even though he continued to discuss CIA interventionism in Central American countries, Goldman adjusted his discourse to his new platform by omitting criticism of U.S. media's coverage of, and the U.S. government's role in, the region. Therefore, the two pieces published in 1995 and 1996 in the *NYT* that I analyze in this section sharply contrast with the ones appearing in *Harper's* during the 1980s and even with "What Price Panama?," published just five years before.

For example, Goldman's "In a Terrorized Country" seemed to want to remind the *NYT*'s readers that Guatemala is still struggling with the effects of a bloody Cold War that was fought in Central America. However, it was published in 1995, after a Democrat finally entered the White House after twelve years of Republican control, and when politics seemed to be in a celebratory mode of post–left/right paradigm, so this piece is cautious in how it sends out that reminder. Rather than focusing on U.S. interventionist politics in the area, Goldman's discourse emphasizes a history of oppression within Guatemalan society. This is a country where a small group has controlled the military and has been terrorizing a majority of indigenous people for five hundred years: "True, Guatemala's modern political situation is the full-blown result of the CIA-sponsored coup of 1954. . . . But the country's problems are rooted in a 500-year legacy of abuse of power and racism toward an impoverished Mayan majority" (A17). Goldman then delves into an in-depth historical analysis that traces political and economic networks between oligarchies—and their military forces—in Central America.

This discursive shift in Goldman's writing during the 1990s leads to another important change: he focuses more on his characters' agency. Goldman portrays the vast region of Central America in a nuanced manner, adding dimension to local issues, and he depicts sympathetic characters who are resisting authority, people with whom a U.S. audience could empathize and even identify. We can see this new emphasis on agency in "In a Terrorized Country," where, after detailing different cases of political intimidation, disappearance, torture, and assassination, Goldman concludes that the ones who are still fighting against the military's impunity are women, and specifically, "poor women, . . . the throngs of Indian women who'd made the journey from the mountains, all of them stopping traffic and clanging pots and pans as if to wake the dead" (A17). It is with these women that Guatemalan and U.S. women professionals form an alliance when they, too, try to find answers after their loved ones were murdered by the Guatemalan military forces. Goldman introduces us to U.S. lawyer Jennifer Harbury, whose husband was murdered, and Rosario Godoy, a Guatemalan leader of a human rights organization, who was tortured and murdered alongside her brother and son. By describing these cases, Goldman's discourse establishes proximity between the *NYT* audience and the victims; "they" are like "us": women, professionals, even Americans. More important, poor and indigenous Guatemalan women are able to acquire a kind of visibility that presents them as complex and relatable subjects with whom American women who read the *NYT* can establish a connection based on gender, due to their position as female agents of resistance against local systems of patriarchal oppression. These are not helpless victims that "we" need to save. Rather, "we" need to support these women who are fighting a battle against terror all by themselves. After all, this terrorized country, Guatemala, is not that far from "us," and this is "our" fight, too. In a context where U.S. international and domestic politics were starting to shift from the Cold War's left/right paradigm toward a focus on terrorism and the figure of the terrorist, Goldman's piece seeks to draw attention to state terrorism, a threat (to Guatemala, Central America, and the United States) that has been created by systemic racism and social injustice.

This is why "we," the ones who are terrorized, cannot proceed with a peace agreement that will involve a complete amnesty for the terrorists. Because of this reason, a year later, Goldman published another *NYT* piece, "In Guatemala, All Is Forgotten," to voice his anger at the process of reconciliation in Guatemala. The Law of National Reconciliation signifies a promise of happiness for the whole country. War has come to an end, and disappearances, tortures, and murders have stopped; "we" can now forgive and forget and start living in a reconciled country. In Guatemala, like in Central America and throughout the continent, the end of the Cold War also meant the elimination of military regimes. As I have discussed, this transition to democracy coincided with a new socioeconomic system: neoliberalism. Therefore, reconciliation, democracy, and neoliberalism guaranteed a promise of happiness for those corners of the world that had been drowning in deadly left/right battles. But what Goldman asks in this piece is: Who will be able to obtain this happiness? And of course: Who will be the unhappy bodies or the killers of joy? The answer to the latter is clear: "Guatemala's majority Maya population," which was "the principal victim of war" (A15).

Goldman alludes to other countries that have undergone similar reconciliation processes (El Salvador and South Africa), where peace usually requires that the guerrillas surrender their arms. This process also usually entails some kind of justice, even if only low- or middle-ranking officials end up paying for crimes against humanity. Nevertheless, as he informs us, in Guatemala, there would not be an opportunity to prosecute criminals. Victims could be named and crimes could be revealed, but the state would not dig into the past and pursue justice in the courts. Therefore, instead of arms, it seems that what guerrilla leaders surrendered, "after a fruitless and horrifying war, is the truth" (A15). This also implies an abandonment, or erasure, of the people who suffered the most at the hands of both sides:

> The army has often been accused of having waged a campaign of genocide against [the Maya population]. But the Indians were used as fodder by guerrillas as well, by their European-blooded and mestizo comandantes. . . . The guerrilla commanders and the army's officers had come to resemble each other. (A15)

This resemblance is a sign of the end of the left/right paradigm, and the incorporation of powerful people (from what used to be "both sides") into the new socioeconomic system, neoliberalism. The promise of happiness will only come for the ones who make the ultimate decision to surrender their arms and forget their victims. For Goldman, this is not cause for celebration, and he directs his anger toward leaders and figures of the left beyond Guatemala: "The Mexico City press has published the glittering list of luminaries—writers, actors, politicians, even Fidel Castro—who are expected to attend as honored guests" (A15). These luminaries are also harvesting the neoliberal promise of happiness, in which the killers of joy—indigenous peoples and peasants—will be forced to migrate for another kind of promise—safety and security in *el Norte*—that will never be fulfilled either.

"FOR THE BELIEVERS," "WE" AMONG "THEM"

In *The Art of Political Murder: Who Killed the Bishop?*, Goldman's decades of reporting on Central America are woven together into a single book. Even though Goldman's focus is Guatemala, and specifically the murder of Bishop Juan Gerardi Conedera, he also examines the Central American context more generally and the ongoing phenomenon of exile. Moreover, we can read *The Art of Political Murder* as a reflection on Goldman's intimate relationship with Central America; his writing is a way to mitigate the pain that he feels maintaining this fraught relationship with the region. After all, this book is the product of more than fifteen years of research and writing by Goldman, in English and in Spanish, about this particular case. Others have participated in shaping his narrative, too; unbeknownst to him at the time, Goldman's work was used in political "pamphlets" that "may have affected the outcome of [2007 Guatemalan] presidential election," according to some, in parts in the interior of the country (367). In this sense, not only does the book's discourse clearly underscore the hybrid place from which the intellectual voice constantly performs cultural translation but, by becoming an itinerant text, *The Art of Political Murder* is also a product that reshapes the borders of geography and knowledge.

Nevertheless, why is Gerardi's case at the center of such a nomadic text? Why does this case evoke a Guatemalan, Central American, and U.S. political history replete with many other nameless victims? At the same time, how does this case permit the intellectual discourse to imprint fearful indigenous and exiled bodies with hope? That is, how does Goldman's writing use Gerardi's case to tell a wider story about the ones excluded from the happiness promised by the Law of Reconciliation and neoliberalism?

Gerardi was a nationally and internationally recognized advocate of human rights. His work documenting, denouncing, and protecting human rights in Guatemala had earned him powerful enemies since the 1960s. As a newly appointed bishop in Verapaz (1967), he "encouraged his priests to learn Q'eqchi'" in order to offer masses in the language spoken by the Mayan majority (Goldman, 2008, 12). The beginning of his career coincided with a reformation of the Roman Catholic Church and, more importantly, with liberation theology in Latin America, which advocated and fought for social justice (11–12). A detail that Goldman points out in describing Gerardi's life and work is that the bishop had already survived an assassination attempt in 1980, the year that El Salvador's Archbishop Óscar Romero was assassinated (12–13). Goldman's account of Gerardi's life gives us a historical perspective about the Central American region and also about a war that has not ended yet, that is rooted in, and continues because of, racial and socioeconomic inequalities. This is an idea that he first develops in an article about the bishop published in *The New Yorker* (1999), a sort of preview of the book, which would not be published for nearly another decade:

> I had come to think of Bishop Gerardi's murder as Guatemala's last great nineteenth-century crime. . . . It had propelled the country's two most influential institutions, the Army and the Church, into their bitterest confrontation since the 1870s. (1999, 77)

Read by a mostly liberal, educated, and upper-middle-class audience, *The New Yorker* sells primarily in the ten biggest urban areas in the United States (Pew Research Center). For Goldman, this audience was not as wide or heterogeneous as the *NYT*'s, but it was similar to *Harper's*, and, therefore, it was familiar to him. Moreover, as he relates in the book, with *The New Yorker* he could negotiate an economic arrangement for a long-form piece that, while not entirely satisfactory, included a U.S. press credential, something that proved to be valuable during his investigation (2008, 65–66). An abridged Spanish-language version of the piece also appeared in Guatemala's *El Periódico*,[5] and the story was translated and published in its entirety in Mexico's *Letras Libres*.[6] These translations demonstrated that the article in *The New Yorker* had gained traction and there was a demand in Latin America (both in Guatemala and elsewhere) for a more in-depth debate about Gerardi's murder. Its publication in *El Periódico* and *Letras Libres* also ensured that it would be widely read in Spanish and sparked prominent debates about the case and about Guatemala among other journalists and even intellectuals, like Mario Vargas Llosa, to whom I will return toward the end of this section.

In the book, Goldman revisits the historical argument he first developed in *The New Yorker* piece, delving further into an analysis of Guatemalan history and positing that the country went straight from the nineteenth century into the twenty-first, skipping the twentieth. His analysis focuses on rigid social structures that were maintained for two centuries without any significant changes, due to military intimidation and political violence. For Goldman, Gerardi's murder was a vestige of an era that was coming to an end, and this advent of change was prompting powerful agents to try to secure their position in the twenty-first century:

> They [the military men that authored and committed the murder] were the defenders of a willfully walled-off culture rooted in local ideas about privilege, status, and the militarism and anti-Indian policies of the nineteenth

5. Founded in 1996, *El Periódico* was José Rubén Zamora's second newspaper, after he had started and left *Siglo Veintiuno* (1990–96). As we learn in the *NYT* article "4 Win Prizes," before *El Periódico*, Zamora already had a high profile in journalism, thanks to various national and international awards recognizing his efforts to defend press freedom. According to its website's "Preguntas frecuentes," *El Periódico* focuses on investigative journalism, editorials, and articles about arts and culture, all of which appeals to an educated and mostly professional audience that seeks an alternative to Guatemala's mainstream press. This may seem like a small sector of the country's population, but, for a newspaper that devotes less than twenty percent of its content to advertising, *El Periódico* boasts fairly strong circulation numbers.

6. According to its website's "Quiénes somos," *Letras Libres* was founded by Enrique Krauze in 1999 and declared itself the heir of Octavio Paz's *Vuelta*, which shut down after the death of the author. *Letras Libres*'s focus is on political and cultural debates, especially between prominent intellectual voices. It enjoys a higher profile in Mexico and Spain, but the journal is read throughout Latin America, mostly by the well-educated. Moreover, although the magazine is associated with an illustrious right-wing group—Krauze is one of the leading voices of the intellectual right in Mexico—, *Letras Libres* has also published articles that contest the same ideas the journal often defends.

century, which had easily metamorphosed into the cold war militarism and massacres of the twentieth. (142)

Therefore, killing Gerardi was, first of all, a political execution that reminded everyone of the power of those rigid social structures. After all, Gerardi had defied these structures by initiating investigations that challenged the Law of Reconciliation and its provision for amnesty for military men. Gerardi was the founder of the Archdiocese's Office of Human Rights (ODHA), which was in charge of the Interdiocesan Recovery of Historical Memory Project (REMHI) that produced *Guatemala: Never Again!*, a four-volume report about violations of human rights since the 1960s, documenting the identities of more than fifty-two thousand of the estimated two hundred thousand civilians who were killed or forcibly disappeared.

Killing Gerardi was also a symbolic gesture that strengthened the socio-economic position of military men within the new democratic and neoliberal system. If right/left political conflict no longer justified a militarized society, military men needed to foment another kind of war that they could benefit from: drug and human trafficking. Goldman's discourse establishes this connection through three stories: the forced migration during the 1980s civil war, a witness in Gerardi's trial who had to seek political asylum in Mexico, and a prison revolt over the control of trafficking routes. By retelling the child-hood and youth experiences of ODHA's lawyer Mario Domingo, the intellectual voice centers on the 1980s displacement of the Popti people, indigenous inhabitants of the Río Azul Valley, close to the border with Chiapas, Mexico. Civil war and army massacres forced Domingo's family into exile in Mexico, where they lived in "refugee camps and settlements" and where many in their community were rejected at the border or put in jail (336). Two decades later, Guatemalans continued to seek political asylum, and Goldman illustrates this phenomenon through the story of Rubén Chanax, who testified against the military men who had planned and executed Gerardi's assassination. Even though he was under the protection of the UN Refugee Agency, and the prosecutors in the Gerardi case covered his rent in Mexico City, Chanax only found work that paid him "barely enough to live on" (276). The legacy of the human rights crisis in Guatemala continues to have dire consequences for the region and for the United States. Writing about the Gerardi's case against the military men for human rights violations is also, for Goldman, an opportunity to write about how, even in prison, these men were able to control the gangs (like the *maras*, also known as *cholos*) that emerged in Central America and in the exile community in the United States during and after the 1980s wars (281–87). The power held by these former military men led to a crisis in governability, too: "Legal authorities were too frightened of the Limas [father and son that planned and executed Gerardi's assassination] and their allies [inside and outside of prison] . . . to expose their illicit prison activities" (285). By highlighting the ongoing pattern of political exile and forced migration from Guatemala, Goldman makes his readers aware of a space of catastrophe—neoliberalism—in which military forces have been able to find a new purpose. This is the reason why the intellectual voice states: "Everything about the Gerardi case—perhaps even the murder itself—was a continuation of the war by other means. The war wasn't over" (241). As I discussed at the beginning of this chapter, by 2014, the presence of unaccompanied Central American children at the U.S.-Mexican border also underscores that the war is not yet over.

Moreover, the migrant and refugee bodies, imprinted with fear and hate by discourses cultivated in the center of the U.S. empire, come from a context of war, where they were already traumatized by a culture of fear and hopelessness. In *The Art of Political Murder,* memories of fear and sadness emerge when Goldman reflects on his time living and writing in Guatemala in the 1980s. Reading the book as a cultural production that comes into dialogue with other discourses in the Guatemalan context, Ileana Rodríguez has analyzed Goldman's literary resources (hyperbole, metonymy, and anaphora) as a way to represent a "senseless psychotic history that produces phobic states" (91). While Rodríguez follows a theoretical framework anchored in psychoanalysis, I want to examine fear as a cultural emotion that entails specific body politics in social space, that is, from a material perspective.

After recalling an incident where he and another journalist were followed and threatened by armed men on the street, Goldman remembers the fear that prevailed in his everyday life and in everybody else's, too:

> I'll never forget those months. There were incidents in which "they" broke into homes or apartments and horribly mutilated their victims. . . . I rigged up homemade alarms in my grandmother's house [where Goldman was living alone]: glass bottles on chairs beneath every window, an escape rope leading into the patio. I lost about thirty pounds just from nervousness, and developed a tic in my cheek. This time of fear and sadness—but also of unforgettable intensity—stayed inside me like a dormant infection that can sometimes be stirred back to life, even by a glance. (145–46)

Fear cuts through the body and takes up residence there. Fear becomes a very well-known sensation that can be mistaken for a kind of protective shield but that, in reality, cuts off the body's ties to the world.

Almost two decades later, the infection of fear is still festering in Guatemalan society. When he first arrives in Guatemala to research and write about the Gerardi case, Goldman finds almost no one who wants to even talk about the murder. On a Sunday afternoon, walking the streets of Guatemala City's downtown, he goes into an almost empty church, and the fear becomes, once again, unbearable. He merely exchanges glances with an indigenous woman, and her fear "revives" his:

> Her fear ignited, or rather revived, mine, like the disease the Indians call *susto*, a "fright" that you can catch like a cold, fear leaping from someone's glance into your own, a low-grade contamination that felt so familiar that it was just like stepping back into the past, into the Guatemala of the war years and its suffocating atmosphere of paranoia. (69)

By resorting to the specificity of the word *susto* and the cultural explanation that binds it not only to the Spanish language but also to indigenous traditions, Goldman's discourse lets "us" into the communal experience of fear that persists in Guatemala. This communal experience, of course, is imprinted on the bodies that have been exposed to it, the suspicious ones—like the indigenous woman or the "foreign" reporter asking too many questions—who have been terrorized again and again for many years. In this context, fear is understood, exchanged, transmitted, and magnified when these bodies find each other, because they are not supposed to expose themselves in the public sphere and/or to others. They are supposed to shrink and disappear.

Therefore, in this "terrorized country," as Goldman had described Guatemala in previous publications, living fearlessly becomes a tool of resistance. In this sense, *The Art of Political Murder* goes beyond Rodríguez's proposition, a representation of a "senseless psychotic history that produces phobic states." Rather, there is an explicit, and even more urgent, intention to disarticulate the cultural politics of fear. This is why, for example, it was important to talk about Gerardi's bold character and how he chafed against the imposed terror:

> One Sunday afternoon, a few hours before he was bludgeoned to death in the garage of the parish house of the church of San Sebastián, in the old center of Guatemala City, Bishop Juan Gerardi Conedera was drinking Scotch and telling stories at a small gathering in a friend's backyard garden. Bishop Gerardi's stories were famously amusing and sometimes off-color. He had a reputation as a *chistoso*, a joker. . . . Guatemalans admire someone who can tell *chistes*. A good *chiste* is, among other things, a defense against fear, despair, and the loneliness of not daring to speak your mind. In the most

tense, uncomfortable, or frightening circumstances, a Guatemalan always seems to come forward with a *chiste* or two, delivered with an almost formal air, often in a recitative rush of words, the emphasis less in the voice, rarely raised, than in the hand gestures. Even when laughter is forced, it seems like a release. (3)

Daring to laugh and make others laugh—that is, laughing together—becomes a release for fear, despair, and isolation. According to Sigmund Freud, there are certain kinds of jokes that become a source of pleasure because they rely on rediscovering something familiar (1960, 120). Since there is a "close connection between recognizing [the familiar] and remembering [it]," for Freud, when we laugh at these jokes, "the act of remembering is in itself accompanied by a feeling of pleasure" (122). In a "terrorized country," where memories are often associated with painful traumas, making the act of remembrance pleasurable is revolutionary. Also, jokes that refer to the familiar, as analyzed by Freud, enable us to connect our domestic or everyday lives with abstract or "remote" realms of politics (123). Therefore, making jokes and laughing at them is a way of daring to speak up, that is, breaking through a culture of imposed silence. In her argument about the relationship between humor and political activism, Majken Jul Sørensen alerts us to how humorous pockets of resistance "can be attacks in the *discursive guerrilla war* which cannot be easily ignored" (2). In this sense, laughing together becomes a collective tool that opens up time and space within a society, like the Guatemala described by Goldman, where every word, gesture, and movement is being controlled.

This openness, according to Goldman's intellectual discourse, also symbolizes a break with the traditional narrative of Guatemala's history and culture, too:

Guatemalans have long been known for their reserve and secretiveness, even gloominess. "Men remoter than mountains" was how Wallace Stevens put it in a poem, "alien, point-blank, green and actual Guatemala." . . . In 1885, a Nicaraguan political exile and writer, Enrique Guzmán, described the country as a vicious, corrupt police state, filled with so many government informers that "even the drunks are discreet"—an observation that has never ceased to be quoted because it has never, from one ruler or government to the next, stopped seeming true. (3–4)

A small circle of friends telling *chistes* and laughing is evidence of another kind of history, one that starts with this small and quotidian act. Very much in line with what Benjamin explained about the storyteller, in the introduction to his study on jokes, Freud notices that a "new joke acts almost like an event of universal interest; it is passed from one person to another like the news of the latest victory" (1960, 15). This collective retelling of another kind of past also offers hope for a possible alternative future; one in which subsequent generations laugh more and speak louder, finally bringing an end to the culture of silence and fear and the rigid societal hierarchy. Killing Gerardi was also an attempt to kill that possibility.

Nevertheless, in Goldman's writing, Gerardi's political murder is not only significant for people in the "terrorized country." Goldman also seeks to provoke a sense of urgency and outrage from his U.S. audience about the murder. By using, translating, explaining, and historicizing *chiste/chistoso*, Goldman invites the reader to cross over a perceived linguistic and cultural barrier, just like he did with the word *susto*. This invitation is echoed by the reference to Wallace Stevens's poem "Arrival at the Waldorf" (1942), a reference probably familiar to U.S. readers, which Goldman seems to use as a promise that he will help them understand the "alien" Guatemala that so baffled Stevens. He also seems to vow to decipher the silence that so frustrated Enrique Guzmán. These two references—to Stevens and to Guzmán—show U.S. readers that the intellectual voice guiding them into the story of Gerardi's murder knows both worlds very well, "ours" and "theirs," the United States and Guatemala.

Moreover, it is precisely because Gerardi—and others like him who worked for justice in Guatemala—served as a bridge between the country and the rest of the world that Goldman spent a decade researching and writing about the case. While Gerardi publicized his work abroad in order to make progress toward ending the war and bringing the military to account for its crimes, Goldman's writing aims to vindicate Gerardi—whose legacy was tainted by authorities and lawyers who tried to sully his name during the murder investigation—and recognize those who fought to solve the case and prosecute the killers (366). It is in this sense that I think we should interpret Goldman's book, as a celebration of the ones who work every single day for a future yet to come and still unseen. Even in the book's dedication, "*Por los que creyeron*. For the believers," *The Art of Political Murder* seems to be foretelling that all hope—including his own—relies precisely on the actions of those who actively hoped in the past (*creyeron*). Furthermore, Goldman's dedication establishes an arc between their work in the past and his work in the present and, from there, a continuous trajectory of active believing, of having hope, in the future. As I have discussed previously, the performance of this communal and extended action of hoping opens up an interstice where Goldman's discourse reaches out to an imagined transcontinental audience and invites it in while also asking to let "us" (both those plagued with fear and the fearless, hopeful ones) be part of "your" world.

Nevertheless, returning to Lewis's *The Politics of Everybody*, whenever there is a push for "us" to be included in the world, there is a "they" that feels threatened and fights back. While the Gerardi case ended with the imprisonment of a few military men—a victory for many Guatemalans, as it gave them a taste of true justice—, the societal inequities that have historically preserved a racial and economic hierarchy remain unaltered. Furthermore, "their" judicial loss was felt as an affront that needed to be avenged nationally and internationally in order to keep everyone "in place." Goldman understands this intention of keeping everyone in place as a "third stage" of "the art of political murder": it is "a continuation of the murder itself. . . . [And it includes a set of methods] to subvert the courts . . . and also the crucial role of misinformation, especially disseminated through the media, used to discredit opponents and create confusion" (301). "They" also have voices that will emerge from a powerful locus of enunciation and will compete with "us" in our attempts to persuade an audience in the discursive battle.

Goldman's Moro hybrid space will have to compete against European journalists Maite Rico and Bertrand de la Grange, who defended the accused military men in Spanish-language texts published in Mexico and Spain. His Moro hybrid space will also have to face Mario Vargas Llosa's famous name and widely circulated column in Spain's *El País*, which is also reprinted in numerous Latin American newspapers, where the Nobel Prize winner described the accused military men as "innocents" who were sacrificed for the gain of Rubén Chanax (Goldman, 2008, 267–68). Chanax, the witness for the prosecution who had to go into exile in Mexico for his own protection, was a homeless man of indigenous ancestry. It is upon this body, to keep him in place, that Vargas Llosa's discourse will etch disgust and hate. As Goldman recounts, Vargas Llosa focuses on how Chanax had gone "from living on nothing and in the streets to being maintained and protected abroad by the state, . . . [while his actions] throughout this story are supremely suspicious, to say the least" (268). Goldman's story about Chanax's life, developed through interviews with him, reveals a complex character who does not evoke pity or total empathy; after all, this is an ex-military man who had a part in the surveillance and murder of Gerardi. Nevertheless, Chanax's life in exile, where he is languishing in poverty and drowning in fear, complicates Vargas Llosa's description. Furthermore, as I explained before, Goldman's discourse uses the narrative of Chanax's life in exile to trace a historical trend of forced displacement. His narrative follows Chanax's already racialized and impoverished body as it becomes a vulnerable migrant body, yet still refuses to succumb to fear and dares to testify and, furthermore, to live. While Vargas Llosa's discourse tries to move the audience away from Chanax (and the rest of "us," fearless ones) by directing disgust and hate toward the ones who dare to "move up" from their assigned places, Goldman's narrative bestows respect on the vulnerable ones who dare to act and to hope.

IN VULNERABILITY, "WE" STILL RISE

By 2015, seven years after the publication of *The Art of Political Murder,* Guatemalan President Otto Pérez Molina, one of the suspected masterminds behind Gerardi's murder, resigned. Succumbing to weekly protests against corruption in his administration and overwhelming national and international pressure, the corrupt ex-military man and politician surrendered to the authorities. Nevertheless, he still appealed to the "Guatemala *profundo,*" the silent majority of the countryside, asking them to intervene in his defense, which was interpreted by Goldman as "an implicit threat from a former general who famously had been elected President . . . by promising a 'stern hand' as the solution to the country's problem" (2015). The countryside of Guatemala—and across Central America—is home to all the bodies "buried in clandestine graves in the mountains, victims of the military's 'scorched-earth' strategies, and especially of the massacres of rural Mayan communities" (2015). Goldman traces a history that once again takes the reader through decades of crimes against humanity and, this time, establishes an explicit connection between that era, when Pérez Molina was "a young officer [and] commanded a military garrison in Nebaj, in the Ixil region, an area among the hardest hit by the violence," and the present, in which a war criminal could become a corrupt president: "Pérez Molina represented a perfect union of Guatemala's past terrors and its current model of power" (2015). The happiness promised by the peace accords of 1996 never arrived for the victims of the civil war; moreover, the neoliberal space of catastrophe pushed the military toward newly transnational import/export products, the source of the Pérez Molina corruption scandal.

Therefore, the Guatemalan *profundo* that the corrupt president appealed to had already woken up years ago—and not in his favor. By 2008, Goldman had received news that his book was being circulated throughout rural parts of Guatemala. Young people in the countryside had translated parts of the book and "made stacks of photocopies that they passed out to the crowds at the entrance of the cemetery on the Day of the Dead," a reader told Goldman's publisher via e-mail (2008, 367). Goldman further explains that the Guatemalan mainstream media "no longer dominated the countryside" and that people were becoming connected to other sources of information through Internet cafés and thanks to the vast network of "relatives and friends living and working in the United States" (367). Therefore, the Guatemalan countryside had also become emboldened from its place of exile. Moreover, from the refugees' vulnerable position abroad, where they were often subject to exploitation, the Guatemalan *profundo* stood up and fought against fear. In 2015, when Goldman learns about the urban protests calling for Pérez Molina's resignation and prosecution, he realizes that, finally, the Guatemalan countryside has also transformed the conservative and silent nature of the cities. With this epiphany, Goldman joins "the believers" to whom he had dedicated his book, as he says: "I found myself finally believing that Guatemala—though much still remains to be done before we can say that the country has truly changed— really will never be the same again" (2015). And yet, any reader who has followed his work knows that, throughout his years as a journalist in Central America, he was constantly taking action in a transcontinental public sphere: researching, retelling, teaching, and translating. He was bridging imagined communities through his active hoping and, yes, he had always believed.

FIGURE 2. *Monumento a las mujeres víctimas de la dictadura* [Monument to the Female Victims of the Dictatorship] (Santiago, Chile, 2007). Author's photo.

CHAPTER 3

Pedro Lemebel's Queer Intellectual Discourse or *la loca*'s Angry, Enamored, and Melancholic Call

TOURING THE CITY of Santiago in 2007 and 2008, I encountered numerous monuments, memorials, exhibitions, movie posters, and conferences dedicated to discussing and honoring the victims of Pinochet's dictatorship (1973–89).[1] Some of these gestures of memory from the Chilean state, like the *Monumento a las mujeres víctimas de la dictadura* (hereafter, *Monumento*), designed by the architects Emilio Marín and Nicolás Norero, are located in Paseo Los Héroes in downtown Santiago, where monuments tell us about different historical events. As with other official sites, Marín and Norero's project sought to document and acknowledge the disappearance of thousands of people—in this case, women—with some kind of permanent record.

The monuments and memorials are the official question and answer to a sociopolitical conflict, as described by Aldo Rossi, but they also represent cracks in the public space where other interpretations of the events they attempt to signify can be debated (59). They are "archi-textures," as Lefebvre understood them, open bodies that mark the social domain with their presence, but at the same time, they are exposed to the mark of those who use them (1991, 118). In Chile, as in other Latin American countries that have had

---

1. Conservative estimates place the number of disappeared detainees in Chile during the dictatorship at 1,209. For more information, see *Proyecto Desaparecidos: Chile* and the Facebook page of the "Agrupación de Familiares de Detenidos Desaparecidos."

to struggle with their dictatorial pasts and their consequences in the present, architextures have been sites of/for debate. When examining their importance in the context of Uruguay, for example, Hugo Achugar follows Nora's ideas (discussed in chapter 1) and documents that much of the new construction after the transition to democracy are malls that serve as centers that push to the periphery, or even swallow up, the *lieux de mémoire* (Achugar, 221). Similarly to Avelar (discussed in chapter 1), in Achugar's text there is a fear that market logic devours everything, erasing the categories of time and space and replacing memory with constant newness (221). Although, yes, "we" shall never forget, as Susana Draper states, "when addressing postdictatorial geographies, it is important to problematize the 'we' that one is assuming when addressing memory practices" (4). When talking about the politics of memory, or about the events they relate to, nothing comes out clean and clear. After all, there will always be pieces, bodies, that remain lost.

In 1973, the bombing of La Moneda, Chile's presidential house, by Chilean military forces marked perhaps the most outrageous moment of the military coup under Pinochet against President Salvador Allende's government and his party, the Unidad Popular. From this moment on, through the seventeen years of military dictatorship, the Chilean state was crushed and reinvented. Control over the physical aspects of social space—daily life and bodies—, as well as over the public sphere, was demonstrated through the murder, kidnapping, torture, disappearance, and exile of political dissidents; the militarization of public space; control over mass media; the writing of new laws; and the neoliberal economic model, just to name a few examples (Moulian, 229). Nelly Richard calls this historical period *la catástrofe* (1998, 15) [the catastrophe]. Nevertheless, following Lefebvre's ideas, discussed in the introduction, I would say that the dictatorship was a violent transition toward a space of catastrophe.

After the 1989 referendum that paved the way for the return of a democratic government, the state's primarily goal was to whitewash Chile's dictatorial past in order to debut the country as the product of an economic miracle. One of the most iconic symbols of this whitewash was a giant iceberg pulled from the South Pole to become the Chilean pavilion at the 1992 World's Fair in Seville, Spain. As other critics (Richard, 1998, 174–75; Moulian, 34–36) have argued, the iceberg symbolized the new democratic state: raw, pure geography, without a trace of the crimes committed by the dictatorship, and ready for new investments and enterprises. The continuity between dictatorship and democracy, however, is evidenced in the official government policy for military crimes—reconciliation, social amnesia, and consensus—and in the neoliberal economic model imposed by Pinochet and continued by all governments after the transition.

First, new democratic governments had to accept the condition of amnesty imposed by Pinochet and the military. In order to conceal this tacit agreement between the new democracy and the military, the Commission for Truth and Reconciliation was established—with representation from the dictatorship but not from the victims—in order to investigate the excesses of violence between 1973 and 1989. In 1991, the Commission published a document entitled *The Rettig Report,* in which the word *justice* did not appear even once. This document acknowledged the excesses of some military and police members, and, after very quick trials, some of them were sentenced to brief jail time. Newly elected president Patricio Aylwin—but not any military figure—had to offer the only official apology to the families of the victims.

Second, the social domain continued to be dominated by the shadow of the dictatorship in the form of its neoliberal economy and its laws. As Tomás Moulian argues, a new kind of citizenship emerged; the credit-card citizen was controlled by deferred-payment consumption (103). Therefore, if the Chilean dictatorship is a clear example of a space of catastrophe where there was destruction and reappropriation of geography, institutions, and imaginary space, postdictatorship governments made no move to change the inherited social space, as would have been expected by the majority of Chileans who fought for democracy. The space of catastrophe became the Chilean social space.

In terms of the political imagination, after the democratic transition, there was a battle between different tales of memory that competed to appropriate the official historical narrative surrounding the dictatorial past. Three fundamental stories took shape: that of the military ancien régime and the sectors of the extreme right; that of the victims of the dictatorship; and that of the recently elected government of democratic transition. The first was based on a patriotic nationalist discourse: the events that took place had the salvation of Chile as their objective, and, of course, they benefited the country. From this perspective, the military became heroes and were absolved of any attempt at prosecution (Moulian, 33–34). The second sought to open spaces that had been closed by the dictatorship for sustained reflection about what had happened. It took the form of victims' testimonies, art and literary representations, and intellectual discourses on truth, justice, and ethics (Richard, 2000, 10). The third, which became the official history, moved between the other two under the panacea of reconciliation. In turn, the reconciliation formed the myth of consensus. After *The Rettig Report* and the iceberg, the subject of memory was brought to a close by Chilean governments: the dictatorship's horrors had already been remembered and reconciled; now they should be tossed aside in favor of national progress.

Returning to the *Monumento,* a critical examination shows that, if there is no official historical discourse on, and no justice process for, the dictatorships' crimes, monuments become monolithic empty gestures that reflect nothing but silence back to us. Unveiled in 2006, the *Monumento* rises up as a small wall of glass on a metal platform, a design whose intention is to evoke the image of the protests by families that demand from the state truth and justice for their family members who are still classified as disappeared detainees. As architect Marín explains, the project achieves this evocation through a representation of a series of motifs associated with these protests: candles placed on the ground as a spontaneous act of remembrance and posters of the disappeared detainees worn by their family members on their chests (Basulto). Therefore, the monument focuses on the inscription of a struggle fought primarily by women within the public space, where they created ephemeral memorials (like the combination of photos, candles, and flowers) for practicing a continual, repetitive mourning.

According to Freud's definitions in "Mourning and Melancholia," for many in Chile, the work of mourning has become a melancholy that associates the loss of the external "other" with an excision of the self, which, therefore, cannot process the loss—in this case, the disappeared body. In their melancholy, the families of the disappeared ones mark the space with temporary memorials that contain metonymies, a kind of specter of the missing bodies, which serve to suspend the present and return to an imprecise time in the past through an allegorical flash of memory, as Benjamin described in his "Theses on the Philosophy of History" (255). In this way, the improvised memorials serve as an unexpected—even shocking—reminder for other inhabitants of the city of the absentee ones and of an imprecise moment and place that was practiced or intervened by those bodies' everyday life in Santiago.

The potentiality of ephemeral memorials relies on their allegories, which resist the imperative to be fixed in symbols, myths, or absolute meanings. I wonder, then, whether the allegorical call of the ephemeral memorial can be sustained by the permanent nature of the monument that freezes, within its image, the melancholic action of those who take to the public space to remember. On the one hand, both in the proposal of its image and in the materials and design used, the *Monumento* tries to become a site that is open to interpretation about the memory it summons. In this sense, it does not dictate a set story about an event, but, rather, it represents a break in the apparently stable discourse present in the rest of the monuments in Paseo Los Héroes. On the other hand, although it seeks to question that fixed historical story represented by the rest of the monuments, the placement of the *Monumento* remains dislocated from the rest of the urban network; that is, very far from the central Plaza Valdivia and in a secondary location within the Paseo itself. Also, the lack of an official action—justice—that could support the gesture this monument carries makes of this *lieu de mémoire* an empty place, a void.

This is evidenced by the graffiti it carried in 2007, indicators that the daily life of the city maintains an active interaction with the *Monumento*, but also that this interaction has no relation to the discussion about the women who were victims of the dictatorship, the families who keep fighting for truth and justice, or the memory debate in Chile. I suspect the best way to read it is captured in the words exclaimed by the person using the monument when I took photos of the site: "*¡Esto no sirve para nada!*" [This is worthless!]. This is perhaps because, although the allegory of the ephemeral memorial *can* bring into play a phantasmagorical presence that underlines the absence of the disappeared body, the permanence of a monumental symbol ultimately requires the univocal referential force of an official action and its story.

The *Monumento*, then, like the monuments of the postmodern city described by M. Christine Boyer as fragments of a forgotten past, is incapable of summoning the memory it seeks to evoke, since its function and purpose are erased by the everyday practices of urban subjects (19). Hence, returning to the ideas of Nora and Achugar, although the logic of the market has had considerable influence on our practices of memory and forgetting, I agree more with Huyssen's analysis, in which he shows that the conception of *lieux de mémoire* constructs an extremely divided reality, where the monument functions as a supplement or a crutch that attempts to fill the void or the silence of official discourse (23–24). It is in this sense, too, that Draper has interpreted the transformation of the dictatorships' prisons and detention centers into memorials or malls as a "museification of memory" that even naturalizes "certain forms of violence" by reformulating a traumatic past into something we are ready to resolve and leave behind, sealed by the act of the monument (3). In Chile, the museification of memory directs us straight to the Museum of National History, which, in 2007, narrated and organized Chile's national history into a neat story that went all the way from the first indigenous groups that inhabited the territory to the military coup d'état on September 11, 1973—and there it stopped.

This inability to construct a narrative after 1973 evidenced a reluctance to address and act upon the dictatorship's crimes from the various democratic governments since 1989. In terrible accord with that missing story, all across the city are scattered the monoliths that circumvent the void—omitting it, denying it, censoring it—, and thus the different administrators of the so-called transition to democracy try to protect themselves behind a feeble admission that the crimes did indeed occur. At least that much, since *The Rettig Report* in 1991, has been acknowledged. The monolithic silence, or empty gesture, points us right toward two clear catastrophic manifestations of the neoliberal transition to democracy in Chile. The first is at the material level: the absence of bodies in space (the disappeared detainees). The second is at the level of the political imagination: the official silence, in the face of the crimes perpetrated by the dictatorship, which refuses to create a historical narrative that seeks and commemorates justice, instead of violence.

LA LOCA'S VOICE, HER TRANSVESTISM, AND HER EMOTIONS

Within this space of catastrophe, the chronicler and performance artist Pedro Lemebel developed a project of memory during the 1990s. The project began in 1994 with the radio program *Cancionero*, where Lemebel aired chronicles accompanied by songs, and continued in 1998 with the book *De perlas y cicatrices*, in which he collected the stories he had aired on the radio and added some more along with a series of images. In these, Lemebel related events, described characters, and gave testimonies (his and others') about the years of the Unidad Popular, the dictatorship, and the transition to democracy. More specifically, many of his pieces were dedicated to recalling disappeared detainees in detail through the narration of their everyday lives before they were kidnapped, and the feelings that survive among their families and friends. Lemebel aired *Cancionero* again in 2002, just when Pinochet's case reopened the debate that *The Rettig Report* had tried to bury. Since then, several pirated archives with the recordings have emerged on the Internet, like the one I will be using for my analysis of four of the radio chronicles, "Pedro Lemebel— *Cancionero*: Crónicas en Radio Tierra," uploaded to *YouTube* by a user named "Virgo". In addition, in 2010, the author published a reedition of *De perlas y cicatrices*.

If we consider Lemebel's project of memory from within the context of Santiago, inscribed by the monolithic gesture of official silence, what potentiality can the ephemeral nature of the performance of the voice in *Cancionero* have, as opposed to the permanence of the monument? Furthermore, keeping in mind the shift of the radio program *Cancionero* to the book *De perlas y cicatrices*, how is this transition between the logics of orality and writing problematized? What does each format contribute to Lemebel's project and its intended effects?

When thinking about the different kinds of historical narrative that the 1992 iceberg and Lemebel's *De perlas y cicatrices* propose, Martina Bortignon establishes that, although both gestures include a kind of "transparent" element in their relationship with memory (the ice or the voice), the former seeks a sanitized transparency in the past while the latter's "ether" character still misses what has been lost (74). In my analysis, I would like to push Bortignon's idea further by adding that, when comparing the element of *Cancionero* to the iceberg, we can also see that both are ephemeral in their performative gesture of memory; both were intended to happen once and to fade away afterward. Nevertheless, going back to what others have said about the iceberg, the political intention was to wash out the past, to disappear it along with the iceberg, and to launch the myth of Chile as a democratic nation. In contrast, the ephemeral character of *Cancionero* relates to the ghost and the flash of memory, a piece of the past that cannot be apprehended but to which we still sustain an intimate relationship.

As I will discuss, the performance of the voice in *Cancionero* is in reality the performance of *la loca*'s voice. *La loca,* a pejorative name for homosexuals and, particularly, for transvestites across a large part of Latin America, has been reappropriated and placed center-stage by Lemebel. *La loca* is the narrative voice in his first two collections of chronicles, *La esquina es mi corazón* (1995) and *Loco afán* (1996), and is also one of the main characters, along with the *péndex,* as they call any impoverished youth with no future prospects in Chile. In these books, *la loca*'s performance is what invigorates and amplifies a critique of the Chilean transition and neoliberalism. And, as I will argue, in *Cancionero* and *De perlas y cicatrices,* the intellectual locus of enunciation resides in *la loca*'s desire and emotions, a combination of love and anger that will inject specific tones into stories full of melancholia.

While the void of meaning resides at the center of the permanent gesture of monuments, the ephemeral performance of *la loca*'s voice evoked the aesthetics and politics of the ephemeral action of improvised memorials. Although the ephemeral flash of memory forces the acting subject to look toward the past in order to refuse the official imperative to forgive and forget, like Benjamin's "angel of history" in "Theses on the Philosophy of History" (257–58), the performance practiced by Lemebel is anchored in the present and feeling a full force to open possibilities into the future. In this sense, I agree with Carl Fischer when he states that "the *loca* also embraces the future in Lemebel's writing, and thus stands apart from the larger, leftist agenda of mourning the past" (203). After all, *la loca* is an ongoing character in Lemebel's chronicles who navigates the city guided by her desire and emotions in relation to what she witnesses in the present. Furthermore, even though the power of the ephemeral performance of the voice—as well as other elements of the aural—was lost in the chronicles' transcription and publication, *De perlas y cicatrices* seems to perform an extended and continued intervention of the public space by *la loca*'s stories. As I will explain, in her sexuality and her writing, there is an intersubjective movement that breaks the dichotomy between the self and the "other." This movement, I will argue, hopes to reach out to an affective "we" that shares *la loca*'s emotions and that continues to add other "others" into the collective as the project keeps operating into its multiple stages.

An analysis into these ideas needs to consider, first, how some of the elements at play in Lemebel's project of memory—transvestism, performance of the voice, and chronicle—enter in dialogue with the aesthetics and political proposals already initiated by the author in his work with *Las Yeguas del Apocalipsis,* a performance art collective created in conjunction with Fernando Casas.[2] Also, it will be fundamental to examine the literary style and intellectual enunciation in relation to his previously published collections of chronicles.

The collective *Las Yeguas del Apocalipsis* was born during the 1980s, and, for them, performance was an act and an intervention that represented the taking of the public space and of the body (Domínguez Ruvalcaba in Blanco, 2004, 124). For this collective, performance was also a way to create a common cause with activist groups (for example, feminists and families of disappeared people) in the demand for the disappeared body. Their performance focused on the blurring of the categories of gender and sexuality, following their ideology of empowerment of bisexuals, homosexuals, lesbians, and transgenders (Blanco, 2004, 52). *Las Yeguas* emphasized the pain of the body for the public denunciation of military control over bodies. Furthermore, *Las Yeguas*'s performance, as well as Lemebel's continued performance during the 1990s, underlined the staging of the eroticized body's victimization (Blanco, 2004, 125). In addition to continuing to highlight the dictatorship's unsanctioned violence, as he had in the 1980s and throughout the 1990s with *Las Yeguas,* Lemebel's artistic and literary work traces a link between the dictatorial past

---

2. *Las Yeguas del Apocalipsis* is related to the work that the *Escena de Avanzada* had begun to develop at the end of the 1970s. The *Escena* was an artistic and literary movement in which a wide variety of voices and expressions participated and which took the arts and urban space by storm. Their artistic aims broke down the barriers between a variety of art disciplines and, in addition, disrupted the boundaries between "art" and "not art" to make art out of the everyday and to turn art into an everyday experience, to culminate in a utopian fusion of art and life (Richard, 2007, 16). By (re)taking public space through their artistic actions, the *Escena* also put the body in motion by reinserting it into a web of contact with other bodies, and in close relation to the city.

and the neoliberal present with respect to the violation of the body at the hands of the market and conservative hegemonic discourses.

In terms of his literary work, Lemebel defined it as a "bastard genre" that combines popular songs, biographies, testimonies, interviews, and a diversity of voices (Lojo). He also declared:

> Digo crónica por decir algo, por la urgencia de nombrar de alguna forma lo que uno hace. . . . Te digo crónica como podría decirte apuntes al margen, croquis, anotación de sucesos, registro de un chisme, una noticia, un recuerdo al que se le saca punta enamoradamente para no olvidar. (Blanco and Gelpí, 93)

> I call it chronicle just to call it something, because of the urge to name what one does in some way. . . . I say chronicle the same way I could say notes in the margin, sketch, list of events, gossip or news, a memory lovingly sharpened so as not to forget.

With these words, Lemebel highlights the importance his written work assigns to three literary characteristics: the ability to create a story that people will repeat, as Benjamin describes in "The Storyteller," discussed in chapter 1; the melancholy that prevents forgetting, divides the self, and insists on demarcating empty places throughout the city and the story; and the love and sexual desire that acts as a creative force as long as it is tied to absence, that is, the melancholy precept of *no olvidar*.

When analyzing the author's writing style, Luis E. Cárcamo-Huechante has compared it to a flea market, where different codes operate simultaneously, in specific, literature, popular culture, and urban languages (162). This is a metaphor that summarizes what many other critics have often said: Lemebel's literature is affiliated with the baroque. For example, Juan Poblete has described Lemebel's style as a "popular baroque" that works as a cultural translation between popular culture and literature, as well as between the local and the global (2006, 291). For Monsiváis, Lemebel's style can be described as an "out-of-the-closet baroque" that combines a skilled use of the metaphor, the kitsch, the grotesque, and the parody (2009, 28). A "genuine poet," according to Monsiváis, Lemebel knows how to use this combination of literary processes as an "ideological weapon" (28). This is why, when presenting the author's work at the *Semana de Autor*—a week (November 21–24, 2006) dedicated to Lemebel—in Havana, Cuba, Jorge Fornet said that this is a literary style that exhibits itself and risks it all in order to achieve one of the most aggressive and seductive literatures in Latin America (68). It is out of the *bar-*

roco desclosetado, out of the combination of aggressiveness and seductiveness, that Lemebel gives life to *la loca.*

In speaking of *la loca,* Richard finds the potentiality of the constant movement between identities: "It could be that the 'peripheral persona' of *la loca,* with her roaming metaphor of superimposed and interchangeable identities, presents one of the most potentially subversive challenges confronting systems of univocal characterization of normative identity" (2004, 52). *La loca* cross-dresses and, through that action, is constantly moving, regulated only by her desire. For Ben Sifuentes-Jáuregui, Lemebel's literature brings back José Donoso's *la Manuela,* the transvestite woman in *El lugar sin límites,* with a renewed political force (2014, 116). Nevertheless, even if *la Manuela* served as a model for *la loca,* in Lemebel's texts there is a necessity to "name and rename" his characters—it is never one single *loca,* but a multitude of *locas*—in order to "legitimize the transvestite" (121). Just like other critics already mentioned, Sifuentes-Jáuregui talks about Lemebel's literary style, but he focuses on how particular characteristics help this process of legitimization; the "Baroque allegory, the act of extending the name metaphor *ad infinitum,* to twist and turn the name so that it gets baptized continuously" (122) constitute the ways by which *la loca* becomes, more than a character, the literary voice and, therefore, the one who guides the readers into the narration. Furthermore, for Efraín Barradas, Lemebel's readers are guided through the voice and gaze of "la loca mala" [a bad *loca*], who delights in irony and verbally attacking others and, in turn, creates a counterbalance for the weak victims, that is, *locas* like Donoso's *la Manuela* (74). For Barradas, *la loca* in Lemebel is bad and strong, and I will argue that she is angry, too.

I want to deepen this analysis a little more, following Sifuentes-Jáuregui, who declares that transvestism is an act "that penetrates and tampers with those who witness it" (2002, 2). In other words, in the act of cross-dressing, not only is the subjectivity that performs it invested (vested/inverted) but also the subjectivities that watch it. Sifuentes-Jáuregui's theoretical reflection brings up a very important point for my study of Lemebel's voice when he compares what transvestism means for the "outside viewer" with what it does to the cross-dressed subjectivity. For the former, "transvestism is about representing the other, . . . occupying the place of the Other, . . . (re)creating the figure of the (m)other" (3). For the latter, "transvestism is about representing the Self, . . . becoming the Self, . . . (re)creating the Self" (3). Thus, in her intersubjective movement, the transvestite—like *la loca* in Lemebel's chronicles—blurs the dichotomy between self and "other" and, in so doing, she destabilizes all identitary categories and rarefies the gaze of those who witness it.

Moreover, in Lemebel's *Cancionero,* one must also keep in mind that *la loca*'s performance of the voice will also resort to a transvestism of voices and emotions in the told stories. As I will show later in this chapter, *la loca*'s voice will perform desire and lovelornness for the *péndex*'s [young male's] body in the chronicle "Ronald Wood." She will cross-dress into the voice of a grand-mother telling an everyday family story in "Claudia Victoria Poblete Hlaczik." She will sound as a collective voice of the women crying over the absence of their partners as they dance the *cueca sola*—a modification of a traditional Chilean couple dance—in "El informe Rettig." She will also cross-dress into the voice of a young rape victim in "La leva." Between the "I," the "you," and the "we," the intersubjective movement will elongate *la loca*'s desire and emo-tions toward the past and into the present and the future.

CANCIONERO'S REPERTOIRE: *LA LOCA'S* ANGRY, ENAMORED, AND MELANCHOLIC CALL

Punctually, if briefly, *Cancionero* aired for ten minutes twice a day, Monday through Friday, and Lemebel shared a song and an urban chronicle with his audience. Voice, radio, music, and literature were the elements used by this intellectual to make himself heard in the public realm, to disagree with official policy, and to contribute to new dialogues. In addition, these elements mag-nified the irruption of *Cancionero*'s repertoire into the daily life of the radio audience and brought together a community already united in spirit by the emotions of love, anger, and melancholy.

In describing *Cancionero* as a repertoire, I follow Diana Taylor's conceptualization:

> [an] embodied memory: performances, gestures, orality, movement, dance, singing—in short, all those acts usually thought of as ephemeral, nonrepro-ducible knowledge. . . . The repertoire requires presence: people participate in the production and reproduction of knowledge by "being there," being a part of the transmission. . . . The repertoire both keeps and transforms cho-reographies of meaning. (20)

To better understand how *Cancionero*'s repertoire operates on different aes-thetic, social, and political levels, I will itemize and study how each of its com-ponents function, that is, how each of them reinforce the effectiveness of the radio program.

I consider the element of the voice to be fundamental to Lemebel's purpose, since in its sound resides the imprint of the body in language. In addition, keeping in mind that, over time, this project will shift between the domains of orality and writing, the focus on the voice—and not on orality per se—can break the false dichotomy between those two domains (Ong; Zumthor). As Adriana Cavarero notes, the voice is the instrument that reveals the unique character of the speaker: "The typical freedom with which human beings combine words is never a sufficient index of the uniqueness of the one who speaks. The voice, however, is always different from all other voices, even if the words are the same, as often happens in the case of a song" (2005, 3). If the voice is also what shows the shifts between the uniqueness of "I" and of "you," then its main function is to relate subjectivities. This is Cavarero's main point: "The act of speaking is relational: what it communicates first and foremost, beyond the specific content that the words communicate, is the acoustic, empirical, material relationality of singular voices" (13). In the chronicler's voice in *Cancionero*, we encounter the urge to communicate an experience that collects other experiences and emotions shared between an "I" and a "you" who are then united to recreate haunting memories about things both lost and disappeared. In this sense, the spectral voice broadcast through the radio evokes a missing body and thus the phantasmagorical experience of the disappeared ones, who have left their mark on the memories of those who still love them.

When evaluating radio as a broadcast medium, besides considering its capacity for recreating the spectral effect of the voice, we must keep in mind that *Cancionero*'s repertoire sought to interpellate the residents of the poor neighborhoods of Santiago by telling stories pertinent to their daily lives and memories. Throughout its history, radio has been the most accessible mass medium for the poor masses for many reasons: it did not require literacy to use it, the equipment itself was cheap, there were large numbers of radio stations broadcasting across the country, and portable radios permitted mobility. Lemebel's choice of medium was very deliberate, as he explains in one of the chronicles added to *De perlas y cicatrices*:

> La radio ha logrado permanecer casi intacta frente al chispazo televisivo. Pero sobre todo la onda larga, que es el lugar vital de la radiotelefonía. Allí se mezclan horóscopos, noticias en chunga, brujos, meicas, evangélicos que alharaquean con su mensaje apocalíptico. Sobre todo en las mañanas, la radio AM es el espejo de un cotidiano popular que enfiesta de circo el inicio del día. Casi al final del dial, la Radio Tierra enmarca el rostro de una mujer que borda palabras en el aire. Es una voz afelpada que atraviesa la ciudad en alas del cambio. (205)

Radio has managed to remain almost intact in the face of television's spark. But above all, the long-wave [radio], which is the vital place of radiotelephony. There, horoscopes mix with sensationalist tabloid news, witches, herbalists, evangelists who exhort their apocalyptic messages. Especially in the mornings, AM radio is a mirror for the working-class daily routine that enlivens the start of their day like a three-ring circus. Almost at the end of the dial, Radio Tierra frames the face of a woman who embroiders words in the air. It is a velvety voice that travels the city on wings of change.

Across the jumbled noise of the AM dial, aimed primarily at the Chilean *poblaciones* or *poblas*—the poorest urban neighborhoods—, the flash of memory activated by Lemebel's song and voice seeks to find its own space within the listening routine of the "murmullo compañero de esas tardes calurosas" (204) [murmur that accompanies those warm afternoons]. The flash effect of *Cancionero* is augmented, in fact, by using the medium that reproduces "la imagen a través de la voz, la narración, la música, el relato de [una] confidencia modulada por el timbre sedoso de ese locutor invisible" (204) [the image through the voice, narration, music, the story of [a] secret modulated by the silky timbre of that invisible announcer]. That is, the noise of the AM band serves as a stage for the sudden appearance of a spectral voice become song and story that demands to be heard.

Moreover, the characteristics noted above also made the radio, particularly the AM band, the most used medium in case of emergencies. As Lemebel reminds us, "en los temblores, lo primero que se agarraba en el apuro era la radio" (204) [during earthquakes, the first thing we would grab in our panic was the radio]. During Pinochet's coup—a national emergency—, the military rapidly took control of television broadcasting, but it took longer to gain control of the airwaves. While the television channels aired cartoons, the radio was divided between stations already seized by the military, which broadcast public announcements notifying the population of the progress of the coup, and stations that resisted longer (Eltit, 20). For example, President Allende broadcast his last message to the Chilean nation via radio, an act that, for Diamela Eltit, went beyond being a "dramatic historical document" as it called for workers to continue the country's democratic transformation (19).

Lemebel's choice of radio as a medium for his project, then, is not simply for expediency but rather to make a political gesture. It is a choice that marks an emergence—as a response to a new emergency state caused by imposed neoliberal consensus—in the final space of dissidence in the face of the coup of 1973. Furthermore, we must consider how Lemebel affiliates with the radio dissidents throughout the dictatorship, and how he analyzes its vital importance:

> Durante la dictadura, la memoria de emergencias guarda intacta el timbre de Radio Cooperativa. Su tararán noticioso hacía temblar el corazón de la noche protesta. . . . También surgieron como callampas las radios clandestinas, que con un transmisor y un alambre de antena, contagiaban las poblaciones de afanes libertarios. Histórica es la Radio Villa Francia, perseguida, casi detectada, pero siempre fugándose con su nomadismo comunicador. Estos sistemas radiales caseros aún subsisten. Algunos agrupados como Organización de Radios Clandestinas, otros siguen errantes, transmitiendo una hora a la semana, con el auspicio del almacén de la población. (204–5)

> During the dictatorship, the memory of emergencies kept alive Radio Cooperativa's distinctive chime. The news humming used to shake the heart of that night of protest. . . . Underground stations also sprang up like mushrooms; with a transmitter and some antenna wire, they filled the *poblaciones* with the desire for freedom. Radio Villa Francia was historic: pursued, almost found, but always escaping with its nomadic transmitter. These homegrown radio systems still survive today. Some have grouped together as the Organization of Underground Radios, others are still roaming, transmitting an hour a week, with the support of the *población*'s bodega.

A place of solidary dissidence, secrecy, and wandering, in the context of 1994, the radio allows *Cancionero* to attend to another catastrophe: amnesty and the attempt to erase the memory of those who survived the terrible events and those who must confront the empty space of a disappeared loved one.

In 1994 *Cancionero*'s repertoire could still only be mobilized effectively from a station like Radio Tierra. As Poblete explains (2006, 322–23), Radio Tierra appeared at the beginning of the 1990s as a feminist initiative of La Morada, a feminist group, thanks to financing from KULU, a Dutch agency. While for KULU it was important to create a space of communication where different community organizations could express themselves freely, without intellectual mediation or intervention, La Morada was more interested in taking advantage of the space to disseminate feminist ideas in Chile. Although there may have been conflicts between the two visions, the basic mission was the same: to create a space for public journalism, that is, to move the public discussion closer to the daily experience of the listeners. Also, this combination of visions made it possible for both Radio Tierra and Lemebel's *Cancionero* to take advantage of local and global languages and tools. For Poblete, both projects are the result and the promoters of global discourses (2009, 292). Therefore, for *Cancionero*, Radio Tierra was the possibility to be located within a larger project privileging a heterogeneity of voices and the right to information and to inclusive public debate.

Even more, in the production of *Cancionero*, it is important to recognize the central role played by the network of affects that also made up a part of Radio Tierra, as Lemebel acknowledged in *De perlas y cicatrices*:

> Este libro está dedicado a Violeta Lemebel, Pedro Mardones P., Paz Errázu-riz, Soledad Bianchi, Jean Franco y a todas mis compañeras de Radio Tierra, quienes en todo el tiempo de su mensajera elaboración, aportaron con su cariño para que este proyecto se viera realizado.
>
> Han pasado casi dos años, desde que Raquel Olea y Carolina Rosetti me dieron un lugar en la programación de esta emisora de mujeres para que echara a volar estos textos en el espacio "Cancionero." (5)

> This book is dedicated to Violeta Lemebel, Pedro Mardones P., Paz Errá-zuriz, Soledad Bianchi, Jean Franco, and to all my comrades at Radio Tierra, who, the whole time of their communication craft, contributed with their affection so this project could be carried out.
>
> Almost two years have passed since Raquel Olea and Carolina Rosetti gave me a spot in the programming schedule of this women's station so that I could let these texts fly into the "Cancionero" space.

In this sense, Lemebel chose to ally himself with a feminist agenda, because he well understood that Radio Tierra was a vehicle for pointing out the Chilean patriarchal system that had sustained the dictatorship and the transition guided by amnesty. This becomes evident when he narrates events that link the violence against women and sexual minorities with the violence of the dictatorship and also with the sociocultural context of the Unidad Popular. What is more, he recognized the feminist-affective force generated through the technical execution of the program; this was a communal kind of project, in which each member contributed to its execution.

It would be precisely through that feminist-affective force that the intentionality of the program would be strengthened: to call a heterogeneous community of public debate joined by emotions. When examining the book part of the project, *De perlas y cicatrices,* other critics have pointed to the book's tone, which alternates between "tenderness and outrage" (Bortignon, 74) or between "rage and heartbroken homage" (Ojeda, 157). Others have also commented about its "bitter and passionate character" (Mateo del Pino, 133), because it "claims justice for the ones who lost" everything (Olea). Many have also noticed irony, sarcasm, parody, and satire as the combination of resources that infuse the discourse with dark, even sinister, humor (Mateo del Pino, 139; Ojeda, 157–58). When listening to some of the pieces in radio format, the combination of love and anger administers a particular character to the melancholic voice. It is important to conceptualize each of the emotions at play in order to conduct an in-depth analysis of how each one works on its own and in conjunction with the others within Lemebel's intellectual project.

From Radio Tierra, the affective force of *Cancionero* was projected by plugging into the nostalgia that the selected songs attempted to induce. Specifically, Lemebel sought to highlight the artistry quality of the popular song, especially of the romantic variant. By choosing this kind of music to be intertwined with his chronicles, the author legitimizes it and requests all listeners—including literary critics—to devote their attention to the songs as well as to the texts he reads. Therefore, I coincide with J. Agustín Pastén in that Lemebel approaches history from a narrative formed by this kind of repertoire, and, in this sense, he is able to transmit the pain and worries experienced by those—generally from the working class and the dispossessed—who have always enjoyed songs that are despised by most of the middle class and the privileged (115). Some pieces were instrumentals whose melodies inspired sadness, as is the case with the chronicle dedicated to Ronald Wood. The rest were chosen from a wide variety of musical genres: bolero, rock, *nueva trova*, and cumbia, to name just a few. What they all had in common was their effect: many evoked an earlier era, since they were songs from previous decades; and all had popular-culture appeal, since most of them had been hits in their respective times. In this sense, *Cancionero* sought to provoke the typical reaction of listeners who, while searching for a station, suddenly heard a song that would take them back to a long-ago moment in their past that they still yearned for.

Even when the nostalgic feeling has had or still has very negative connotations in contemporary thought, according to Svetlana Boym, nostalgia also breaks with the modern idea of history as always progressive and also with the idea of the constant, always-new present of neoliberalism. Nostalgia, in its search for the utopic, looks to the past, certainly, but it can also help to analyze critical situations of the present and to move it toward a future full of possibilities: "Nostalgia is not always about the past; it can be retrospective but also prospective. Fantasies of the past determined by needs of the present have a direct impact on realities of the future. Consideration of the future makes us take responsibility for our nostalgic tales" (xvi). The melancholy in *la loca*'s voice added a political inflection into the nostalgic music repertoire.

Listeners were hooked by an evocation that opened the door to the telling of the chronicle by a voice that was also enamored of the victims and their families, while, at the same time, it expressed anger at the official agreement to forget. Love and anger are both shared emotions by the audience Lemebel was reaching to; and, although the two may seem opposites, in *Cancionero,* they operated in conjunction to potentialize nostalgia and melancholia into opening up possibilities for the future.

Different from the imperative of national love, which I have discussed in other chapters, in *A Lover's Discourse,* Roland Barthes proposes that we think of the solitary discourse of the lover as a series of implosions or fragments that do not follow the instructions of the *logos* (science or technique) and that are, rather, "figures." These figures should be understood in their choreographic sense: "[The lover] struggles in a kind of lunatic sport, he spends himself, like an athlete; he 'phrases,' like an orator; he is caught, stuffed into a role, like a statue. The figure is the lover at work" (4). In the performance of the chronicler's voice in *Cancionero,* we are shown the figures of the lover's discourse that Barthes enumerates: *la loca's* performance of the voice moves from the "I" to the "you," working through the radio waves, carrying with it the imprint of her enamored and desiring body, which thus speaks and makes figures of love to "you," wishing to become a "we."

Like love, anger is an emotion that groups the "I" and the "you" together in a "we"; but it also needs to be against a "they," an element that puts this emotion close to the ideas Lewis explained about "the politics of everybody," discussed in the introduction. An emotion closely related to love, but that needs antagonism, anger has been deeply analyzed in feminist discourses, especially by African American feminism. Looking into Audre Lorde's conceptualization of the relationship between hatred, pain, and anger is particularly helpful when examining histories inscribed by systemic abuse. After all, "every woman has a well-stocked arsenal of anger potentially useful against those oppressions, personal and institutional, which brought anger into being" (127). For Lorde, it is not only women who experience anger as a defense against oppression; people of color, lesbians and gay men, and poor people feel constant "virulent hatred" that is attached to their identities, their existence, their inhabitance of the world (128).

In several interviews, Lemebel talked about the anger or the rage that is engraved in his writing. In 2003, he commented, "Yo extraño esa rabiosa insolencia de mi infancia primitiva" (Nachon) [I miss that angered insolence from my primitive childhood]. Missing being as angry and insolent as he was as a child is also acknowledging that, since early childhood, the emotion of anger was present in his life. This recognition tells us that there is a "primitive" force in anger that allows us to survive the hatred that the antagonistic "they" inscribed on our skin. It seems that anger was still a force needed in his adulthood, in his writing, as he explained again in the following statement he made a year later: "La rabia es la tinta de mi escritura, pero no la rabia hidrofóbica del hombre perro, puede ser una rabia con pena, rabia con cuentas pendientes en el tema Detenidos-Desaparecidos, una rabia macerada y en espera de su pronta ebullición" (Costa) [Rage is my writing's ink, but it is not the dog man's hydrophobic rage, it can be a rage with sadness, rage with old scores to settle on the issue of the Disappeared Detainees, a tenderized rage that is waiting for its prompt boiling]. By distinguishing his rage from the one expressed by the abusive heterosexual male (the *hombre perro*), Lemebel is defining his emotion as a system of defense, rather than offense. Going back to Lorde's ideas, she explains further the difference between "their" hatred and "our" anger: "Hatred is the fury of those who do not share our goals, and its object is death and destruction. Anger is a grief of distortions between peers, and its object is change" (129). In Lemebel, there is a type of rage that emerges out of pain and sorrow, *pena,* that is also an aged *pena,* on the verge of acting violently, if the *cuentas pendientes* are not settled once and for all. Could these *cuentas pendientes* be settled? Is this only about the specificity of the disappeared detainees?

Anger grants survival while also fueling melancholia for the ones who did not survive hatred (Lorde, 129–32). Therefore, *la rabia de la tinta* in Lemebel's intellectual voice, that is, in *la loca's* voice, gives him "information and energy" (Lorde, 127) to critically examine the past and to fully experience the present. Moreover, when turning back to Lorde, Ahmed dwells on the possibilities that anger can open up for the ones who are stuck together in pain, and, she says, "anger is not simply defined in relationship to a past, but as an opening up for the future. . . . [Because] being against something is also being for something, but something that has yet to be articulated or is not yet" (2015, 175). Just like love and the combination of nostalgia and melancholy, anger works into the future.

I suspect that, especially in the chronicles that went from *Cancionero* to *De perlas y cicatrices,* the intellectual voice's anger is not only directed toward the dictatorship and neoliberalism but, rather, toward the "Chilean way," as Fischer has denominated the patriarchal, capitalist, and racist system that generated a kind of hatred and violence that escalated to the point of a dictatorship and that continues to nourish the neoliberal democratic regime in Chile (1–19). This is why in the continuity of Lemebel's project of memory, throughout the years of transmissions, transcriptions, reeditions, and archiving, *la loca's* melancholic, angry, and enamored voice continues to look back while anchored in the present and moving into the unknown future.

AN UNSTABLE ARCHIVE AND AN INVITATION TO SIN: FOUR TALES, FOUR MEMORIES FROM *CANCIONERO*

My analysis of *Cancionero*'s chronicles depends on the archive, not on the repertoire. I did not listen to Lemebel's texts while they aired in Radio Tierra in 1994 or in 2002. According to Taylor, in relation to the repertoire, the archive functions as a memory that is in constant interaction with the present moment:

> Archival memory works across distance, over time and space. . . . What changes over time is the value, relevance, or meaning of the archive, how the items it contains get interpreted, even embodied. . . . Insofar as it constitutes materials that seem to endure, the archive exceeds the live. . . . What makes an object archival is the process whereby it is selected, classified, and presented for analysis. . . . Individual things—books, DNA evidence, photo IDs—might mysteriously appear in or disappear from the archive. (19)

Throughout the years, every time that I have searched for *Cancionero* on the Internet, I have found different sites that contain a varying selection of chronicles from the original corpus. Therefore, the appearing/disappearing effect of the archive is radicalized by the instability of the Internet, especially in websites (like blogs) or channels (like YouTube) whose maintenance depends on personal efforts and/or whose contents can be censored or removed by administrators. And, yet, thanks to anonymous listeners/readers of Lemebel, *Cancionero* always reemerges somehow, on a different site and with a different structure. Reminding us of Lemebel's reasons to select Radio Tierra for his project, the precariousness, persistence, and resourcefulness that his avid listeners/readers have demonstrated on the Internet recreate some of the aspects of what the author admired about the AM radio station.

Each one of the chronicles in *Cancionero* begins with the song "Invítame a pecar," by Paquita la del Barrio, which serves as background to the voice of the announcer presenting Lemebel's program.[3] I believe that the selection of this particular bolero *invites* us to join the performance of remembering, and, in doing so, of *sinning*: "Invítame a pecar, quiero pecar contigo, no me importa pecar, si pecas tú conmigo" [Invite me to sin, I want to sin with you, I don't care if I sin, if you sin with me]. Participating in the act of memory, and specifically in a memory that demands a collective remembering, is a sin

---

3. In this analysis, I rely on "Pedro Lemebel—*Cancionero*: Crónicas en Radio Tierra" to examine sound elements (voice, noise, and music). On the other hand, I have taken all quotes from the textual version (*De perlas y cicatrices*) to facilitate references.

because it inflicts the official law of forgetting on that neoliberal logic set in motion by the transition to democracy in the 1990s. Precisely, my selection of four particular chronicles within *Cancionero* responds to a memory trail that I have weaved together through the four texts and that brings us from the beginning of the 1970s to the mid-1990s. The choice, then, also outlines the social structures that "disappear" political and sexual dissidence and that now forbid "our" memory, "our" sin.

The story "La leva" is an example that shows that the melancholic voice is interested in publicly discussing not only events related to crimes of the dictatorship but also social conventions that provide the necessary context in which a dictatorial-military-patriarchal regime can be articulated. In this chronicle, the focus becomes the *machismo* made possible by a social attitude that commits, condones, and justifies crimes against subjects who dare to depart from the patriarchal norm. This is the case of *la chica de la moda* [the fashionable girl] who is gang-raped by men from her *población* but gets no help from her female neighbors. It is interesting that *la loca*'s angry voice focuses on a poor neighborhood in Santiago, a scene normally viewed through an enamored gaze in most of Lemebel's other books. "La leva" warns us that it is impossible to idealize and that the social networks that make an authoritarian regime viable extend horizontally and vertically.

The chronicle begins with barking that stops when the 1961 song "Linda muchachita" by Connie Francis is heard. Francis's song serves as background throughout the narration of the text, although it does occasionally achieve prominence when the volume is turned up. The barking and the song function as metaphors for a patriarchal system in which women must follow the conventions of their assigned gender roles. Specifically, the song acts as a dictation to be memorized—repeated ad nauseam like greatest hits on the radio—, and the barking is a warning aimed at all those women who would disobey this dictum:

Linda muchachita, . . .
Voy a preparar
la aguja y el dedal,
porque tienes que coser
el vestido azul matrimonial
con el que te quiere ver.

Pretty little lady, . . .
I will prepare
the needle and the thimble,

because you have to sew
the blue wedding gown
he wants to see you in.

While in the background the song continues to describe the archetype of the woman-child whose only desire should be to stay at home to maintain the fictional heteronormative marriage, in the foreground *la loca*'s voice narrates a grotesque scene:

> Al mirar la leva de perros babosos encaramándose una y otra vez sobre la perra cansada, la quiltra flaca y acezante, que ya no puede más, que se acurruca en un rincón para que la deje tranquila la jauría de hocicos y patas que la montan sin respiro; al captar esta escena, me acuerdo vagamente de aquella chica fresca que pasaba cada tarde con su cimbreado caminar. (Lemebel, 1996, 36)

> When I see the gang of slobbering dogs climbing all over the tired bitch, the skinny, panting stray, over and over, until she can't take it any more, crouching in a corner, hoping the pack of slavering, pawing animals who keep mounting her over and over will leave her alone, I vaguely remember that cheeky girl who sashayed past every afternoon with her hips swaying.

The antithesis created between the song and the narration summons the memory of *la chica de la moda,* who did not adhere to the conventions of feminine gender performance and was punished by her own *población*: "Ella era la única que se aventuraba con los escotes atrevidos y las espaldas piluchas y esos vestidos cortísimos, como de muñeca, que le alargaban sus piernas del tobillo con zuecos hasta el mini calzón" (36) [She was the only one who had the nerve to wear such plunging necklines and open backs and those very short dresses, like a doll's dress, that made her legs look so long, all the way from her flat shoes to her bikini underwear]. Although her outfit challenges gender performance, for *la chica de la moda,* those who criticize and harass her are part of her familiar environment, to the point that they even set the tone of her walks through the neighborhood:

> En aquellas tardes de calor, las viejas sentadas en las puertas se escandalizaban con su paseo, con su ingenua provocación a la patota de la esquina, siempre donde mismo, siempre hilando sus babas de machos burlescos. La patota del club deportivo, siempre dispuesta al chiflido, al "mijita rica," al rosario de piropos groseros que la hacían sonrojarse, tropezar o apurar el

paso, temerosa de esa calentura violenta que se protegía en el grupo. Por eso la chica de la moda no los miraba, ni siquiera les hacía caso con su porte de reina-rasca. . . . Tan creída la tonta, decían las cabras del barrio, picadas con la chica de la moda que provocaba tanta envidiosa admiración. Parece puta, murmuraban, riéndose cuando el grupo de la esquina la tapaba con besos y tallas de grueso calibre. (36)

On those hot afternoons, the old women sitting in their doorways were scandalized to see her stroll by, shocked by her innocent provocation of the gang on the corner. They were always in the same place, always drooling over her, always mocking. The gang from the sports club, always whistling and flirting with her, sending crude comments her way that made her blush, stumble, or hurry past, fearful of the mob's violent arousal. That was why the fashionable girl didn't look at them, she didn't pay attention to them, little miss frost queen. . . . The little idiot is so stuck-up, said the neighborhood goats, angry at the fashionable girl who roused such envious admiration. She acts like a slut, they whispered, laughing when the group on the corner showered her with kisses and obscene gestures.

Although grating, this was the normal daily setting of la chica de la moda's life; and, although intimidating and aggressive, this was the only community she knew. With her clothes, her walk, and her attitude, she knew very well how to successfully confront this familiar violence.

Nevertheless, when late at night all the everyday noises stop and a strange silence suddenly falls—reinforced in the radio narration by the pause in the song "Linda muchachita," and by the sound of footsteps on asphalt—, la chica de la moda does not know how to act and senses that something is wrong:

Curiosamente no se veía un alma cuando llegó a la esquina. Cuando extrañada esperó que la barra malandra le gritara algo, pero no escuchó ningún ruido. Y caminó como siempre bordeando el tierral de la cancha, cuando no alcanzó a gritar y unos brazos como tentáculos la agarraron desde la sombra. . . . Ella sabe que aulló pidiendo ayuda, está segura que los vecinos escucharon mirando detrás de las cortinas, cobardes, cómplices, silenciosos. (37)

Oddly, she saw no one when she got to the corner. Surprised, she waited for the gang of delinquents to shout something at her, but she didn't hear a sound. And as she walked, as always, along the dusty edge of the lot, she didn't even get a chance to scream when arms like tentacles snaked out and grabbed her from the shadows. . . . She knows she wailed a cry for help, she is sure the neighbors were listening, watching silently from behind their curtains, cowards, accomplices.

The former was a matter of daily, familiar violence, something she experienced every day, but the latter, in an unfamiliar setting (at night and alone), became sinister and wild. Although just before the attack, the song "Linda muchachita" stops, as soon as the narration of the scene ends, the song starts back up in the background. When it returns, the song—a metaphor for the social conventions of gender—enhances the sinister mood.

La loca's voice concludes the story with an ideological evaluation: "Pienso que la brutalidad de estas agresiones se repite impunemente en el calendario social. Cierto juicio moralizante avala el crimen y la vejación de las mujeres, que alteran la hipocresía barrial con el perfume azuceno de su emancipado destape" (37–38) [I think these brutal crimes are repeated with impunity every day. A certain moralizing judgment supports the crime and the humiliation of women, who disrupt the neighborhood hypocrites with the floral perfume of their emancipated state of undress]. In this way, Lemebel's work shows us that violence under the dictatorship cannot be thought to be isolated from a system of identification that is imposed on the subjectivity of gender and sexuality. This system, like the *tentáculos* that trapped *la chica de la moda,* is entrenched in every sector and, through its indoctrinating repetition, permeates everyday life, becoming at once familiar and sinister.

In "Ronald Wood ('A ese bello lirio despeinado')," *la loca*'s voice takes us to the 1980s and guides us with an enamored and desiring inflection to the body of a young man murdered during the dictatorship. On May 20, 1986, in downtown Santiago, Ronald Wood, a resident of the section of town known as Cuatro Álamos de Maipú and a student at the Professional Institute of Santiago, was killed when the army fired on a student protest against the dictatorship. Wood's murder sparked numerous demonstrations, a wave of community and organizational support, memorial services in his honor, and this chronicle in *Cancionero.* In the text, "rescatar" [rescuing], "encontrar" [finding], "pensar" [thinking], "evocar" [evoking], and "soñar" [dreaming] about Ronald Wood, or "ese bello lirio despeinado" [that beautiful tousled lily], among "tanto joven acribillado en aquel tiempo de las protestas" [so many young people gunned down in that time of protests], stems from the need to remember him in his daily life and through an intimate moment, the one she shared with Ronald, or Rony (1996, 95).

For this special moment, *la loca,* always in love with the *péndex,* will remember the teacher/student bond that she and Rony once had. When examining the relationship between *la loca* and *el péndex* in Lemebel's chronicles, Barradas sees it as a "complicada relación de miedo y atracción, de inferioridad y superioridad, de conveniente uso del uno y del otro" (76) [complicated relationship between fear and attraction, inferiority and superiority, of convenient use of one and the other]. Even the chosen term to describe the subject of attraction, *el péndex*, expresses the combination of "cariño y superioridad" [endearment and superiority] that *la loca* feels toward this type of young man (76). The teacher/student bond falls within this kind of complicated interaction.

In *Cancionero*, the chronicle opens with music—a soft, melancholic duet between a piano and a flute—that will continue throughout the narration and even after the voice stops at the end of the story. The voice also moves slowly from word to word, sober and sorrowful. At the beginning, music and voice reinforce the spell of a memory that "golpea en el pecho [de la voz narradora]" [hits (the narrating voice) in the chest] with intermittent flashes of Rony's face and smile:

Quizás, sería posible rescatar a Ronald Wood entre tanto joven acribillado en aquel tiempo de las protestas. Tal vez, sería posible encontrar su mirada color miel, entre tantas cuencas vacías de estudiantes muertos que alguna vez soñaron con el futuro esplendor de esta impune democracia. Al pensarlo, su recuerdo de niño grande me golpea el pecho, y veo pasar las nubes tratando de recortar su perfil en esos algodones que deshilacha el viento. Al evocarlo, me cuesta imaginar su risa podrida bajo la tierra. Al soñarlo, en el enorme cielo salado de su ausencia, me cuesta creer que ya nunca más volverá a alegrarme la mañana el remolino juguetón de sus gestos. (95)

Perhaps it might be possible to rescue Ronald Wood from among so many young people gunned down in that time of protests. Perhaps it might be possible to find his honey-colored gaze among so many empty eye sockets of dead students who once upon a time dreamed of the future greatness of this democracy of impunity. When I think of him, the memory of him as an overgrown child hits me in the chest, and I watch the passing clouds, trying to see his profile in those cottony wisps scattered by the wind. When I remember him, I can't imagine his laugh rotting underground. When I dream about him, in the overwhelming heartbreak of his absence, it's hard to believe that never again will his playful ways brighten my morning.

If we consider that after his death Wood became a symbol of the student resistance and that of the *poblaciones* against the dictatorship during the 1980s,[4] this chronicle could well be read as a metonymy of *tanto joven acribillado*. However, *la loca*'s remembrances are not shared to evoke the symbolic aspect of Wood's death, but the intimate memory of the relationship between the narrator-teacher and the teenaged boy who was her student: "Sería lindo volver a encontrar al Ronald en aquella comunidad de Maipú donde yo le hacía clases de artes plásticas en la medialuna yodada de los setenta" (95) [It would be wonderful to meet Ronald again in that neighborhood in Maipú where I taught him art in the rusty yellow arena from the seventies]. In recounting that story, the voice carries us through modulations that playfully emphasize each syllable in certain sentences, describing the uniqueness of that "payaso del curso":

Güeviando toda la hora, derramando la témpera, manchando con rabia la hoja de block, molestando a los más ordenados. . . . Insoportablemente hiperkinético, aburrido con mi cháchara educativa, lateado, estirando las piernas de adolescente crecido de pronto. Porque era el más alto, el pailón molestoso que no cabía en esos pequeños bancos escolares. El payaso del curso que me hacía la clase un suplicio. (95)

Wasting the whole hour, spilling tempera paints, angrily staining the block medium, bothering the more orderly students. . . . Unbearably hyperactive, bored with my educational chatter, annoyed, stretching out those overgrown adolescent legs. Because he was the tallest, the annoying clumsy one that did not fit in those small desks. The class clown that made my class torture.

Within the narrative of the chronicle, this relationship between teacher and student will find complicities in the agreement in their political opinions. The *payaso del curso,* we are told, becomes the most engaged student in the class when, through the art of the Roman Empire, the teacher brings the discussion around to an examination of Chile's dictatorship. The teacher/student relationship becomes more personal through their dissident dialogue:

Yo aproveché esa instancia de atención para meter el discurso político, riesgoso en esos años cuando era pecado hablar de contingencia en la educación. Y el Ronald tan atento, participando, ayudándome en esa compartida subversión a través de la ingenua asignatura de las artes plásticas. (95–96)

---

4. The library of the neighborhood Cuatro Álamos de Maipú is named "Ronald Wood." This *población* emerged under the Unidad Popular as a working-class community.

> I took his moment of attention to insert political discourse, risky in those years when it was a sin to talk about possibilities in education. And Ronald, so attentive, participating, helping me in that shared subversion through the innocent subject of art.

What interests me about this quote is the use of the word *pecado,* especially in relation to that complicity. On the one hand, the narration tells us about an infraction of the dictator's martial law prohibiting, pursuing, and punishing subversion. In this case, the sin is not only on the part of the teacher but also of the student who "participates" and "helps." That is, the sin exists both in the act of subversion and in the relationship that supports the act.

On the other hand, the narration suggests that the sin was also defined by the game of seduction between teacher and student. The loving description of Ronald's body brings us to the moment when "[se] sellaba nuestra secreta complicidad" [our secret complicity was sealed]:

> Al terminar la clase, cuando todo el curso salió en tropel a recreo, al levantar la vista del libro de asistencia, el único que permanecía sentado en la sala era Ronald en silencio. . . . [S]in decirme nada, me miró con esos enormes ojos castaños, estirándome la mitad de su manzana escolar, como un corazón partido que sellaba nuestra secreta complicidad. (96)

> At the end of class, when all the students trooped out to recess and I raised my eyes from the attendance book, the only one still in his seat was Ronald, sitting silently. . . . Without saying a word, he looked at me with those enormous brown eyes, offering me half of his apple, like a broken heart that sealed our secret complicity.

It is this *corazón partido* that keeps bringing us back to *La esquina es mi corazón,* Lemebel's book full of those *péndex,* to whom *la loca* addresses her enamored and desiring voice. Moreover, in this sense, the sin of their complicity is doubly political: in its antidictatorship expression and in its queer desire.

Thus, within the memorial narrative of the radio chronicle, the student's death is more than a symbol of the fight against the dictatorship. It is about the death of the desired body: "Tenía apenas 19 años esa tarde cuando una maldita bala milica había apagado la hoguera fresca de su apasionada juventud. . . . Había agonizado tres días con su bella cabeza hecha pedazos por el plomo dictatorial" (96) [He was barely nineteen years old that afternoon when a damned soldier's bullet extinguished the fresh fire of his passionate youth. . . . He suffered for three days with his beautiful head shattered by the dictator's lead]. With the memory of Ronald comes the memory of the doubly sinful complicity of teacher/student, of intimate moments that died with the young body and that survive, like a ghost, in the traces of *la loca*'s desiring voice: "Lo sigo viendo florecido en el ayer de su espinilluda pubertad. . . . Sus grandes ojos pardos, aquellos lejanos días de escuela pública cuando me regaló en sus manos generosas, la manzana partida de su rojo corazón" (96) [I keep seeing him thriving in the yesterday of his pimply youth. . . . His big brown eyes, those long-ago days of public school when he gave me, from his generous hands, the split apple of his red heart]. Ronald's uniqueness survives, then, in the melancholic desire made literature through *la loca*'s lovelorn and angry voice.

La loca's voice cross-dresses in the intimate love of family in the text "Claudia Victoria Poblete Hlaczik (o 'un pequeño botín de guerra')," which begins its broadcast with Mario Cavagnaro's song "Osito de felpa." The song tells the story of a father who talks to his dead son's stuffed bear. The teddy bear becomes personified through his dead son; the father shares his sorrow with the toy, which animates it and returns the sadness like a reflection. While the father misses his son, the bear misses his friend. For the father, the teddy bear becomes a prosopopoeia of his relationship with his son: "Osito de felpa, / yo sé que lo extrañas, / dame tus manitas. / Yo que fui su padre, / tu amigo seré" [Teddy bear, / I know you miss him, / give me your little hands. / I, who was his father, / will be your friend]. At the same time, the work of the prosopopoeia preserves the child's memory.

Although the song opens the radio space for the story about Claudia Victoria Poblete Hlaczik, an eight-month-old girl disappeared during the Argentine dictatorship, her photo in the book *Mujeres Chilenas Detenidas Desaparecidas* is what inspires the story in the chronicle:

Al mirar su foto y leer su edad de ocho meses al momento de la detención, pienso que es tan pequeña para llamarla Detenida Desaparecida. Creo que a esa edad nadie tiene un rostro fijo, nadie posee un rostro recordable, porque en esos primeros meses, la vida no ha cicatrizado los rasgos personales que definen la máscara civil. (1996, 83)

Upon seeing her photo and reading her age of eight months at the time of detention, I think she is so small to be calling her [a] Disappeared Detainee. I think at that age nobody's face is set, nobody has a memorable face, because, in those first months, life has not scarred the personal traits that define the civil mask.

Based on this photo, the narrator will tell pieces of a family history that destabilizes the categorical identity of [the] disappeared detainee. This family history opens on the night of November 28, 1978, in Buenos Aires, when soldiers entered the house of Chilean José Poblete and Argentine Gertrudis Hlaczik and kidnapped them along with the baby. From there, the narrator goes on to tell the story of the relationship between José and Gertrudis, filling it with daily details, the same ones she would like to share with the disappeared child:

> Se hace imposible recuperarla [a Claudia Victoria] para decirle la verdad, contarle un viejo cuento que se inició en Santiago de Chile, en el barrio de La Cisterna, cuando José Poblete, lisiado de las dos piernas, emigró a la Argentina para rehabilitarse. Y allí conoció a Gertrudis Hlaczik, con quien formó un hogar y tuvieron una niña que crecía cada día más linda, mientras él estudiaba sociología y se movía entre los pasajeros de los trenes en su silla de ruedas vendiendo cosas. (84)

> It is impossible to recover [Claudia Victoria] to tell her the truth, to tell her an old story that began in Santiago de Chile, in the neighborhood of La Cisterna, when José Poblete, crippled in both legs, emigrated to Argentina for rehabilitation. And there he met Gertrudis Hlaczik, with whom he made a home and they had a baby girl who grew prettier every day, while he studied sociology and moved among the passengers on the train in his wheelchair, selling things.

This is an impossible story, because it does not have the desired interlocutor, Claudia Victoria, to whom *la verdad* must be told. However, the intersubjective void left by Claudia Victoria becomes an object of interpellation, like the teddy bear in the song that opens the chronicle. In speaking to that void, the narrator is speaking to the prosopopoeia of Claudia Victoria's death or the death of a possible Claudia Victoria, who can only be imagined through the remains of the family history. In this impossible making of the story, the listeners—and, later, the readers—figure as witnesses of the process and also as replacements for Claudia Victoria. *La loca*'s voice angrily demands that "we" take over that empty place and listen from it. Even if "we" know about our impediment to filling that space—that is, "our" lack of experience—in the performance of *la loca*'s voice, "we" share her anger and manage to become witnesses for Claudia Victoria, the absent witness.

After bringing us through the family's daily life and its abrupt cessation by the military kidnapping, the story opens again to include Claudia Victoria's grandmothers:

Las abuelas de la niña dejaron los zapatos en la calle, buscando, pregun-
tando por ellos [José, Gertrudis y Claudia Victoria] en Campo de Marte, el
Olimpo y Puente Doce. . . . Por eso la abuela chilena de la niña se integró
a las Abuelas de Plaza de Mayo; solamente ella, porque la abuela argentina
sucumbió en la inútil espera. Se suicidó en Buenos Aires, justo a los tres años
de ocurrido el hecho. (84)

The child's grandmothers left the shoes in the street, searching, asking about
them [José, Gertrudis, and Claudia Victoria] in Campo de Marte, in Olimpo,
and in Puente Doce. . . . That was why the child's Chilean grandmother
joined the Abuelas de la Plaza de Mayo [Grandmothers of the Plaza de
Mayo]; only her, because the Argentine grandmother succumbed to futile
hope. She committed suicide in Buenos Aires, exactly three years after it
happened.

With those shoes left in the street, Claudia Victoria's grandmothers pointed
out the absence of the disappeared bodies. Thus the shoes remained as metaphors for the grandmothers' children and grandchild, bearing bits and pieces
of the family history and wanting to tell it to anyone who would listen. *La
loca*'s voice cross-dresses into another *abuela,* as she joins her voice with hers,
the only grandmother who survives the loss.

Toward the end of the chronicle, the narrator returns to a contemplation
of the child's photo and says, "Su amplia sonrisa dibujada en el papel es la
misma cicatriz que une a los dos países [Chile y Argentina]. La misma costra
cordillera que hermana en la ausencia y el dolor" (85) [Her wide smile drawn
on the paper is the same scar that joins both countries (Chile and Argentina).
The same mountainous scab that unites through absence and pain]. While
in the union of the grandmothers a family history to be told to Claudia Victoria was obtained piecemeal, in the enigmatic smile of a child that might
never hear that riven story, the chronicler locates a geographic symbolism
(the Andes) that, read as such, tells us about many family histories cut short
in both Argentina and Chile. It also tells us of national histories that are broken, unspoken, enigmatic, that point to the great void of absent bodies, and
of those who have to visit them day after day in their memories and their
everyday lives.

The chronicle about Claudia Victoria, especially in the daily action of the
grandmother who bears and represents the memory, can be linked to the last
chronicle, "Recado de amor al oído insobornable de la memoria," set in the
context of 1990s Chile. Its protagonists are the women who make up the Association of Families of Disappeared Detainees. In some of their demonstra-

tions, a number of women dance the *cueca sola*. In the traditional *cueca*, a couple stages a game of seduction by uniting, separating, and reuniting to the rhythm of the music while fluttering white handkerchiefs. However, in the *cueca sola*, a woman goes through the steps and flutters her handkerchief alone. Staged this way, the *cueca* makes no sense. The steps of the dance take the women around the floor as if they were dancing around someone who is not there, and both the steps and the fluttering handkerchief underline that absence in the dance. It could be said, then, that, during the few minutes that the *cueca sola* lasts, we are witnessing the index of the absent body both in the empty space and in the steps that are missing to complete the story of the dance.

In *Cancionero*, the music of the *cueca* begins the "Recado de amor al oído insobornable de la memoria" where *la loca*'s voice takes on a kind of angry manifesto tone and cross-dresses in a "we" to tell us about the difficult experience of surviving the absence of the loved ones disappeared during the dictatorship. Surviving the absence means resisting the urge to deny their disappearance, to forget:

> Y fueron tantas patadas, tanto amor descerrajado por la violencia de los allanamientos. Tantas veces nos preguntaron por ellos, una y otra vez, como si nos devolvieran la pregunta, como haciéndose los lesos, como haciendo risa, como si no supieran el sitio exacto donde los hicieron desaparecer. . . . Nos decían: otra vez estas viejas con su cuento de los detenidos desaparecidos, . . . nos hacían esperar horas tramitando la misma respuesta, el mismo: señora, olvídese, señora, abúrrase, que no hay ninguna novedad. (1996, 102)

> And there were so many kicks, so much love broken open by the violence of the forced entries. So many times they asked us about them, time after time, as if throwing the question back at us, acting like they were the injured parties, like [they were] mocking [us], as if they didn't know the exact place where they made them disappear. . . . They told us: again these old women with their story about the disappeared detainees, . . . they made us wait for hours while processing the same answer, the same: ma'am, forget it, ma'am, quit pestering us, there is no news.

In *De perlas y cicatrices*, the chronicle is titled "El informe Rettig," with the phrase "Recado de amor al oído insobornable de la memoria" as a subtitle, as if it were questioning the authority of the official report. Surviving the absence, then, means holding the hand of the disappeared loved one through that performance of the *cueca*, not only offering tribute to them and saying that their memory lives on, but telling them—through music and dance—that they have never been alone, that "we" share their experience and their anger:

> Tuvimos que aprender a sobrevivir llevando de la mano a nuestros Juanes, Marías, Anselmos, Cármenes, Luchos y Rosas. Tuvimos que cogerlos de sus manos crispadas y apechugar con su frágil carga, caminando el presente por el salar amargo de su búsqueda. No podíamos dejarlos descalzos, con ese frío, a toda intemperie bajo la lluvia titiritando; . . . dejarlos solos, tan muertos en esa tierra de nadie, en ese piedral baldío, destrozados bajo la tierra de esa ninguna parte; . . . dejarlos detenidos, amarrados, bajo el planchón de ese cielo metálico; . . . dejar esos ojos queridos tan huérfanos. . . . No pudimos dejarlos allí tan muertos, tan borrados, tan quemados como una foto que se evapora al sol. (102–3)

> We had to learn to survive by holding the hands of our Juans, Marias, Anselmos, Carmens, Luchos, and Rosas. We had to grab them by their brittle hands and bear their fragile weight, walking the present through the bitter salt flats of our search for them. We couldn't leave them barefoot, in that cold, in all that bad weather, shivering in the rain; . . . leave them alone, so dead in that no-man's land, in that rocky, barren land, destroyed beneath that nowhere land; . . . leave them prisoners, tied up, under the ice field of that metallic sky; . . . leave those beloved eyes so orphaned. . . . We couldn't leave them there so dead, so erased, so burned like a photo that evaporates in the sun.

If the authorities denied their absence for so long during the dictatorship, then, during the new democracy, the monumentalism of The Rettig Report—as with the other rushed gestures to seal the memories in the forgetfulness of reconciliation—buries the uniqueness of each one of the human singularities in the imposed identity of *disappeared*. In the voices of the family members who call the names of those who disappeared, there is also a demand to remember who they were before they were taken:

> Tuvimos que rearmar noche a noche sus rostros, sus bromas, sus gestos, sus tics nerviosos, sus enojos, sus risas. Nos obligamos a soñarlos porfiadamente, a recordar una y otra vez su manera de caminar, su especial forma de golpear la puerta o de sentarse cansados cuando llegaban de la calle, el trabajo, la universidad o el liceo. (103)

Every night we had to rebuild their faces, their jokes, their gestures, their nervous tics, the triggers for their anger, their laughs. We were forced to stubbornly dream them, to remember over and over again their way of walking, their special way of knocking on the door, or of falling exhausted into a seat when they returned from being out, at work, at college, or at school.

Dancing the *cueca sola,* a ritual of less than ten minutes, like each of the chronicles of *Cancionero,* is a performance that stages the everyday memory, stubborn and ephemeral. Every practice of everyday life, with its concomitant materiality, can lead to the moment when an unexpected memory returns. It appears and disappears phantasmagorically, but its trace persists in everyday tasks:

Aprendimos a sobrevivir bailando la triste cueca de Chile con nuestros muertos. . . . Con nosotros viven y van plateando lunares nuestras canas rebeldes. Ellos son invitados de honor en nuestra mesa, y con nosotros ríen y con nosotros cantan y bailan y comen y ven tele. Y también apuntan a los culpables cuando aparecen en la pantalla hablando de amnistía y reconciliación. (103)

We learned to survive by dancing the sad Chilean *cueca* with our dead. . . . They live with us, and our rebellious gray hair is increasingly speckled with silver. They are guests of honor at our table, and they laugh with us and sing and dance and eat and watch TV with us. And they also point at the guilty people when they appear on the screen speaking of amnesty and reconciliation.

Put this way, surviving not only refers to the memory that witnesses phantasmagorically, in the name of the material absence of the body, but also to the possibility of continuing a life that is still here, that of the family member. In this sense, daily life and memory are needed to make note of the singular human presence that is now missing. The song and *la loca*'s voice, her ten minutes on the air evoking lives lived, is, then, a performance of what the family members of the disappeared live every day. As with her intimate memory of Ronald Wood, for those who remember/live their own memories:

Nuestros muertos están cada día más vivos, cada día más jóvenes, cada día más frescos, como si rejuvenecieran siempre en un eco subterráneo que los canta, en una canción de amor que los renace, en un temblor de abrazos y sudor de manos, donde no se seca la humedad porfiada de su recuerdo. (103)

Our dead are more alive every day, younger every day, fresher every day, as if they were always being rejuvenated in a subterranean echo that sings them, in a love song that gives birth to them anew, in trembling hugs and sweating hands, where the obstinate moisture of their memory does not dry up.

It is a phantom that is only perceived through the materiality of human contact and daily life and that is conjured through dancing the *cueca sola* or through the angry love song of *la loca*'s voice.

THE WRITTEN ARCHIVE OF THE VOICE: *DE PERLAS Y CICATRICES* AS RELIQUARY AND OMEN

The conjuring that Lemebel did with his voice became a flash of visual memory through photography when, four years after *Cancionero* aired, he published *De perlas y cicatrices*. The book is divided into eight parts, with a series of photographs added like a photo essay. For Ángeles Mateo del Pino, *De perlas y cicatrices* exhibits its aural origins in its discourse's rhythm, the reference to songs and singers, and the musicality or melodic play with words in the chronicles' titles and subtitles (135). Both Francine Masiello and Marta Sierra coincide in their description of the book's particular kind of literary voice as a voice of everything popular (Masiello, 2001, 192; Sierra, 126). Masiello goes on to state that the powerful voice that we could almost hear in the book is due to what Lemebel developed in *Cancionero*, "a testimony to the power of the oral-aural exchange, a seduction through the ear of the anonymous other" (300, n3). It seems that some traits of orality persist phantasmagorically within the elements of the book; and, moreover, I consider that the book functions as a written and visual archive in which the letter-image shelters the voice-body of the untellable story, in other words, of experience.

Following the clue in the title—*De perlas y cicatrices*—and in the title of the section housing the photo essay—"Relicario"—, the pearls and the scars refer to the wound that remains as a synecdoche of the trauma, while the reliquary holds the remains of a venerated past. Talking about the title of the book, Raquel Olea, one of the first critics to approach the new publication, explained that pearl and scar are a product of the same defensive operation by a body; they perpetuate the indelible. For me, if in *Cancionero* the voice-body remained as the metonymic mark of the disappeared ones and the broken past, the letter-image in *De perlas y cicatrices* becomes a prosopopoeia through which the voice-body is represented and can "speak" again, even if through the written word.

In this sense, furthermore, the letter-image in Lemebel's project functions as "truncated texts of memory," defined by Richard as diffuse signs of stories cut short or shattered visions that circle around what is absent (2000, 11). The pearls and scars in the reliquary of chronicles and images accentuate what is *cut* and *shattered* from a project in two stages, the first of the voice-body and the second of the letter-image. Apart from the repetitive gesture of remembering and pointing to an empty place, the relation between the first stage and the second one operates as a *mise en abyme,* since the letter-image archive refers to the voice-body repertoire.

In his "A modo de presentación," Lemebel clarifies that the book does not try to trap "el espectro melódico, . . . el gorgoreo de la emoción, el telón de fondo pintado por boleretos, rockeados o valseados contagios [que] se dispersó en el aire radial que aspiraron los oyentes" (1996, 5) [the melodic spectrum, . . . the trill of emotion, the backdrop painted by the contagious beat of boleros, waltzes, and rock [that] the radio spread through the air breathed by the listeners]. Rather, *Cancionero*'s repertoire is defined as a kind of vanguard whose continuation was promised in the archive of *De perlas y cicatrices*: "El espejo oral que difundió las crónicas aquí escritas fue un adelanto panfleteado de las mismas" (5) [The oral mirror that disseminated the chronicles written here was a pamphlet-preview of them]. It is worth noting that Lemebel postulates *Cancionero* as a project of voice and sound—that is, a project of form rather than content—and *De perlas y cicatrices* as a type of documentation that supports *juicio* [judgement] and *homenajes* [homages] never carried out in the Chilean social sphere:

> Este libro viene de un proceso, juicio público y gargajeado Nuremberg a personajes compinches del horror. Para ellos, techo de vidrio, trizado por el desvelaje póstumo de su oportunista silencio, homenajes tardíos a otros, quizás todavía húmedos en la vejación de sus costras. Retratos, atmósferas, paisajes, perlas y cicatrices que eslabonan la reciente memoria, aún recuperable, todavía entumida en la concha caricia de su tibia garra testimonial. (6)

> This book comes from a process, a public, spitting Nuremberg judgment of characters who were accomplices in the horror. For them, a glass roof, shattered by the posthumous revelation of their opportunistic silence, tardy homages for others, with scabs perhaps still tender from being picked at. Portraits, atmospheres, landscapes, pearls, and scars that link recent memory, still recoverable, still numb in the crude caress of its lukewarm testimonial talon.

In this way *Cancionero*'s structural pattern announced the documentation to come in *De perlas y cicatrices*. That announcement—what came before—survives in the book, and the traces of his voice linger in many other aspects than the already mentioned: the anecdotal, everyday nature of the chronicles; the poetic, irreverent, local language; the spontaneity that rambles and breaks out into unexpected sentences; the stretching of the past into the present, marked by the length of the sentences and his uses of punctuation; and the evocation of an almost audible emotion—whether it be love, anger, or melancholy. Therefore, it could be said that there is a bidirectional relationship between both stages of the project. Furthermore, this repetition achieves an effect of intermittent continuity, just like that of memory, as Richard noted, *cut* and *shattered*.

On the cover of the book, the photo (taken by Paz Errázuriz) of Lemebel's performance "Devuélveme el corazón para matarlo" (Teatro Mauri, Valparaíso, 1994) underlines the double metaphor of memory in pearls and scars. His chest appears naked and shaved, with a necklace made of razors. With the top of the image cut off, all we see is his closed mouth, serious and enigmatic. Thus, instead of a pearl necklace, we have razors that shave the skin, stripping it of any protection; the skin willing to be exposed to the cold, to pain, and to the beauty of the experience. The closed mouth guards the enigma of this experience and hints at the possibility of (re)broadcasting the story to us through the voice that emerges.

Right in the middle of the eight parts into which the book is divided, there appears the photo essay "Relicario" with the epigraph: "Sus ojos de vidrio no saben del llanto" (1996, 105) [His eyes of glass know nothing of tears]. This line, from the song "Osito de felpa," refers to the chronicle "Claudia Victoria Poblete Hlaczik (o 'un pequeño botín de guerra')." We can see how, in the context of the image archive, the teddy bear to whom the father talks in the song is a metaphor for the reliquary of *De perlas y cicatrices*: the bear and the reliquary are synecdoches for the disappeared times and people, and, through that, they become prosopopoeias for death.

Mateo del Pino highlights the religious character of the book, not only because of the name of "Relicario," but also due to how the group of short chronicles and images resembles a "rosary" or a "litany" that is an invocation of memory, too (136). I would also add that the act of remembrance is a religious act for the one who honors the memory of those who are not with us anymore. It is also a pious act, an act of devotion, that requires dedication and work, just like the religious ceremony, which, like memory, is a repetitive ritual. Furthermore, if the rosary—like other prayer devices—conducts to a trance state where communication with the divine is possible or, in other words, we can transcend our human condition, the constancy of the short chronicles and the images (like religious stamps) could serve the purpose of activating our memory and connecting to the past.

The photos that appear in "Relicario" are related to the texts of the chronicles in their presentation of protagonists, events, or places in some of the stories. The presentation follows a chronological order that begins in the years of Unidad Popular and ends in the 1990s. It might seem that Lemebel proposes a strange conversation in juxtaposing photos that appear to be unrelated, but I believe that the apparent randomness indicates a subjective linking of memories that has a meaning only for the emotions of the one organizing this reliquary. Furthermore, all of the photos seem to be asking "us," the spectators: What are the pearls and scars possessed by these bodies, exhibited as models of or threats to a system? And where do they point us in the brokenness of their stories?

I propose that the last photo of "Relicario" functions as an artifact that speaks to us, not only about the content of Lemebel's project of memory but also about the operation of its structure. The photograph depicts a performance of the *cueca sola* demonstrated by the women of the Association of Families of Disappeared Detainees. In this scene, a woman has stopped the dance to dry her tears of grief with the white handkerchief that is fluttered during the dance. In the background, other women hold up the photos of disappeared family members. It seems to me that, in closing his image archive with this performance, Lemebel is signaling the empty place. In preserving this staging of the act of memory, "Relicario" warns us that there is no ending for this story told through images. Likewise, it would seem to tell us that *De perlas y cicatrices* is not an attempt to close the project of memory, since it marks the impossibility of tracing a coherent, unique story. Just as *Cancionero* announced a second documentary part in *De perlas y cicatrices,* this stage of Lemebel's project of memory presaged a continuation, however uncertain and intermittent.

"SOLOS EN LA MADRUGADA" OR THE "WE" IN LEMEBEL'S INTELLECTUAL QUEER DISCOURSE

Leading into the conclusion of this chapter, I want to comment on "Solos en la madrugada (o el pequeño delincuente que soñaba ser feliz)," a chronicle that Lemebel did not read in *Cancionero* but is included in *De perlas y cicatrices.* It is an autobiographical text in which the author tells us about a night when an ex-convict *péndex* approaches him with the intention to mug him but stops when he hears Lemebel's voice, recognizing it from the radio show that he used to listen to in prison: "Me busca conversa y de pronto se interrumpe. De pronto se queda en silencio escuchándome y mirándome fijo. . . . Tú hablai en la radio. ¿No es cierto?" (147) [He starts a conversation, and he suddenly stops. Suddenly he gets quiet and listens to me while staring at me. . . . You talk on the radio, right?]. What does it mean to know someone by their voice? In this case, Lemebel's voice is a voice that had accompanied the *péndex* in prison, that had even provided some solace during difficult times: "Yo agarraba la radio cassete y la ponía bien bajito debajo de las frazadas pa' escucharte" (148) [I grabbed the radio cassette player and played it very low, under the blankets, to listen to you]. Lemebel's voice represented a moment of intimacy for a man who was under extreme surveillance.

For Barradas, this chronicle is an example of the most powerful motif that guides Lemebel's literature, the relationship between *la loca* and *el péndex* (76). I agree, and yet, this interpretation needs to be complicated, because *la loca*'s voice in *Cancionero* is a narrative device, but here, in this chronicle, the author becomes a character. Moreover, we could say that the author has become *la loca,* if we notice that this text is part of a book section entitled "Quiltra lunera," which begins with a quote from José Joaquín Blanco's *Función de medianoche*:

> Esas locas preciosísimas, que contra todo y sobre todo, resistiendo un infierno totalizante que ni siquiera imaginamos, son como son valientemente, con una dignidad, una fuerza y unas ganas de vivir, de las que yo y acaso también el lector carecemos. Refulgentes ojos que da pánico soñar. (qtd. in *De perlas y cicatrices,* 143)

> Those extremely beautiful *locas,* that against all odds and above all, resisting a totalizing hell that we cannot even imagine, are the way they are courageously, with an amount of dignity, force, and will to live that I, and maybe the reader too, lack. Splendid eyes that we are afraid to dream about.

By becoming *la loca,* right here, in *De perlas y cicatrices,* Lemebel wants to associate his voice with her voice, the voice of *Cancionero.* And he wants to underline the courage it takes to be a *loca,* yes, and also to become *la loca* and, with her voice, speak his intellectual ideas and emotions, a brave act by itself. She gave us her voice through the radio, and, in this written chronicle, the author is underlining the fact that she also gave us her body, which is his body, too. Finally, it is not only *la loca* the one who lives courageously; the *péndex* does, too. In the story, he continues to struggle and survive within a system that would do everything to crush him. And he is not afraid to say that the intimate relationship with *la loca*'s voice has meant the opening of a small and brief space of possibility, of another kind of world.

My analysis, at this point, is engaging with what Poblete has thought about *De perlas y cicatrices* in relation to some of Lemebel's other books. For Poblete, Lemebel's books demonstrate a literary movement that started with *la loca*, a locally recognized character that had a distinctive voice, and ended with the superstar, a national and international notorious author that also became a character (2009, 289–90). After classifying *La esquina es mi corazón* and *Loco afán* as the two books that best represent the first literary period, and *Adiós mariquita linda* and *Serenata cafiola* for the second one, Poblete establishes that *De perlas y cicatrices* is an intermediary publication between the two stages. According to the critic, *la loca* is "notoriously absent" in this book; thus, Lemebel's chronicles become, for Poblete, a "hardened and flat time," moving between the immediacy of the dictatorship-transition's events and the nostalgia for older and better times (2009, 293). I understand how *De perlas y cicatrices* is very different in its style, format, and even its political effect when compared to *La esquina es mi corazón* and *Loco afán*. In *De perlas y cicatrices,* the express and only purpose is to conduct an open trial in order to accuse, condemn, absolve, and restitute.

Nevertheless, as my selection and analysis of chronicles have demonstrated, the project does not direct the open trial solely to condemn villains of the dictatorship or the neoliberal transition; nor is there a kind of nostalgia that wishes to return and stay in the past. This is a project that is intended to judge "the Chilean way," the patriarchal, racist, and capitalist structure that has made possible all the horrors lived in the past and the present. Also, in order to understand the complexities of time, space, and body involved in *De perlas y cicatrices,* it is necessary to take *Cancionero* into consideration. There is a constant movement in time, space, and body that keeps the voice and the gaze searching for possibilities into the future, what is not here yet. As I have established, this movement is radicalized by the combination of emotions, love, anger, and melancholy that complicates intersubjectivity.

Moreover, as I have argued, it is through *la loca*'s voice and gaze that we access the broadcast/written trial in Lemebel's project. Even in its written component, the performance of memory is *la loca*'s performance, one that here continues to operate through homoerotism and the *cursi* aesthetic. In *Nación marica,* Pablo Sutherland outlines the history of queer political and social movements in the Southern Cone, primarily focusing on those in which the writers of the *neobarroso* participated. The study that Sutherland does of Néstor Perlongher's and Lemebel's literature and of political initiatives like the

Frente de Liberación Homosexual, led by Perlongher in Argentina in the mid-1970s, concludes that there is a "ciudad letrada *queer*" [queer lettered city], that is, of an intellectual (writer or artist) who enunciates from a defiant difference of gender and sexuality. This kind of intellectual goes to great lengths for a "política minoritaria de atentado a la Nación hegemónica . . . [y en la que logran darse] los cruces entre literatura, sexo, política e imaginario popular" (23) [minority politics attacking the hegemonic Nation . . . (and in which are found) the intersections between literature, sex, politics, and the popular imaginary]. This is why, in Lemebel's project of memory, I do not see the fact that the author becomes his character, *la loca,* as detrimental to his literature. On the contrary, I believe that this movement becomes a radical proposition for the intellectual's locus of enunciation and the lettered city, as Sutherland does. For me, though, this city should not be seen as a separate city, because we should not fall into a binarism like the one we already had: real city / lettered city. Lemebel's intellectual discourse breaks through the dichotomy of lettered and real, as well as of queerness/straightness.

Going back to "Solos en la madrugada," there is a necessity to ask about the "you" to whom Lemebel speaks and the "we" that emerges at the intimate moment in which the two bodies connect through voicing/listening. When wondering about Lemebel's intended audience, Monsiváis declares: "Al principio, supongo, Lemebel no imaginaba lectores sino ausentes que van llegando" (2009, 29) [At the beginning, I suppose, Lemebel did not imagine readers but absentees that start to arrive]. Monsiváis's statement can be read as what we could say about almost any writer who, all of a sudden, becomes famous and whose readership diversifies in unsuspected ways. In this sense, Lemebel's writing was not intended for a big and all-encompassing market, and, yet, the editorial industry has had remarkable success with most of his books. Nevertheless, Monsiváis's words can also be interpreted as trying to understand a literary voice that writes about and for the ones who are no longer here and may be conjured up by the writing ritual. Furthermore, the absentees could be seen as the ones for whom not many literary authors write: the broken *péndex* from Chile's *poblaciones,* the *locas* that survive poverty and patriarchy, the women who deal with abuse every day, and all of those who keep fighting for true justice. Once they discovered the literary voice that was talking to them—and not only about them—, these absentees began to arrive at Lemebel's books and constituted his very first audience. I think this is what the author wanted to demonstrate in "Solos de madrugada," that the ex-convict *péndex* is the audience he had and, furthermore, that he is the kind of audience Lemebel had always wanted.

Monsiváis's "ausentes que van llegando" become even more relevant when examining the literary enunciation in Lemebel's chronicles that freely moves between the "I" and the "we." For Monsiváis, Lemebel's texts speak on behalf of a collective, the extended family, and they lose and recover the first-person plural (2009, 29). For Efraín Barradas, the *colectivo* in Lemebel is very specific, the "we" in Lemebel is an oppressed mestizo and indigenous working class that is always against "them," the dominant and white bourgeoisie (72). This cannot be denied. And yet, even if the "we" is very specific, Lemebel's literary style is able to add other kinds of "we," even unexpected ones, because *la rabia de la tinta* can speak to a *colectivo* that can grow endlessly in their shared experience of being abused and being alive to say it and to speak about the ones who no longer can.

CHAPTER 4

Angry Brotherly Love

U.S. Militarized Puerto Rican Bodies and Josean Ramos's filin

AS PART OF his "Mensaje de la situación del Estado," the State address delivered before the Puerto Rican Legislature on February 21, 2012, Governor Luis Fortuño recounted an anecdote about Emmanuel, a Puerto Rican soldier he met in Walter Reed Army Medical Center in Washington, DC, where Emmanuel, whose last name we never hear, was receiving treatment for his severe wounds. The story goes that, while he was serving as the Puerto Rican Resident Commissioner in the U.S. Congress (2004–08), Fortuño went to visit this soldier, who had "su cuerpo severamente mutilado y su conciencia en coma profundo" [his body severely mutilated and his mind in a deep coma] to "susurrarle al oído mi orgullo y mi agradecimiento como puertorriqueño y como ciudadano americano por su entrega y su sacrificio en defensa de la democracia y de nuestra Nación" [whisper in his ear my pride and my gratitude as a Puerto Rican and as an American citizen for his dedication and sacrifice in defense of democracy and of our Nation]. In his whisper, Fortuño commanded Emmanuel, "No te rindas" [Don't give up]. After describing a second visit to Emmanuel in the hospital, in which he repeated, "No te rindas," Fortuño relates that the soldier recuperated several months later and that he returned to meet him again, this time to give him the congressional Medal of Honor. At this point in his speech, the anecdote is interrupted to bring Emmanuel before the Puerto Rican Legislature, which gives him a standing ovation. Then Fortuño concludes,

Emmanuel dedica su vida a enseñarles a otros a no rendirse. . . . En el espíritu de superación que levantó a Emmanuel de su coma, . . . vamos, juntos,
adelante a la gloria que el Creador tiene reservada para nuestra patria.

Emmanuel dedicates his life to teaching others to never give up. . . . In the
same spirit of surmounting obstacles that brought Emmanuel out of his
coma, . . . let us move on, together, to the glory that the Creator has in store
for our homeland.

It is important to note that in 2012, and for four consecutive years by then,
Puerto Rico had been going through a severe economic crisis that after hur-
ricaine Maria (September 20, 2017) and up until now (2018) has only meant
more precariousness for middle- and working-class subjects.

Fortuño's anecdote is constructed to evoke the narrative style of a Chris-
tian parable. The very name "Emmanuel"—which means "God is among us"
and is used by Isaiah to prophesy the Messiah, apart from being a synonym for
Jesus Christ—reveals the religious framing that guides and grandiloquently
concludes the governor's address. The whisper of "no te rindas" and Emmanuel's subsequent recuperation from the coma reminds us of the biblical moment
when Jesus resuscitates a dead man by saying, "Lazarus, arise and walk." If
Lazarus functions as the body on which is written the parable that demonstrates Jesus' divinity on earth, for its part, Emmanuel's body serves to inscribe
a national-state discourse that seeks to show the government's power to work
a miracle of socioeconomic reconstruction. Emmanuel's body becomes the
site of the prophecy; and just like him, under Fortuño's command, Puerto
Rico will also rise again.

Similar to Emmanuel in Fortuño's speech, the bodies of soldiers and veterans, and their stories, have served political purposes in Puerto Rico at previous historical moments. One of the foundational events for the political
mythology of the ELA was the Korean War (1950–53), in which thousands of
Puerto Ricans formed part of the Sixty-Fifth Infantry Regiment. This regiment, composed of Puerto Rican volunteers and trained in Puerto Rico and
Panama during the First World War (1914–18), participated in armed conflict
for the first time during the Second World War (1941–45). Even though the
Sixty-Fifth saw little action on the battlefield during those war years, ever
since then, there evolved a discourse of national honor around the figure of
the Puerto Rican soldier. In Silvia Álvarez Curbelo's view, the Sixty-Fifth was
the proud symbol of an island that was in the midst of an economic transition and political modernization (2003, 4). Specifically, the Sixty-Fifth pride
was used to political advantage in the campaign that initiated the ascent of

the Partido Popular Democrático, under the leadership of Luis Muñoz Marín, the same man who would later establish the ELA in 1952. Now involved in the Korean War, with volunteers and drafted recruits, in Muñoz Marín's speeches the military prowess of the Sixty-Fifth would serve to articulate the epic of the ELA and Operation Bootstrap while keeping the alarming death tolls hidden.

The detail that interests me most about this history is how Puerto Rican *jíbaros'* bodies—like many other bodies recruited from rural areas in the United States—became "hypermasculinized," and therefore "modernized" by the U.S. military forces. All of these bodies "were physically examined, classified, categorized, disciplined, clothed in particular uniforms, sexualized via venereal disease screenings, and subjected to numerous other processes by the military" (Jarvis, 5). In the case of Puerto Rican militarized bodies—similar to other minority groups within the United States and other colonial contexts—there have been other complexities that have intersected the construction and definition of fixed identities based on nationality, ethnicity, and race. Though Truman had already signed an executive order to end segregation practices in the U.S. military forces by the Korean War, in practice, the Sixty-Fifth was the only regiment with blacks and whites fighting together. The majority of these soldiers were Puerto Ricans, "a new racialized group," or U.S. citizens who were conceived of as "culturally and racially inferior," as documented by Álvarez Curbelo (in Rivas-Rodríguez, 113). As such, Puerto Rican war stories emerge from an uncomfortable place of "in-betweenness," being both insiders and outsiders within the larger body of the United States and its troops, and being what Chief Justice White (1922), in his explanation of the status of Puerto Rico within the United States, described as "foreign in a domestic sense" (qtd. in Burnett and Marshall, 13). Notwithstanding, in Muñoz Marín's discourse, the Puerto Rican soldier represented the possibility of a virile state, desperately needed by the island's *criollos,* who saw the colonial relationship with the United States as an index of a flawed masculinity and, hence, of a truncated nation. Therefore, the military transformation of the *jíbaro's* body into a killing machine became the perfect prophecy for a Puerto Rico under the new ELA.

Going back to Fortuño's address, the prophecy for Puerto Rico that is explicitly revealed at the end of the soldier's anecdote tries to leave behind the body and the story it tells us. For Fortuño, as it was the case for Muñoz Marín, only the happy promise of survival must be delivered when times of unrest fill public spaces with angry or unhappy bodies. If the years between the 1930s and 1950s saw the emergence of a threatening Puerto Rican nationalist movement anchored on the sugar cane workers' movement (Denis, 37–41), the austerity politics followed by governments after 2008 have created a spring of very diverse political manifestations, such as university students' strikes (2010 and 2017), protests demanding an audit of the ELA's debt (since 2015), and even individuals, or *tipos comunes,* throwing eggs to political figures (2009). Fortuño's use of Emmanuel's body—just like Muñoz Marín's of the Sixty-Fifth—seeks to constitute an object of feeling that can move a very particular social sector (the upper-middle class, professionals, and religious subjects) toward a symbol of hope. Akin to what I have been discussing in previous chapters, this is a kind of religious hope that asks "us," sticking together with Emmanuel, to endure present circumstances, even to sacrifice ourselves, while waiting for something yet to come. At the end, "we" too will follow "our" leader's command, "No te rindas," and will be strong survivors like Emmanuel. And yet, there is an unhappy body that hides behind Fortuño's parable. It is the body of a war veteran that has been "severamente mutilado y su conciencia en coma profundo." I read this miniscule excerpt as a slippery detail that resists the attempt at domestication that underlies the grandiloquence of the political discourse.

U.S. MILITARISM, COLONIAL NEOLIBERALISM, AND RAMOS'S ANGRY CALLING

What kind of discourse can interrupt the religious hope impressed on the soldier's body by the colonial political imagination? Which are this body's hidden stories of the experience of war? What kind of representation would acknowledge the allegorical power of that body and highlight its capacity to resist and move among significations? In a neoliberal space of catastrophe impressed by war and by a ruling silence about the effects of war, what would be the resources, the desired effects, and the potential interlocutors for a representation centered on Puerto Rican soldiers' and veterans' bodies? In this chapter, I critically read Josean Ramos's journalistic work in *Diálogo* (2000–03), the University of Puerto Rico's (UPR) official periodical, as well as his autobiography *Antes de la guerra* (2005), to continue to understand the relationship between an angry melancholic voice and the love for the absent body that I started in the previous chapter in my analysis of Lemebel's production. Here, I argue that Ramos's public intellectual voice impresses soldiers' and veterans' bodies with, what I call, angry brotherly love and calls for an extended community of friends to dwell on wounds of resistance, like the ones that persist in Emmanuel's body.

Although Ramos had already worked as a journalist for the mainstream and widely read *El Nuevo Día* and for the most prominent left-aligned newspaper *Claridad,* in just three years of working for *Diálogo,* he managed to forge a broad reading public among college students, and his reports earned him journalism awards from the Institute of Puerto Rican Culture and the Overseas Press Club. In my reading of Ramos's journalism in *Diálogo,* I identify three constant themes: the use of space (geographic and social) on the island, militarism, and the implications of the federal clauses included in the Patriot Act for Puerto Rico. It is through *Diálogo* that Ramos begins to cultivate a readership among university students, to whom the autobiographical discourse of *Antes de la guerra* speaks.

In this book, Ramos engages its audience by telling them about an experience that is very familiar to the majority of Puerto Rico's university population: joining the U.S. military forces right before starting college or during the years of a higher education program. Specifically, Ramos joined the U.S. Navy during the 1970s, after the end of the Vietnam War, and his best friend Carlos Carrasquillo accompanied him in this decision. What guides my analysis of this text is the ways in which Carlos's voice joins the autobiographical narration, which switches freely among subjectivities, "I" and "you" and "we." This switching is complicated even more by the incorporation of anecdotes, filtered through the narrator's memory, of his father's experience in the Sixty-Fifth Infantry Regiment during the Korean War, as well as popular songs about the war that are sprinkled throughout and that are sung by Carlos. I propose that this memorial knot sets in motion the allegory of those bodies that have experienced war to engage in a dialogue with college students who live a context marked by the wars in Iraq and Afghanistan and who might feel inclined to sign a military contract. In fact, Ramos would publish the first chapter of *Antes de la guerra* in the pages of *Diálogo* as a teaser for his forthcoming book. This preview of his autobiography managed to hook his target audience, which can be inferred from the book's assignment in Spanish courses at American University and the Carolina and Mayagüez campuses of UPR. Even more importantly, as it was reported in "Diálogo entre estudiantes," the first year it was read in these courses, Ramos's autobiography inspired great enthusiasm among its readers, as evidenced by the staging of the book as a play, performed by students at American University.

In this sense, just like in Lemebel's radio production, in Ramos's writing, a voice calls to others who may feel the emptiness left by the ones who never returned. This voice resorts to music to amplify its melancholic calling, too; but the autobiographical medium, as well as an ongoing history of war, will impart a different effect from the elements at play (urban chronicles and a transition to democracy) in Lemebel's work. Another main contrast will be in the resonance of each voice. While Lemebel's readership has continued to grow nationally and internationally, even after his death, Ramos's has been small and exclusively located in the context of Puerto Rican universities. Even within this context, his work has been more popular among students than among other members of the academic community. This specificity of its appeal, however, makes Ramos's work one of the best to understand the relationship between neoliberalism, war, and the Puerto Rican young male body.

Furthermore, I believe that what makes Ramos's intellectual writing so urgent to study is its ability to denote that ongoing context of war in Puerto Rico by focusing on the effects that it has had on soldiers' and veterans' bodies. As I began to demonstrate in my analysis of Fortuño's address and its use of a Puerto Rican veteran's body, war has been incorporated by the colonial political imagination as a "clean" narrative, that is, as a story that teaches us about survival. Moreover, even though there has been a great deal of Puerto Rican literary, musical, and film production on the experience of war[1]—in contrast with the almost absolute silence that U.S. media representations have devoted to Puerto Rican soldiers and veterans (Avilés-Santiago, 1–3)—, academic discussion has not been prolific on this topic.

Most academic work dedicated to the study of Puerto Rican soldiers and veterans has concentrated on the Korean and Vietnam wars. In the field of history, the topic of the Sixty-Fifth Infantry Regiment (the Borinqueneers) and its intervention in the Second World War and the Korean War counts with the outstanding examinations developed in Álvarez Curbelo's essays. Álvarez Curbelo's work is the most detailed and in-depth in terms of the links between the military intervention of the Puerto Rican soldiers, the populist discourse of the day, and the political constitution of the ELA. It is also worth mentioning the work of José "Ché" Paralitici, who has concentrated on the history of resistance to military recruitment in Puerto Rico. In his book, *No quiero mi cuero pa' tambor,* Paralitici analyzes an archive that reveals a long history of Puerto Rican conscientious objectors to war and military recruitment, which needs to be studied side by side with the other long history of volunteer and drafted military service. As I will argue, Ramos's writings operate within a fine line of (dis)obedience—he talks about the experiences of volunteering, serving, resisting, and objecting—that draws from those two parallel histories of the relationship between Puerto Ricans and the U.S. military forces.

---

1. Literature by José Luis González, Emilio Díaz Valcárcel, René Marqués, and Pedro Pietri were dedicated to exploring the body of the soldier and the experience of war. Also, each of the wars in which thousands of Puerto Rican soldiers participated has its own popular playlist of tropical music. The topic of Puerto Rican soldiers in Korea and Vietnam has also been dealt with in film.

Two concrete events circumscribed the publication of Ramos's autobiography and his journalism in *Diálogo*: the Puerto Rican struggle to close the Roosevelt Roads Navy military base on the island municipality of Vieques (1999–2003) and the terrorist attacks of 9/11, which were used to justify the Patriot Act (2001). This period also marked the return of the U.S. army to extended and very expensive armed conflicts, as well as increased and more active recruiting propaganda for new soldiers among Puerto Rican university students (García Muñiz and Vega Rodríguez, 223–24). In the context of this (anti)militarism, during Ramos's years at *Diálogo* and up to 2005, when he published *Antes de la guerra,* his intellectual discourse intertwines the battle against the militarization of space with an in-depth reflection about the militarized bodies of the poor and the scars they carry. He will be able to trace this link through a passion for the construction of an archive that includes documents, events, personal and family memories, and songs. Most importantly, it is an archive that will only be possible thanks to Ramos's use of the concept of *filin,* both as a reference to the Cuban music genre that inspired so many tropical artists afterward and as a characterization of a kind of singing voice that can vividly transmit *filin* or feeling.

The music of *filin,* developed in Havana, Cuba, during the 1940s, relied mainly on guitars and voices (Ortega). In the midst of the musical productions of big jazz bands and medium-sized groups or *combos* that performed complex arrangements, there was a reformulation of the *trova* from Santiago de Cuba that became this *filin,* a renewal of the traditional song forged in transculturation (Contreras, 46). Composers and singers would participate in *filin* for decades—some examples are Ángel Díaz, José Antonio Méndez, César Portillo de la Luz, and Tania Castellanos—culminating in the *nueva trova,* particularly in the voice of Pablo Milanés (Díaz Ayala, 28). In Ramos's work, however, there is a documentary, literary, and affective interest in tracing a history of Puerto Rican voices that sing popular music with *filin,* that is, the condition of singing with honesty or, in other words, giving oneself back to others (Méndez, qtd. in Ortega). Going back to Cavarero's ideas on the phenomenology of the voice, discussed in the previous chapter, if the voice is what extends between "I" and "you," and within this extension, "our" bodies entangle in an intimate relationship (voicing/listening), the characteristic of *filin* will serve as an amplification of the voice's reach.

Ramos began developing his work on *filin* in his earliest publications: *Palabras de mujer,* a biography of Felisa Rincón de Gautier, the first female mayor of San Juan, and *Vengo a decirle adiós a los muchachos,*[2] a biography

---

2. The title of the book is taken from the first verse of the song "Despedida" by the composer Pedro Flores and popularized by Daniel Santos's voice. The title maintains the original grammatical error in the song (*decirle* [tell him] instead of *decirles* [tell them]).

of Daniel Santos, one of the most important singers of tropical music. While *Palabras de mujer* intercalates fragments of songs (like the bolero "Palabras de mujer," by Agustín Lara) with the story about Rincón de Gautier, *Vengo a decirle adiós a los muchachos* centers on the story of Santos's voice with *filin*: his beginnings, his training, his participation with other musicians, and his final days on the stage. Throughout this last story in particular, there is a narrative fascination with the performance of the singer's voice and how he manages to express *filin*. In *Diálogo*, Ramos published the essay "La guerra en el cancionero boricua," which describes a tradition of tropical music—from the bolero of the 1940s to the salsa of the 1970s—with war themes, expressed through voices with *filin* that sing the experiences of recruits and soldiers of the U.S. armed forces, as well as those of their family and friends. Just like Lemebel in *Cancionero* and *De perlas y cicatrices*, in this essay, Ramos's archive moves the popular into the academic sphere at the same time that it gives life to the allegory of the soldier's body, an allegory bolstered by the *filin* found in that hit parade of tropical music.

Within the context of the early 2000s, Ramos's work constituted the only intellectual voice interested in generating an academic discussion about the connection between the militarization of space and of the body in Puerto Rico. More recently, Manuel G. Avilés-Santiago has broken the silence that dominated concerning Puerto Rican soldiers and veterans of the wars that marked those years, Desert Storm (1991), the war in Afghanistan (2001–), and the second Iraq war (2003–11). Avilés-Santiago's archive brings to the forefront "unaccounted voices and images" of more contemporary Puerto Rican soldiers and veterans as they represent themselves in social networks and other websites and platforms (3). Thanks to his analysis, we can better understand how these subjects negotiate their identities amidst the colonial relationship between the United States and Puerto Rico, the history and contemporary tendencies of Puerto Rican migration, and the racialization of Puerto Ricans in the United States and the U.S. military forces. Nevertheless, beyond Avilés-Santiago's work, I find the Puerto Rican academic silence about these three most recent wars to be disturbing, particularly when we juxtapose it with current statistics on the cost of war for the island: by 2011 there were 150,000 veterans in constant need of medical service,[3] and this number would only continue to increase, because "during the United States' so-called War on Terror, Puerto Rico has contributed more troops in proportion to its population than any other state or territory but one—Nevada" (Avilés-Santiago, 5).

---

3. The number of veterans on the island is an approximation offered in 2011 by Pedro Pierluisi, the Resident Commissioner of Puerto Rico in Washington, DC, during a telephone interview with journalist Yolanda Vélez Arcelay, for Univisión of Puerto Rico, on July 27, 2011.

Finally, this academic silence about soldiers and veterans enters into contrast with the great number of academic publications on the topic of military bases, especially after the civilian struggle against the navy base on Vieques grabbed national and international attention (Rodríguez Beruff; Rodríguez Beruff and García Muñiz; Barreto; McCaffrey; García Muñiz and Vega Rodríguez; Piñero Cádiz).

I find this contrast to be very telling about how militarism has been interpreted by Puerto Rican academia: if it denotes an invasion of "our" island, we need to denounce it; but, if it is about a group of bodies—mostly poor—that are deployed somewhere else, "we" do not want to see it. Arcadio Díaz Quiñones has long thought about a "memoria rota" [broken memory] in the Puerto Rican context, that is, a memory deliberately denied by the political power, or broken by official repression and cultural exclusion (1993, 13). The *memoria rota,* for Díaz Quiñones, is metaphorically equivalent to a perverse occupation that is brutally imposed on everyday life: something dies devoured by silence (84). I believe that, when talking (or not talking) about soldiers and veterans, the *something* that no one wants to see or to name is the allegorical power with respect to the experience of war borne by these bodies, which cannot be assimilated to the fixed categories found in the intellectual debate on colonialism. In Ramos's active work with memory, the *something* referred to by Díaz Quiñones becomes alive.

Moreover, it seems to me that this critical void is the product of the propensity in Puerto Rican studies to read cultural representations of war almost solely within the context of their connection with the event of the U.S. invasion in 1898. Frances Negrón-Muntaner, for example, proposes that many Puerto Rican cultural productions on the island and in its diaspora constitute a discourse of worthiness that attempts to dissolve the shame associated with colonialism, the complex political relationship with the United States, and the American prejudices that have racialized and feminized Puerto Ricans. Although Negrón-Muntaner distinguishes between a "disgrace-shame" (felt by Puerto Rican elites when they are racialized and feminized as Puerto Ricans) and "discretion-shame" (felt by the Puerto Rican majority, which believes that it does not deserve certain "sacred places" based on its difference), many of these supposedly wounded voices speak *"through,* not *despite,"* colonialism (35). Negrón-Muntaner's work has been critical to our questioning and dismantling the myth of 1898 and its construction as a traumatic event. However, in my analysis of Ramos's work, I want to move away from the 1898 set of criticism that has dominated the discussion in Puerto Rican studies in order to study the materiality—soldiers' and veterans' bodies—of war and neoliberalism, a specific space of catastrophe that complicates colonialism.

By moving away from this paradigm, I align myself closely with Juan Carlos Rodríguez's goal to study literature and film devoted to the narration of the trauma of war, instead of just focusing on the trauma of colonialism in Puerto Rican literature. The question that guides his essay is quite similar to my own: What would happen if we were to think of colonialism from the margins of the metastory of 1898? (1145–46). To begin his exploration of the effects of a critique centered on this question, Rodríguez compares the literary narrative about 1898 with the narrative about soldiers and veterans from the 1950s. My reading of Ramos's work, however, goes beyond the representation of trauma to propose an analysis of an angry kind of friendship, or angry brotherly love, as politics of resistance in war scenarios. Therefore, even though I recognize the past inscription of the trauma of war on soldiers' and veterans' bodies, in this chapter, and as I did in chapter 3, I turn to anger as an emotion that demands us to politically imagine the present and the future. Specifically, in *Antes de la guerra*, I identify an angry call to known and unknown friends who have somehow shared the experience of war in the past and/or who may perhaps share it in the future. This call and the potential community it forges are political in their fluidity and in their angry resistance toward national and neoliberal politics of war.

In his classic conceptualization of *nation*, Benedict Anderson proposed to see this "imagined community . . . as a deep, horizontal comradeship" (7). According to Anderson, this feeling of comradeship is what enables so many people "willingly to die for such limited imaginings" (7). Nevertheless, when the moment to die comes for soldiers, the nation—just like freedom or democracy—is still too abstract of an idea. Other material and intimate relationships need to press soldiers forward, toward death, and as Brian Joseph Martin reminds us, friendship between soldiers has been useful for the art of military strategy in the West since Greek and Roman times. As exemplified by *The Iliad, The Banquet,* the *Chanson de Roland,* and literary productions up until the Napoleonic era, military success has historically relied "on solidarity between soldiers and officers, . . . on combat companions and warrior lovers" (5). It is no wonder then that the U.S. Navy, for example, offers new recruits the opportunity to participate in the Buddy Program, which allows up to four friends to stay together during their training and assignment to initial duty station (Navy Recruitment Command).

Within the patronized military fraternity, however, there are other kinds of defiant intimate relationships that contrast—in the performance and effect of their politics—with the imposed rhetoric of national brotherly love. When thinking about the politics of friendship, Derrida argues that there is a potentiality for forming a "community of conspirators" spread across time and space. This idea arises out of his examination of Michel de Montaigne's quote, "O my friends, there is no friend" (qtd. in Derrida, 1). According to Derrida, this phrase signifies friendship as a phenomenon that does not exist in the present, but only as a memory of the past or as a possibility in the future. Moreover, the community of conspirators is brought together through the call made by an "I" that is sent out to a "possible" ("perhaps") "you" whom the "I" does not even know; nor does the "I" know if this "you" will be a friend or an enemy. For Derrida, this call into the past, present, and future entails a responsibility and a commitment:

> I feel responsible towards *them*, . . . therefore responsible before *us* who announce them, therefore towards *us* who are already what we are announcing and who must watch over that very thing, therefore towards and before *you* whom I call to join us, before and towards me who understands all this and who is before it all: me, them, us, you, etc. (39)

Leela Gandhi's decolonial perspective on Derrida's articulation of friendship adds a layer of complexity when examining (post)colonial scenarios such as the one I study here. While colonialism's fantasy is to divide and exclude the "other" as well as to separate the "other" from its "others," Derrida's definition of the politics of friendship as a community can be articulated as a form of resistance. Therefore, in colonial contexts, Derrida's "community of conjurers" often becomes a "conjunction, conjuncture, coalition, and collaboration 'between' the most unlikely of associates," who must have the "capacity for the radical expropriation of identity in face of the other—a capacity, that is, for self-othering" (Gandhi, 20). Thus, in the process of "self-othering," the "I" rejects the identity assigned by colonial discourses and moves towards the "other"—becoming the "other"—instead of following the imperative to mark a differential distance between the "I" and the "other" (or to "other" the "other").

U.S. colonialism has subjected Puerto Ricans and other Latinos to a racialization process that "set them socially and culturally apart from the rest of society as territorial minorities, working-class groups, racially distinct populations, and immigrant communities" (Rivas-Rodríguez and Zamora, 2). Colonialism needs to be complicated by addressing the politics of neoliberalism, too, especially in the most recent war scenarios. For Ana Y. Ramos-Zayas, the economic logic of neoliberalism contributes to static definitions of national love to which every "good citizen" needs to adhere (133). Moreover, neoliberal national love is closely related to the productive capacity of subjects; that is, "only those subjects who can trace their worth or potential worth to conventional measures and meet that criteria are viewed as deserving of compassion and esteem, so that value is ascribed to lives and deaths" (133). In an ethnographic study of the neoliberal affective effects of militarism on racialized communities in Newark, New Jersey, Ramos-Zayas proposes that Puerto Ricans' constant striving to make "our" military experiences visible functions within the neoliberal "politics of worthiness" (137). If Puerto Ricans are worthy because of their military experiences, then their lives and deaths deserve U.S. national compassion and esteem. It seems that "our" worthiness of inclusion within the bodies of love for the U.S. nation moves between becoming visible through "our" difference and through "our" proven capacity for sameness.

I propose that, in Ramos's discourse, angry brotherly love and its affective resistance work against this kind of neoliberal national love and its politics of worthiness. Specifically, in my reading of *Antes de la guerra*, I argue that the "community of conspirators" is forged through the friendship of "Carlos and I" and, from this nucleus and thanks to the voice with *filin* singing tropical music and recounting memories of the Sixty-Fifth, it is extended to past Puerto Rican soldiers and veterans; those who share the experience of militarism and war, and perhaps will listen to the calling of the voice. Furthermore, the melancholic calling carries the intention of angrily warning present and future young college students about the possible consequences of signing a contract with the army. From this affective and intimate knot, there emerges a proposal for a dialogic debate that breaks through the symbolic monolingualism about 1898 and the legal and political trap of the ELA.

RAMOS'S JOURNALISM AND HIS DIALOGUE WITH UNIVERSITY STUDENTS

The university publication *Diálogo* would be the arena from which Ramos would fire his intellectual discourse about diverse experiences of U.S. militarization and militarism in Puerto Rico that go beyond the recruitment of soldiers. *Diálogo* started as a monthly publication in 1986, thanks to an initiative by then UPR President Fernando Agrait and the work of intellectuals and journalists David Ortiz Angleró and Luis Fernando Coss Pontón (Delgado Cintrón). As stated in its website's section "Quiénes somos," one of *Diálogo*'s missions was to provide a workshop in journalism for students in the major; another one was to create a venue in which news contents were considered through and from an academic perspective. Quickly, the monthly paper distinguished itself from other periodicals in Puerto Rico thanks to its constant pieces of investigative journalism and to fostering debates among different academic voices. The long list of awards that *Diálogo* and its journalists have won—listed on the *Wikipedia* entry *"Diálogo* UPR"—demonstrates its quality and relevance to a readership on the island, even beyond UPR, that wants to stay connected to the academic community.

Ramos's journalist work in *Diálogo* was framed by a debate about the force of civilian society in Puerto Rico, specifically in regard to closing the main base of the U.S. Navy, Roosevelt Roads Base, on the island municipality of Vieques. Roosevelt Roads Base operated from 1940 to 2003, and, during all those years, the fishing community of Vieques as well as proindependence groups continually organized uprisings to resist the presence of the navy, due to their training sessions with live rounds, their interference with the schools of fish, and their social and environmental threats to the ecological system of the island. In 1999, the death of a civilian employee at the base, David Sanes Rodríguez, became the event that impelled broad consensus in Puerto Rico, beyond Vieques and political ideologies, to demand that the navy close Roosevelt Roads. The slogan "¡Ni una bomba más!" marked the situation in Vieques as an emergency in the face of which a local and global community emerged—uniting groups and individuals from Vieques, Puerto Rico, the United States, and other places—that was willing to launch a battle based on civil disobedience. Crossing the boundaries of the base and entering the bombing and firing range became a kind of call to which the protesters responded (Santiago, ii). The *call* was heard by the academic community, and in *Diálogo,* Ramos's stories responded to it from different angles.

Ramos's investigative journalism style is characterized by a historicist bent on the topic he is dealing with and an eagerness for documentation that includes incisive interviews, the use of wide-ranging references, and data analysis. Following this style, he published in *Diálogo* a series of articles on a variety of topics, such as resource management and geographical land use in Puerto Rico, mental health, the state of archaeological research, and relations between Church and State, among others. Although he also wrote articles more directly related to the situation in Vieques and the legal consequences of the Patriot Act on Puerto Rico, it is interesting how in all of them—including those that would seem not to be directly related to the topic—Ramos's writing leads to a reflection on the effects of militarism on Puerto Rican social space and bodies.

Thus, for example, in his first contributions in *Diálogo* (August 2000) under the titles "Iglesia y Estado . . . entre la espada y la cruz" and "Encuentros y desencuentros entre dos poderosas instituciones," Ramos constructs a historical tale that takes us, from the final decades of the nineteenth century to the early ones of the twenty-first, through the legal and political relations between the churches and the State in Puerto Rico. Although relations between the churches and the State, as well as among different faiths, in Puerto Rico have been fairly conflictive, particularly throughout the twentieth century (Silva Gotay, 1997 and 2005; Martínez-Ramírez), Ramos's writing traces the origins and possibilities of an ecumenical union that can confront the problems that affect Puerto Ricans' daily life, such as the navy in Vieques and, more recently, the implementation of neoliberal state measures. Through interviews and by explaining the arguments in various studies, he leads up to the idea that the Puerto Rican State cannot promote any religion, but churches *can* intervene in political debates in the public sphere. While he classifies the rise of the Partido de Acción Cristiana for the 1960 elections—when the Catholic Church on the island threatened anyone who voted for another party with excommunication—as "legal and immoral," he describes ecclesiastical participation on Vieques as "illegal and moral." Thus he concludes his articles with a description of the Ecumenical Coalition for Peace for Vieques that evokes a revolutionary/religious discourse:

> La base para el consenso religioso ya estaba establecida cuando se inicia una nueva lucha por liberar a Vieques de la presencia militar. . . . Era una poderosa coalición ecuménica jamás vista, . . . con capacidad de movilizar a miles de siervos al servicio de una causa; evidenciado tras la multitudinaria marcha silenciosa con banderas blancas, convocada por sus líderes a favor de la paz en Vieques. Tal unión evangélica sin precedentes históricos reunió a cristianos de diversas denominaciones en una misma capilla levantada en área de tiro, donde permanecieron solidarios en silentes vigilias de desobediencia civil y obediencia moral. ("Encuentros y desencuentros," 9)

> The basis for religious consensus was already established when a new battle to free Vieques from its military presence began. . . . It was a powerful ecumenical coalition never before seen, . . . with the ability to mobilize thousands of servants in service to a cause; evidenced by the multitudinous silent march with white flags, called by its leaders to push for peace in Vieques. That historically unprecedented evangelical union gathered Christians of various denominations together in a single chapel erected on the bombing range, where supporters maintained silent vigils of civil disobedience but moral obedience.

What interests me about this quote is Ramos's description of a call that is capable of a massive mobilization. The *multitudinaria marcha silenciosa con banderas blancas* speaks of a peaceful response to militarism, a manifestation that supported civil disobedience, and yet it also has tones of war: *lucha por liberar, . . . movilizar a miles de siervos al servicio de una causa,* and *obediencia moral.* Specifically, it speaks of the figure of the martyr, the one who will sacrifice everything, even their life, for a cause. This religious discourse has been used by the Latin American and Caribbean political left for decades, and, in particular, as I will argue in the final chapter, it was the basis for the kind of revolutionary love instituted as nationalism by the Cuban Revolution. Nevertheless, in Ramos's quote and for the context he is addressing, this discourse refers us more to the ideals of liberation theology, according to which the Catholic Church must be involved in the struggle to end oppression. The fundamental point for liberation theology is that this involvement must rely on the guidance of the oppressed, because they are the ones who possess the experience to reform the Church and the world (Rowland, 2–3). In Ramos's quote, the experience that reunites *siervos* from different faiths is the effects of militarization in Vieques. Even though he speaks of *obediencia moral,* without knowing about the effects of militarization from experience, the call and the mobilization would not have been possible.

In later articles, Ramos also links natural resource management and environmental protection with U.S. military presence in Puerto Rico. Therefore, the experience of militarization goes beyond the isolated case of Vieques. In "De espaldas al mar" (September 2002), for example, he examines the economic and ecological potentiality of the island's marine environment and describes how shortsighted and limited the plans to take advantage of this resource have been. Toward the end of the article he reveals and emphasizes how the U.S. Navy has been the organization that has benefited most from this marine resource:

> Históricamente muchas de las investigaciones en el área de la oceanografía y biología marina realizadas en la isla han sido financiadas por la Oficina de Investigaciones Navales del Ejército de Estados Unidos. A principios de la década de los años [19]40, ya la Marina de Guerra norteamericana había auspiciado investigaciones en nuestras costas con fines bélicos. [A lo largo de las décadas] el cuerpo naval comisiona a investigadores de prestigio cuyos proyectos puedan servir sus fines militares. Sin embargo, mucha de la información obtenida es clasificada y ni siquiera les permiten publicar sus hallazgos en revistas académicas. (8–9)

> Historically many of the investigations in the area of oceanography and marine biology carried out on the island have been financed by the U.S. Army's Office of Naval Research. At the beginning of the 1940s, the U.S. Navy had already sponsored research with military objectives on our

shores. [For decades] the naval body commissioned prestigious researchers whose projects could serve military objectives. However, much of the information obtained is classified, and [the researchers] are not even allowed to publish their findings in academic journals.

The navy's rule over the marine environment does not only entail a control over the resources; it also takes charge of all research and, therefore, of geographical knowledge of the island. The connection between the social space's geographical, institutional, and ideological spheres in this quote makes clear a process of militarization that, by 2002, had produced a space of catastrophe that had yet to define new forms of command. The empty space that the navy would leave, and the closing of most military bases by the mid 2000s, is still contested by federal and state agencies as well as by local communities and private interests. And yet, as shown in the movie *Vieques: Una batalla inconclusa*, the most pervasive effect of militarization in Puerto Rico is still inhabiting land and marine resources in the form of military waste and toxic pollution, all the details of which still need to be known by the island's population.

This constant link between militarism and everyday life in Puerto Rico will also lead Ramos to study how the Patriot Act has redefined the social space in Puerto Rico according to a law that privileges a state of war. If in the United States the provisions of the Patriot Act attempted to act against "privacy, the freedoms of speech, association, and religion; due process; and equality" (Herman, 6), for Ramos the territorial condition of the ELA made Puerto Ricans in the island even more vulnerable than the rest of American citizens to the consequences of exercising their constitutional rights. Specifically, taking into account the recent civilian mobilization against the navy in Vieques, Ramos conducts a series of interviews to better understand the impact that the Patriot Act could have on the ability to speak out and take action in Puerto Rico's public sphere. In "Alerta ante la Ley Patriótica" (March 2002), he concludes:

En el caso de Puerto Rico, la ley cobra mayor relevancia dado el número de ciudadanos que han optado por la desobediencia civil pacífica como método de lucha para sacar de Vieques a la Marina de guerra norteamericana. . . . Según redactada la voluminosa ley del USA Patriot Act, estas personas pueden ser objeto de vigilancia telefónica y electrónica sin notificación; así como registros y allanamientos secretos en la casa u oficina. . . . Pese a que tanto la Secretaria de Justicia, Anabelle Rodríguez, como el Superintendente de la Policía, Miguel Pereira, expresaron a *Diálogo* que la ley no iba dirigida a los desobedientes civiles, la amplia definición de "terrorismo doméstico" podría incluirlos cuando el Secretario de Justicia Federal, John Ashcroft, lo considere necesario. (4)

In the case of Puerto Rico, the law takes on greater relevance given the number of citizens who have opted for nonviolent civil disobedience as a means to fight to remove the U.S. Navy from Vieques. . . . According to the voluminous U.S. Patriot Act, these people may be the object of telephone and electronic surveillance without notice; as well as secret searches and forced entry at their homes or offices. . . . Despite the fact that both the Secretary of Justice, Anabelle Rodríguez, and Superintendent of Police Miguel Pereira, told *Diálogo* that the law was not directed at citizens who engaged in civil disobedience, the full definition of *domestic terrorism* could include them whenever Federal Secretary of Justice John Ashcroft, might deem it necessary.

La amplia definición de terrorismo doméstico is still fought today (2018) in the United States, as many documented residents have been denied access to the country in airports across the nation because they are considered potential terrorist threats. For Ramos, it seems that the Patriot Act and its loose definition of domestic terrorism echoes the decades of political surveillance, persecution, retaliation, violence, imprisonment, and assassination that many Puerto Ricans experienced during the Cold War under local and federal authorities (Bosque Pérez and Colón Morera). This long history of extreme policing eroded constitutional rights and has continued to make possible, even at present, "significant human rights violations and an intense social crisis" (Colón Morera, 83). At the time Ramos was writing, and once again today, when thousands of Puerto Ricans participate in different kinds of protest against the dismantlement of the economic and political system of the island under the PROMESA law,[4] the Patriot Act comes as a well-known threat against constitutional and human rights.

Ramos's preoccupation with the impact of the Patriot Act on those who participate in civil disobedience also has to do with his firm belief in the results that civic organization—outside of political parties—can offer in Puerto Rico. Throughout all of his articles in *Diálogo*, his journalism sounds out the effective possibility of different civil actions in the Puerto Rican political sphere

---

4. PROMESA stands for the 2016 Puerto Rico Oversight, Management, and Economic Stability Act, a federal law enacted by the U.S. Congress. The law established an oversight board or *Junta*, whose members were appointed by the U.S. president, to work on a process to restructure the billionaire public debt of the island and to combat future indebtedness. For more details, see "S.2328—PROMESA."

and the rescue of a public sphere that can overtake the actors in the main political parties, who limit public discussion of the formulas for the island's political status. His journalism is also probing his university reading public on various topics that follow some very specific questions: How does U.S. militarism affect everyday life and discussion in Puerto Rico's public sphere? How have civil sectors responded to this militarism? Having cultivated a reading public around questions that revolved around the effects of militarism over geographical resources and the public sphere, Ramos would move on to present his perspective on the impact over soldiers and veterans.

He published the first chapter of *Antes de la guerra* in *Diálogo* (January and February 2003) under the title "Memorias de un recluta," which I will discuss in the next section, and the essay "La guerra en el cancionero boricua," which appeared a year later after the publication of his autobiography (May–June 2006 and August–September 2006) and with which I will conclude my study in this chapter. If the publication of the former baited the hook that announced the coming book, the latter indicated the expansion of one of the fundamental themes in *Antes de la guerra*: the musical *filin* that weaves together a series of shared memories about the experience of war. Again, choosing *Diálogo* for these two publications is no accident: Ramos wants to continue a relationship with that young college audience and remind them again, through daily, intimate experiences, of the dangers inherent in contracts with the armed forces.

ANTES DE LA GUERRA OR AN ANGRY CALL TO SOLDIERS AND VETERANS AGAINST U.S. MILITARISM

"Memorias de un recluta," the first chapter of *Antes de la guerra* that Ramos published in *Diálogo* two years before the autobiography came out, would remain complete and unedited in the book. As was the case with Carlos Monsiváis and Francisco Goldman—integrating their original shorter publications into longer projects—, I believe his wholesale transfer of Ramos's first chapter from one medium to the other was an attempt to preserve its urgent nature. Here the narration's urgent character is designed to alert college students to the *equivocación* of signing a contract with the army (Ramos, 2005, 11), and it will do so through a literary discourse that promptly establishes a complicit intimacy between the autobiographical voice and the listener/reader. This intimacy is presupposed on the sharing of a common background—young people who are impoverished and lost—, and thus the autobiographical "I" opens up to confess his mistakes, while also hoping that the one who listens/reads will embrace the confession in full understanding, without judgement. All anger, the "I" will lead us to agree, must be directed towards U.S. militarism.

This first chapter is constructed as a synthesis of the story: two friends decide to enlist in the U.S. Navy and later plan a series of tactics to desert. While signaling the beginning of the action, the chapter also offers a panorama of the thematic lines that will be developed throughout the rest of the narrative: the innocence of youth and the deceitful propaganda of the army; the violence of military training; the relationship of complicity between friends that forges an angry resistance and a final escape from the army by resorting to mental illness; and an uncomfortable relationship with a paternal figure—which swings between admiration and the desire to be different from him—that, in addition, serves as a pretext for writing the memoir of the Sixty-Fifth Infantry Regiment during the Korean War.

The sense of urgency about the military mark on the body appears from the start of *Antes de la guerra* as it opens with the officer in charge of boot camp shouting at the recruits:

> Cuando aquel oficial alto y jincho de acento sureño me escupió de un grito el primer *motherfucker* muy cerquita de la cara, supe al instante que aquello no era para nosotros. Comprendí que nos habíamos equivocado Carlos y yo al firmar un contrato de cuatro años activos y dos de reserva en la Marina de Guerra Norteamericana, y que de alguna manera había que escapar de allí. (11)

> When that tall, pale officer with the southern accent spat that first "motherfucker" in my face, I knew immediately that that was not for us. I realized that Carlos and I had made a mistake when we signed a contract for four years of active duty and two in the reserves of the U.S. Navy, and that somehow I had to get out of there.

While the aggressive yelling is an indicator of the violence of training, the derisive description of the officer points us toward an emotional response anchored in anger. While the interaction between the officer and the "I" underscores a kind of cultural differentiation that establishes a protective distance; the "us" sticks together in regret. It is a regret that tells us of the mistake made, that is, of a lack of knowledge that led to a bad decision and, at the same time, of a false expectation shattered by the offensive name-calling.

The narration of military violence continues to be detailed in that first chapter. Yelling, humiliations, beatings, and restrictions all work together toward the rupture of a subjectivity that is diagnosed as defective or lacking by the U.S. military forces. The ultimate objective of boot camp must be, then, to turn individuals' defects into a disciplined collective, as the following examples from the narration show:

> Seguiríamos siendo señoritas, decía entre risitas [el Sargento McCalip], mientras ellos se encargaban de hacernos hombres en el *boot camp* durante los próximos tres meses. (15)

> We would keep on being little ladies, said [Sergeant McCalip] snickering, as long as they were in charge of making us men in boot camp over the next three months.

> [McCalip] era experto en hacerse odiar y desalentar la sensibilidad humana en los tiernos reclutas que recibía, como preámbulo a un proceso psicológico riguroso para convertirnos en hombres de guerra entrenados para matar. (17–18)

> [McCalip] was an expert at making himself hateful and at discouraging human sensitivity in the raw recruits he received, as an opener for the harsh psychological process of turning us into men of war trained to kill.

> Los rostros de los demás reclutas se hacían más duros a medida que el Sargento McCalip se paseaba con su insoportable brinquito y nos advertía lo duro que nos haría trabajar en los próximos noventa días, hasta cansarnos como nunca antes y sentir el dolor en músculos que aun no conocíamos. (25)

> The faces of the other recruits became harder with every pass Sergeant McCalip made with his unbearable little jump, warning us of how hard he would make us work over the next ninety days, to the point of exhaustion, the likes of which we had never known, and aching in muscles we didn't even know we had.

> Carlos y yo sentíamos el cuerpo y la mente extenuados, sin haber iniciado aun el temible *boot camp* con sus bajas pasiones humanas. (30)

> Carlos and I felt exhausted in body and mind, and we hadn't even begun the fearsome boot camp with its base human instincts.

Physical subordination through the infliction of pain, as Elaine Scarry explains very well in *The Body in Pain,* sustains the fiction of power, since in physical torture, pain ceases to be felt as something internal. Rather, it is understood, through the external agent, as the power that the "other" has over "me": "Fraudulent and merciless, this kind of power claims pain's attributes as its own and disclaims the pain itself" (56–57). The previous passages describing physical torture must be understood, furthermore, within the context of military training, where the final goal of pain is not to obtain information from the "other"-enemy-prisoner, but to make an "other"-recruit part of an "us"-army. As I explained at the beginning of this chapter, armies have many ways to classify (racialize) and discipline bodies and make them uniform; military training torture is another, more pervasive one. Specifically, this kind of torture seeks to obtain soldiers who will unquestioningly obey the power of military pain, engraved from the first day on their bodies.

In the face of this discourse of military violence, an alternate one of innocence is constructed, anchored in naïve expectations, running through the autobiographical text, and likewise initiated from the very first pages. Before boot camp, the following scene was what they imagined the military experience to be:

> [Carlos y yo] nos imaginábamos estar entonces en Miami Beach, vestiditos de marinos con uniforme de gala y tres rayitas en la manga izquierda, rodeados de chicas rubias y brunettes fascinadas con nuestras aventuras de mar. . . . Me veía de brazos de una linda doncella elegantemente vestida con traje de chifón y seda. . . . A poca distancia veía a Carlos como pez en agua, con micrófono en mano desde el piano bar en penumbras, cantando con filin las *Olas y arenas* de Sylvia Rexach. (11–12)

> [Carlos and I] imagined ourselves, then, in Miami Beach, decked out in Navy dress blues with three stripes on the left sleeve, surrounded by blonde and brunette women fascinated with our adventures at sea. . . . I saw myself arm in arm with a pretty young lady elegantly dressed in silk and chiffon. . . . Not far away I saw Carlos in his element, microphone in hand at the piano bar in the shade, singing with *filin* the song "Olas y arenas" [Waves and Sand] by Sylvia Rexach.

This jarring innocence—jarring because it is so incredible—combines in this imagined scene a series of referents that blend the military, sexual desire, and Puerto Rican culture in the song that enlivens the scene. Nevertheless, I think the incongruity of this discourse of innocence in *Antes de la guerra* has three aims: to achieve a sufficiently destabilizing effect so as to measure up to the horror of the discourse of military violence; to appeal to the sensibilities of the imagined reading public that may be considering enlisting in the armed forces; and to rescue some piece of that past "I"—that innocent youth who enlisted in the navy—who broke under military training.

Furthermore, the efficacy of this jarring innocence is made possible by the autobiographical genre, in which the "I" attempts to use confession and honesty about a series of experiences that have constructed his subjectivity. Autobiographical candidness, then, manages to make that subjectivity empathetic, and even representative or exemplary, as it "becomes the blueprint for others;" after all, in "its capacity to be representative, autobiography oversteps the line which separates literature and reality by referring to the reader's involvement and considering the implications of the text upon lived experiences" (Lynch, 211). Thus *Antes de la guerra* is being forged within a didacticism that functions by example. It will be important for that example to be constructed on a reciprocal empathy: from the readers to the subjectivity that exhibits itself, and from the narrator that tells the story in the present to the young "I" of the past, who is also imagined as representative of the innocent readers who are considering the military option.

In the autobiographical exercise, the narrative voice continues to justify the errors and contradictions of that innocent "I" of the past. The first contradiction is the protagonist's decision to volunteer for the armed forces, even though he had leftist political leanings and was aware of his own father's experience as a soldier in the Korean War. To justify this contradiction, the narrator explains in detail the political and socioeconomic context of Puerto Rico between 1976 and 1977, when the young protagonists were students at UPR and the academic institution was experiencing a workers' strike, supported by the students, which was one of the key struggles in the midst of the ideological battle rocking the island. The narrator describes it this way in the second chapter:

> Eran tiempos de mucha agitación política y sindical en el País. Se escuchaba hablar de los movimientos ambientalistas para contrarrestar los avances de la industria petroquímica, que contaminaba la Isla como una escuadra de soldados, por aire, tierra y mar. Había confrontaciones violentas entre grupos de izquierda y derecha, entre patronos y obreros; protestas contra el Servicio Militar Obligatorio y la presencia militar en la Isla; atentados contra las figuras identificadas con el socialismo y la independencia para Puerto Rico, imprentas y periódicos alternos. . . . Para peor de males, el año coincidía con la entrada al poder de uno de los más hábiles políticos maquiavélicos, empeñado en convertir a Puerto Rico en un estado más de la nación norteamericana a fuerza de su mano dura, desplegada con toda su furia en los

asesinatos del Cerro Maravilla dos años más tarde. El ambiente que se respiraba en la Universidad era tenso, con mítines de huelguistas en las distintas facultades, donde se repartían boletines y propaganda alusiva a los reclamos de los trabajadores y las demandas de los estudiantes, al acecho de la Guardia Universitaria y la Fuerza de Choque.[5] (33–34)

It was a time of great political and union unrest in the Country. There was talk of environmental movements to counteract the advances of the petrochemical industry, which polluted the Island like a squadron of soldiers, by land, sea, and air. There were violent confrontations between leftist and rightist groups, between employers and employees; protests against Selective Service and the military presence on the Island; assassination attempts against figures identified with socialism and independence for Puerto Rico, alternative presses and journals. . . . To make matters worse, the year saw the rise to power of one of the cleverest Machiavellian politicians, determined to turn Puerto Rico into one more of the United States by dint of his iron fist, [which was] unleashed in all its fury in the assassinations at Cerro Maravilla two years later. The atmosphere at the University was tense, with meetings of the strikers from different schools, where they distributed bulletins and propaganda alluding to the workers' complaints and the students' demands, to the spying of the University Police and the Riot Police.

The polarization of the political context is combined with the lack of economic opportunities for the narrator and his friend Carlos, who had abandoned their university studies because of the impasse between protesters and the administration. Thus, the narration of the search for work and the description of the lines of unemployed people are the backdrop for a military recruiter's appearance on the scene. If joining the military was the only economic way out left to young people with the desire and the need to work, the military propaganda was what fed the hopes for a guaranteed future:

Recién había terminado la Guerra de Vietnam, y el reclutador vociferaba que ahora era el momento de asegurar un futuro digno y honrado, con oportunidades de estudio y empleo garantizado, bonos y beneficios para la esposa

---

5. The *político maquiavélico* was Carlos Romero Barceló, governor of Puerto Rico between 1976 and 1984. During his eight years in office, there were disappearances and assassinations of people affiliated with the proindependence movement and with socialism on the island. Also in this quote from *Antes de la guerra* are mentioned the "asesinatos del Cerro Maravilla," which was the most notorious case of political assassinations in the 1970s. At Cerro Maravilla, an isolated mountain area in the heart of Puerto Rico's countryside, two proindependence young men, Carlos Soto Arriví and Arnaldo Darío Rosado, were assassinated by the police.

e hijos, seguro de vida, los mejores servicios médicos y hospitales, viajes y
aventuras por el mundo en tiempos de paz. Sonaba atractivo lo que decía,
sobre todo a los oídos de jóvenes pobres, inmaduros y ahora desempleados.
(37)

The Vietnam War had just ended, and the recruiter bellowed that now was
the time to secure a decent, honorable future, with opportunities to study
and guaranteed work, with bonuses and benefits for the wife and kids, life
insurance, the best medical services and hospitals, trips and adventures
around the world in peacetime. What he was saying sounded attractive, particularly to the ears of poor young people, immature, and now unemployed.

Even better, beyond a guaranteed education, work, and marginal benefits in
"peacetime," the narrator's attention was caught by the propaganda pamphlets,
"with color photos" that showed how "los del Navy navegaban en barcos y
portaviones enormes con sus característicos uniformes blancos con lazo y
franjas azules; o figuraban de visita en ciudades exóticas a orillas del mar,
rodeados de hermosas chicas con cara de admiración" (37) [navy men sailed
on huge boats and aircraft carriers wearing their iconic white uniforms with
blue neckerchiefs and stripes; or they were shown visiting exotic seaside cities,
surrounded by beautiful girls smiling in admiration]. Based on this propaganda, the friends built their fantasy that combined military life, sexual desire,
and Puerto Rican culture in perfect harmony.

So, when the violence of military training had fractured that fantasy, and
with it the protagonist's innocence, the narrator's memory would recover the
pieces to justify again and again his decision to join the navy. For example, he
confesses in the third chapter:

Personalmente, quería ser un marino sin perder la sensibilidad, que era
como hablar de Dios en la casa del Diablo. . . . Pero mi error fue suponer que
tal actitud bélica [la del entrenamiento militar] se daría nada más en tiempos
de guerra, sin imaginar que era una característica indispensable de las fuer-
zas armadas aun en tiempos de paz. Más aun, comprendí que en el ejército
no hay tiempos de paz porque sería una contradicción a su razón de ser, que
es la guerra, por aquello de hacer la guerra para preservar la paz. (80–81)

Personally, I wanted to be a sailor without losing my sensitivity, which
was like talking about God in the Devil's house. . . . But my mistake was
in thinking that such a military attitude [that of military training] would
be necessary only in times of war; I never imagined that it was an essential

characteristic of the armed forces even in peacetime. What was more, I came to understand that in the army there is no peacetime because it would be a contradiction to its reason for being, which is war, having to make war to protect peace.

And yet, the innocent "I" of the past already had intimate knowledge of his father's experience in the army. He knew, from both his parents' stories, that the army had changed him profoundly:

> Después del ejército [mi padre] no fue igual, decía mi madre, algo extraño le hizo la guerra que me lo cambió para siempre y ya nunca más fue el mismo que conocí. . . . Ese proceso militar psicológico que transformó a mi padre en lo que había conocido, empezaba a verlo ahora delante de mí en sus primeras manifestaciones, y así lo entendí desde el principio para enfrentarlo con prudencia y evitar que me afectara más allá de los gestos. Después de todo, lo menos que deseaba era parecerme a mi papá, era lo opuesto. (19)

> After the army [my father] wasn't the same, my mother said, the war did something strange to him that changed him forever and he was never again the same person I [she] had first met. . . . That psychological military process that changed my father into what I had known, I began to see now before me in its beginning stages, and that was how I looked at it from the start to face it carefully and prevent it from affecting me beyond the [facial] expressions. After all, the last thing I wanted was to look like my father; just the opposite.

This knowledge warned him about some of the changes that soldiers would experience while also confirmed his refusal of that transformation, of becoming his father. Therefore, the experience of training will also be a bridge to join the everyday memories and anecdotes of his father in the narration. It seems to me, then, that the preservation of his jarring innocence—sheltered behind his contradictory justifications—also tries to maintain a piece of the past "I," as well as a piece of his father's experience. It is from these pieces that an angry calling for a community of soldiers and veterans against militarism will rise.

The first call of this intellectual discourse will be for his friend Carlos, and it is full of angry love since the dedication opening the text: "Para Carlos Carrasquillo, arquitecto del plan, víctima de la aventura" [For Carlos Carrasquillo, architect of the plan, victim of the adventure]. As Cavarero explains it, autobiographical writing is born of the need to tell the story that gives testimony of "my" existence in the world and "my" relationships with others. But, for that story to be told, there needs to be an "other" to narrate it, and an "other" to listen to it. In the narrative process, that "other" becomes an intimate "you," first in the development of the "I," between the narrator in the present and the character of the past, and second, in the process of confessing intimate details to an imagined "you" to whom it is narrated. It is only through these intimate relationships with a "you" that the narrated identity becomes *bios* (social or human life) instead of *zoe* (natural or bare life). In the case of *Antes de la guerra*, the existence of the autobiographical-relational being is complicated even more, because this is not just the narration of a past "I," but also of Carlos, an intimate "you" to whom is told the story of the "I," the story of the "you"-Carlos, and the story of the "we"-Carlos and I, "the inassimilable, the insubstitutable, the unrepeatable; . . . a unique existent that no categorization or collective identity can fully contain; . . . the *you* [*tu*] that comes before the *we* [*noi*], before the plural *you* [*voi*] and before the *they* [*loro*]" (Cavarero, 2000, 90). In the narration that insists on telling us about "Carlos and me," Carlos is the "you" that comes first, the biographical absence to whom the story must be told. Only in this way, relationally, can the stories of the "I" and the "we" come out.

Carlos's absence, announced in the epigraph, further suggests a narrator who functions as a witness of the witness to an experience not survived, who can turn into language the final experience lived by the one who can no longer give testimony, as thought by Agamben (discussed in chapter 1). As studied in the previous chapter, the witness of the witness speaks from the site of a melancholic anger, loading their story with information about the past that establishes a series of alliances, as Lorde and Ahmed explained. From the first time he gives a more detailed description of Carlos, the narrator includes the revelation of the end in what will be a process of transformation for his friend, and with it, he underlines his anger about Carlos's absence in the present, and the relation of such absence to the experience of military training:

> [Carlos] era un espíritu libre y cómico que provocaba con sus chistes las delicias del público, ingenioso y alegre por demás, lleno de ocurrencias para cada ocasión. Llegaba a un lugar aunque le fuera extraño, y al poco rato ya tenía a varias personas cautivas a su derredor, riéndose a más no poder y embrujados de aquella alegría pasajera, que en el fondo mitigaba su penar. Nadie jamás hubiera imaginado aquel trágico destino que le deparaba la vida años después, tras la traumática experiencia militar que lo llevó a la locura. (42)

> [Carlos] was a free and comical spirit who delighted the public with his jokes, extremely witty and happy, full of humorous comments for every

occasion. He would go to a place, even if he'd never been there before, and in no time he had several people around him captivated, laughing until their sides hurt, and enchanted by that fleeting joy that eased their pain deep down. Nobody could have ever imagined that tragic fate that life would hand him years later, after the traumatic military experience that drove him crazy.

In fact, reading it through the character of Carlos, *Antes de la guerra* relates a process of military transformation that results in physical and mental illness. And it will be from the space of insanity that Carlos and the narrator will come up with the tactic to get out of military training. Even though in *Literatura y paternalismo en Puerto Rico* Juan Gelpí analyzes the use of the metaphor of illness in several canonical Puerto Rican literary texts and proposes that this image points to what was diagnosed by those texts' authors as a deficient masculinity of the colonized in confronting colonialism, I believe that Ramos's autobiographical discourse takes advantage of the undefined and uncertain space of madness, seeing it as a potentiality rather than as a peril for the two young male recruits.

It could be said then that, in *Antes de la guerra,* illness is proposed as a tactic of "el arte de bregar," as conceptualized by Díaz Quiñones for the Puerto Rican context: *bregar* refers to a code that allows us to take action by resorting to a negotiation that evades open confrontation and great acts of heroism (2000, 22–23). For Díaz Quiñones, the meaning and action of *bregar* relate to everyday life and literary/intellectual discourses. In Ramos's autobiography, Carlos's mental illness is, first of all, an angry resistance to military training. Secondly, it is the *bregar* a way out of the signed contract. Finally, it is what makes the start of something new possible. In this last sense, Carlos's mental illness appropriates military discourse to perform a different kind of masculinity from the one the army wants for its soldiers.

If in military logic the recruit's transformation during basic training must lead to the optimization of his physical abilities and military aptitudes and in this way make up the disciplined body of the army, in Carlos's case, right from the moment of receiving his military haircut—one of the first physical changes—we can see that his physical and mental weakness does not match up with the hardening expected by the army:

Aparte del cambio por el recorte, Carlos se notaba raro y se veía decaído y deteriorado, algo enfermo. . . . Alcancé a ver desde el lado izquierdo su semblante desfigurado, los hombros caídos y un juego en las rodillas, ida la mirada en un semblante de pena que me recordaba a su mamá. (88–89)

> Beyond the change because of the haircut, Carlos seemed odd and he looked depressed and worn, a little ill. . . . From the left I got a glimpse of his contorted expression, his shoulders slumped and a wobble in his knees, his gaze vacant, and a sorrowful expression that reminded me of his mom.

Madness, a terrain associated with the feminine, will also be for Carlos a way of somehow becoming his mother, who suffered from a mental illness (56). Specifically, when the recruits are subjected to watching images of torture as part of their training, the narrator comments on Carlos's reaction: "Cesó la tortura con una foto desgarradora que provocó un gemido a mi lado; era Carlos en estado de *shock* y las manos cruzadas temblando de espanto, con huellas en su rostro de la imagen que había dibujado en la arena un rato antes" (139) [The torture ended with a heartbreaking photo that drew a moan from my side; it was Carlos, in a state of shock and with his hands crossed, trembling with fear, with traces on his face of the image he had drawn in the sand a little earlier]. It was an image that reminded the narrator of the face of Carlos's mother.

Since the end of the Middle Ages, according to Michel Foucault's *Madness and Civilization,* madness has had an assigned place, whether it be exile, police surveillance, medical treatment, or family supervision (38–64). In its relation to the discourse of reason, the discourse of delirium has been one of passions and dreams, and also of poetry and literature (85–116). Speaking about gender roles, Sandra M. Gilbert and Susan Gubar's *The Madwoman in the Attic* analyzes how certain female authors appropriate the metaphor of madness to sharply criticize the subordinate role of the feminine in patriarchal society (45–92). In Caribbean literature, *Wide Sargasso Sea,* by Jean Rhys, is the best text to exemplify what Gilbert and Gubar studied in U.S. and English literary traditions. After all, in this novel, the "madwoman in the attic"—the character of Bertha Mason in *Jane Eyre,* by Charlotte Brontë, called Antoinette Cosway in Rhys's text—is recuperated to cast a postcolonialist look at the relation drawn by Western patriarchal discourse between madness and racial/ cultural "otherness." Precisely, in *Antes de la guerra,* I propose to see Carlos's madness working against a military machine that has been the product of patriarchy and colonialism. Also, Carlos's performance of mental illness will be one of the fuels of the *filin*—or artistic passion—in Ramos's autobiographical discourse.

It seems to me that, if madness is the place of the tactic of *bregar,* the friendship of that "we," "Carlos and I," is what sustains the intellectual discourse developed in *Antes de la guerra.* The two friends share details that unite them, as the text indicates, even from before their military experience:

both are students at a paralyzed university, from working-class families in the Caguas area, and have no job prospects. Moreover, their recruitment in the army occurs "bajo los beneficios del plan *buddy partners,* que nos garantizaba permanecer en la misma base a lo largo de nuestros años de servicio, como estímulo para reclutar a los amigos inseparables de dos en dos" (58) [under the benefits of the "buddy partners" plan, which guaranteed that we would always be on the same base for our whole enlistment period, as an incentive to recruit inseparable friends two at a time]. Going back to Martin's ideas about Napoleonic friendship, it is no wonder that the friendship of "Carlos and I" is taken, accepted, and encouraged by the navy.

Nevertheless, in *Antes de la guerra,* the friendship of "Carlos and I" will serve as shelter in the face of the violence of basic training and, therefore, as a relationship that will oppose military fraternity. This kind of oppositional friendship flourishes "when overarching identities are fragmented, . . . when lives are lived at odds with social norms" and offers the involved friends "the possibility of developing new patterns of intimacy and commitment" (Weeks, 51). The friendship of "Carlos and I" constitutes an intimate, committed relationship, strengthened by knowing they are united in angry love by their cultural and emotional difference, which works against the imposed military fraternity. In this sense, the nucleus of "Carlos and I" can be seen as a "romantic friendship," that is, as a very intimate relationship between two lovers that is never expressed physically and relies on the sharing of "emotional, intellectual, and . . . *spiritual* aspects" (Nissen, 8). And yet, intimate relationships between men throughout history can also be studied from the structure of desire, as Eve Sedgwick does in *Between Men.* For Sedgwick, desire is better than love to describe these intimate relationships, since the former implies "affective or social force, the glue . . . that shapes an important relationship" (2). This is why I view the friendship between "Carlos and I" as a nucleus, intimate and committed, while also romantic and desiring, which angrily defies the notion of the military body affiliated fraternally.

So important is this romantic and desiring friendship that, when the narration tells us about the day of the friends' departure for boot camp, the "I" confesses that without Carlos—who was late to the appointment—it would not be possible to fulfill the contract he had signed:

Pasaron quince minutos y ya la espera [por Carlos] se hizo insoportable, al extremo de que opté por no jurar bandera e irme para mi casa aunque me fueran a buscar arrestado. Era la compañía de Carlos, precisamente, uno de los atractivos de la aventura, y no estaba dispuesto a irme solo, porque no sería igual. (58)

Fifteen minutes passed and the wait [for Carlos] became unbearable, to the point that I decided not to pledge allegiance to the flag and go home even if they came to arrest me. Carlos's company was, in fact, one of the attractions of the adventure, and I was not willing to go alone, because it wouldn't be the same.

Later, Carlos's performance of insanity, which led him to pretend not to understand English, will be followed by the "I," who admits he cannot finish boot camp alone:

Tenía que decidir mi futuro militar en las próximas fracciones de segundos, y aunque no sabía qué se traía Carlos con tal actitud [negarse a seguir las órdenes del oficial porque supuestamente no sabía inglés], tampoco quería quedarme solo en ese mundo tan distinto al mío, de manera que decidí al instante. (90)

I had to decide my military future in the next fractions of seconds, and although I didn't know what Carlos had in mind with such an attitude [refusing to follow the officer's orders because he supposedly did not understand English], I also didn't want to be alone in such a different world from mine, so I decided right away.

Like Carlos, he tells the officer that he does not know English.

It could be said, then, that without Carlos the autobiographical story would not exist. In the end, it is Carlos who bears the *filin* in his voice, who has the bohemian soul, who has been the witness, and who is now capable of transmitting the experience. Since that fantasy the two friends had had before boot camp, in which Carlos would be singing Rexach's "Olas y arenas," Carlos's voice was the one leading the adventure and the autobiographical tale. Moreover, the *filin* in Carlos's voice keeps rearticulating military training into something different from war:

Aspiraba a ser el primer cantante piloto en la historia de la aviación, para deleitar a sus pasajeros con la rítmica melodía de la Vereda Tropical. "Vuelve al ritmo de la voz que acaricia," sería el lema de sus excursiones aéreas, decía Carlos, y por las noches haría lo propio en los distintos night clubs de las grandes ciudades, buscando un escape a su alma de bohemio. (41)

[He] aspired to be the first singing pilot in the history of aviation, to delight his passengers with the rhythmic melody of the *Vereda Tropical* [Tropical

Way]. "Come back to the rhythm of the voice that strokes," would be the slogan of his aerial excursions, Carlos used to say, and at night he would do the same in the different nightclubs of the big cities, looking for an escape for his bohemian soul.

Therefore, *la voz que acaricia* in *Antes de la guerra* is Carlos's voice, and it is the one that drives the autobiographical subject's voyage of memory. In this sense, and following the ideas that Cavarero develops in analyzing the story "A King Listens," by Italo Calvino, "As long as the ear shows its natural talent for perceiving the uniqueness of a voice that is alone capable of attesting to the uniqueness of each human being, the one who emits that voice must remain invisible" (2005, 3). Carlos's absence, his no longer being in the autobiographical subject's present, is what allows the *filin* in his voice—that is, his unique character—to guide the story. Even more, it is that voice that makes the action in the past possible. After all, it will be the *filin* in Carlos's voice that devises the tactic to escape from basic training. For example, in response to a military cadence, Carlos's voice turns to the lyrics and rhythm of the song "Vas bien" by El Gran Combo:

> —Al que se llevaron pa' Vietnam fue al hijo de Armando, y como cosa natural, él iba temblando . . .
> —¡Oye, no puedes cantar en español aquí, sólo en inglés!—le decía el mexicano, pero Carlos lo ignoraba y seguía.
> . . .
> —De pronto, una sombra se movió y el chico asustado, puso pies en polvorosa y ¡fuá! salió disparado . . .
> —A Yankee Doodle, do or die . . .
> —["]¡Búsquese a otro hombre!["], gritaba en plena carrera, ["]pues lo que es a mí no me cogen, ni amarrao' con cadena . . . ¡Qué va! . . . ["] (101–2)

> —The one they took to Vietnam was Armando's son, and of course, he went trembling . . .
> —Hey, you can't sing in Spanish here, only in English!—the Mexican told him, but Carlos ignored him and kept singing.
> . . .
> —Suddenly, a shadow moved and the frightened boy took off running and BOOM! He took off like a shot . . .
> —A Yankee Doodle, do or die . . .
> —"Look for another guy!" he yelled, running flat out. "Cause you won't catch me, or chain me down . . . No way! . . ."

The selection of this song is not accidental. It tells the story of a drafted Puerto Rican soldier that deserts the Vietnam War. El Gran Combo's "Vas bien," in Carlos's voice with *filin*, becomes an angry resistance to the military cadence that punctuates their training. It is also the *canto* [singing] that dialogues with the experience of past Puerto Rican soldiers who have resisted militarism somehow. It is, finally, an angry calling—potentialized by the popular salsa song—to other Puerto Rican soldiers who may come afterward.

In fact, romantic friendship, the military experience, and Carlos's voice with *filin* work together to open a window through which to look into the relation of the "I" with the "you"-father. If their relationship had been tense because of the father's military character, the violence received in boot camp opens a dialogue with the "you"-father to sound out the disaster of the war on his body: "Pensé en mi padre que recién se había retirado, precisamente, como *clerk* del Correo Federal, tras una condición en los bronquios y los nervios adquirida como combatiente en la Guerra de Corea y la Segunda Guerra Mundial" (38) [I thought of my father, who had recently retired, in fact, as a clerk at the Federal Post Office, after a lung condition and the nerves developed as a fighter in the Korean War and the Second World War]. Thus begins in the story a move toward the compassion that will be offered to more Puerto Rican veterans of the U.S. armed forces.

What is more, the intimate knowledge of family experiences and of friends keeps forming a community of debate among the new Puerto Rican recruits regarding the U.S. military forces. Above all, in this debate, the remembrance that the autobiographical memory rescues is the one that weaves the affective history of the Sixty-Fifth Infantry Regiment, which begins to be formulated in the second chapter, when, in the recruiting office, the protagonist meets Betancourt, another Puerto Rican recruit who knows military history inside and out. While Betancourt narrates the performance of the Sixty-Fifth in Korea, guided by history books written by generals, the narrator turns to the intimate memory of his father's story, and tells the personal history of a soldier in the midst of war: "Esa parte de la guerra [cómo había podido sobrevivir su padre en medio de la gran cantidad de bajas en Corea] no la conocía Betancourt, ni sabía tampoco que mi padre había sido el último soldado en abandonar el puerto de Hungnam" (49) [That part of the war (how his father was able to survive among the huge number of casualties in Korea) Betancourt didn't know, nor did he know that my father had been the last soldier to leave the port of Hungnam]. Later, when Betancourt analyzes the result of the court martial of many Puerto Rican soldiers of the Sixty-Fifth—stripping them of their colors, disbanding the regiment, and many of them having to spend years in prison—, the narrator again turns to his father's memories:

Mi padre me había contado que les quitaron los colores injustamente y los fueron incorporando en calidad de reemplazos a otras unidades del Army, porque el sargento a cargo del regimiento [65 de Infantería] de valerosos boricuas combatientes, tenía por costumbre plantar la bandera monoestrellada en lugar de la norteamericana, en cada territorio conquistado. (50)

My father had told me that they stripped them of their colors unfairly and kept assigning them as replacements for other units of the Army, because the sergeant in charge of the [Sixty-Fifth] regiment of courageous fighting Boricuas had the habit of planting the single-starred flag instead of the American flag, in every territory they conquered.

Finally, in the seventh chapter, when the protagonist gets involved in a long discussion about details of the actions of the Sixty-Fifth and the consequences they had, we can see that this autobiography cannot—nor does it want to—survive without questioning the "you"-father, since it is what brings him to tell the experience of the community of Puerto Rican soldiers in the Korean War that survives, through the narration, in the experience of the young recruit:

[Mi padre] también me contó que bajo esas condiciones discriminatorias y de maltrato por los suyos, muchos soldados boricuas se cuestionaban su participación en la guerra, preguntándose qué hacían allí lejos de su familia y hogar, siendo el blanco de la artillería pesada china, hasta comprender que estaban ahí para morir por una patria que no les agradecía el sacrificio. (185)

[My father] also told me that under those discriminatory conditions where they were mistreated by their own, many Boricua soldiers questioned their participation in the war, wondering what they were doing there so far from their families and homes, being the target of Chinese heavy artillery, to the point of understanding that they were there to die for a country that didn't thank them for their sacrifice.

The affective network among angry Puerto Rican recruits and soldiers is woven, then, around a community spread across time and space. It is thanks to the *filin* in Carlos's voice, the absent friend, that the autobiographical subject's memory can return to his experience at boot camp and also establish an intimate dialogue with the experience of the "you"-father. It would be a community united around the call of a voice, that of the absence of Carlos's body, which is strengthened through the autobiographical exercise, that is, in the spell of his own memory and that of others. The possibility of this community network is found, at last, in the anger of knowing themselves to be "others" within the homogenizing discourse of the U.S. military "we."

However, there is also the danger of knowing oneself to be excluded and (in)visibilized in the hegemonic political discourse of the Puerto Rican "nation" and in the abstract debate over colonialism. As Álvarez Curbelo discusses, Puerto Rican soldiers circumvented the ELA state's and U.S. military's hegemonic discourses and constructed their own stories; they would survive wars by turning to a Boricua world of their own making (1995, 103). In this sense, the community network that is concocted in Ramos's text has little to do with designing a national Puerto Rican "we" that might put itself before the U.S. military "we." Little or nothing, then, does this affective community have to do with what Anderson called the "imagined community." The *bregar* resorts more to the intuition of tactics in search of life than to the strategy of a national imaginary that might compel death.

ANGER AND THE CALLING FOR LIFE

A year after the publication of *Antes de la guerra*, Ramos returned to *Diálogo* to continue his work on militarism. In "La guerra en el cancionero boricua," his journalistic style once again resorts to enormous amounts of research and documentation while also pursuing an anecdotal bent full of memories in order to replace the holes in the official history. In this case, memories come through testimonies made into songs, or "archivos de la memoria" as the author calls them in his essay (24). His interest is centered particularly on the decades of the 1950s and 1960s, just when there were more Puerto Rican soldiers who "regresaron traumatizados por los horrores de la guerra, humillados en su trato discriminatorio por ser boricuas" (20) [returned traumatized by the horrors of war, humiliated by their discriminatory treatment for being Boricuas]. It is precisely in this vulnerable historical moment when Ramos detects a great musical effervescence in Puerto Rico:

> Por su pertinencia en la vida de todos los puertorriqueños, el conflicto militar que más composiciones había de inspirar entre nuestros autores, fue la Segunda Guerra Mundial, donde participaron 65,000 soldados boricuas, de los cuales regresaron unos 340 en cajas de plomo selladas. [Esto] coincidía con el inicio de la gloriosa época musical de los años cuarenta, protagonizada por los géneros del bolero y la guaracha, con la voz de nuestros máximos intérpretes, e inspirados por los mejores compositores de todos los tiempos. (24)

Due to its pertinence in the lives of all Puerto Ricans, the military conflict that inspired the most compositions among our authors was the Second World War, in which sixty-five thousand Boricua soldiers participated, of which some 340 returned in sealed lead boxes. [This] coincided with the start of the glorious musical era of the [19]40s, featuring the genres of bolero and *guaracha*, with the voices of our greatest singers, and inspired by the best composers of all time.

The allusion to the literary production of the same era can be seen in the mention of the "cajas de plomo selladas"—in reference to José Luis González's emblematic short story "Una caja de plomo que no se podía abrir"—, which I also interpret as Ramos's intention to place popular music side by side with literature. Even if this specific musical production has received no critical attention, for Ramos, there is an urgency to study it academically. After all, these songs about war experiences document the feelings of the people, that is, "los engaños, temores, prejuicios y estereotipos de la época" (25) [the disappointments, fears, prejudices, and stereotypes of the era]. Seen through this particular archive of memory, the topic of war is full of contradictions, where patriotic sentiment about going to war is combined with resistance to recruitment, and also the pain of the soldier's departure with the revelry of his return. Ramos does not hesitate to present the most melancholic of tones together with more humorous notes to allow this document to speak to us of a moment when one part of the debate around the war took place "a través de las ondas radiales y en las velloneras de bares y cafetines" (24) [through the radio waves and on the jukeboxes of bars and cafes]. This is the kind of discussion that Ramos wants to have with *Diálogo*'s readership. Through his journalism, his voice builds a place within the bond between ideas and feelings; and, from this bond, his voice will immerse itself in this topic that is so uncomfortable and indomitable for the Puerto Rican government and academia.

As my reading of *Antes de la guerra* demonstrated, Ramos's intellectual voice is full of anger because of the experience of war, and I believe that "La guerra en el cancionero boricua" searches for other kinds of cultural productions carrying that experience in order to historicize a manifestation of such anger. As I have argued, his insistence to speak to a very localized audience—university students—has to do with an urgent and angry calling toward the ones who perhaps may share the same experience he and others have had. As it was the case for Lemebel, for Ramos, popular and melodramatic music is the way to amplify his intellectual voice. In this specific context, as I have said, the intellectual voice is interested in establishing an academic debate that can break through the symbolic monolingualism about 1898. Anger is the emotion that best helps him undo such monolingualism and actively hope for an alliance with the most vulnerable ones for the right to live and against the neoliberal machine of war. After all, this is a struggle that keeps going on; and the calling needs to extend into unforeseen years to come.

CHAPTER 5

Afro-Cuban Cyberfeminism

Love/Sexual Revolution in Sandra Álvarez Ramírez's Blogging

LOVE IS an oft-invoked emotion in revolutionary discourses in Cuba. From Fidel Castro's "Palabras a los intelectuales" (1961) to Ernesto "Che" Guevara's "El hombre nuevo" (1965), the discourse of love seeks to unite a collectivity around a single ideal, whether *la patria* or *la revolución*. Interestingly, this ideal is imagined as a feminine object, a mother or a lover, surrounded by devoted men. Of course, this prosopopoeia is not exclusive to Cuban or Latin American political discourses, and it can be traced back to nineteenth-century romanticism and nationalism.[1] In the case of Cuba, as Guillermina De Ferrari has proposed, the narratives of the Cuban Revolution illustrated those devoted men through a series of rhetorical devices portraying male friendship, a fraternity that was supposed to be "masculine and equal, rather than patriarchal" (3). Nevertheless, the fraternity manifested here, convening around a shared love for a female object, also deploys this emotion as a pretext and a justification for violence that renders the present meaningless. As we have seen, national discourses always contain a promise of happiness. In the cases of Guevara's and Castro's texts, love for *la patria* or *la revolución* is disillusioned with the present situation; instead, love fights and waits for its fulfillment in the future. And the future will only be secured thanks to the efforts

---

1. For an interpretation of the interplay between fraternity and women's bodies in European national discourses, see George L. Mosse's book. The same topic in the Latin American context has been studied in pivotal books by Mary Louise Pratt, Francine Masiello (1992), and Licia Fiol-Matta.

of true revolutionaries that, as these discourses and the Cuban context show, are mostly white males.

In this final chapter, I want to focus on the dynamics of (dis)embodiment between national love and the love for the Afro-Cuban woman's body, a body that has remained outside of the racist and patriarchal revolutionary structure, unless it becomes useful as a commodity and/or an empty signifier. This very discussion lies at the center of Sandra Álvarez Ramírez's blog *Negracubana tenía que ser* and propels her writing into an articulation of the black woman's body as an ideal in itself, employing narratives that include a documentation of black women's political actions in both the past and the present. In this sense, if the national promise of happiness determines the flow of bodies in social space and categorizes them as happy or unhappy, according to their adherence to determined norms (Ahmed, 2010, 11–12), as I will explain, in Álvarez Ramírez's discourse, black women's unhappy bodies stick together and seek to form another kind of (more fluid) "we," gathering together around expressions of their bodies' enjoyment. Specifically, Álvarez Ramírez's intellectual interventions impress the black woman's body with love and assemble a community whose members share the cyberfeminist goal of a love/sexual revolution that radicalizes body politics (gender, race, and sexuality) thanks to (dis)embodiment processes in virtual space. Therefore, *Negracubana*'s cyberfeminism takes back the representation of the black woman's body and constitutes it into an agent of history. Furthermore, contrary to the utopian love promise of the Cuban Revolution, the black feminist love/sexual proposition is that of enactment in the present, in everyday life—in both the physical and virtual realms.

Most importantly, Álvarez Ramírez's Afro-cyberfeminist stance relies on the fluidity of polyamory, that is, the possibility of being in love with more than one person at the same time. My main argument for this chapter is, then, that polyamory's fluidity, as conceptualized in *Negracubana,* works against the utopian love promise of the official revolution in several ways. First, because it refuses a sole commitment, polyamory disrupts the notion of the revolution as the ultimate promise. Second, the advocacy for fluidity in this blog puts black women's necessities at the center of social discussions, which operates contrary to what should be the perfect revolutionary's (white male's) ideal, that is, the eternal sacrifice for the love of the revolution. Third, since there is an acknowledgment of intersectionality (of different kinds of oppressions, resistances, and associations) in the philosophy and practice of fluidity, Álvarez Ramírez's understanding of polyamory defies the requirement of a single political affiliation, as requested by the revolution (as well as by the groups that preach antirevolution politics). Finally, the Afro-cyberfeminist discourse on polyamory deconstructs two binaries: love/sex and public/private. In terms

of the former, her blogs often fuse love (as an emotion) and sex (as a pleasurable practice) to better understand the complicated necessities of (black
women's) bodies. Regarding the latter, she insists on public discussion of love/
sex practices that are thought to be private, and, moreover, she conceives of
these supposedly private matters as key to revolutionizing social space. Both
binaries find their shortcomings in Castro's and Guevara's texts. As I will discuss later on, if for them there were two kinds of love (the revolution's tran-
scendental one and the ordinary), *Negracubana* brings the discussion of love
back to the black woman's body and refuses to disassociate this emotion from
its concrete needs.

I want to examine these ideas by looking into *Negracubana*'s revolutionary matrix, which I believe is to be found in the blog's networking, that is,
an active agenda to connect Cuban black women's voices with other voices
around the world. Starting with its platform, WordPress, the blog is presented
as an effort that relies on collaboration and open sharing. It does not include
ads, and its objective is to educate and advocate for black women. Álvarez
Ramírez uses social media to promote *Negracubana*, which has 6,344 followers. Therefore, this is a small community, and most entries have one or two
comments, even though there are a few, like some I study here, that have up to
fourteen reactions. Many followers are other Cuban and Caribbean bloggers
and academics—some of them contribute their pieces to *Negracubana* from
time to time—, but there is a diversity of women among this group, too, that
also take the time to leave their comments, as I will explain in my analysis of
one of the blogs.

Thus, the format and concept of the blog can be seen as another way in
which Álvarez Ramírez exercises her polyamory philosophy. Small and intimate networking is vital to the subsistence of this open project. When talking
about networks, however, I am not only referring to the possibilities of previously unimaginable associations that the Internet has created; I also want us to
think about how networks have always been fundamental for the production
and transmission of intellectual ideas. One of my tasks in this chapter will
be, then, to establish an intellectual network between Álvarez Ramírez and
some of the canonical (patriarchal) voices of the Cuban Revolution in order
to identify concrete points of struggle concerning the representation of the
black woman's body. Another of my proposed networks presents a dialogue
between the dissident discourse of *Negracubana* and Cuban literary productions referenced therein, such as Virgilio Piñera's *La isla en peso* and Nancy
Morejón's "Mujer negra." I will also pursue an intellectual reflection on the
experience of black bodies through networking Frantz Fanon's, Audre Lorde's,
and Álvarez Ramírez's ideas on the topic. Finally, Álvarez Ramírez's appropriation of cyberfeminist ideas and actions provides us with another context for

reflecting on, with respect to what feminist Donna J. Haraway and the Australian cyber collective VNS Matrix have envisioned, the kind of community she has intended to build through her blog. All of these proposed dialogues have prompted my analysis to consider the importance of *Negracubana* for the Cuban (virtual) context as well as for comparative race and feminist studies. In this sense, even though the blogger does not have the visibility that any of the other mentioned figures have, I see her work as a crisscrossed network that allows us to discuss Cuba within local and global perspectives. Furthermore, as I discuss later, Álvarez Ramírez is probably one of the best examples to talk about a new kind of intellectual figure that has emerged post-1989 in Latin America and the Caribbean.

In post-Soviet Cuba, many authors have also ventured into digital networking and have worked with different notions of community that could break through the traditional socialist proposition of a masculine lettered city (De Ferrari, 2–3). In Álvarez Ramírez's case, *Negracubana* has come to occupy a central place in the Cuban blogosphere because of her constant experimentation with diverse media and because of the network the blog has built beyond the island, extending to other contexts in the Hemispheric Americas and Europe. As her brief and concise introduction says,

> Nací en La Habana en 1973, un día después de los sucesos en el Palacio de la Moneda, Chile. . . .
> Trabajé por casi 10 años como editora del sitio web *Cubaliteraria,* portal de la literatura cubana; al tiempo que me convertí en periodista y webmaster.
> Realizo esta bitácora desde junio del 2006. . . .
> Como ciberfeminista negra participo del Proyecto Arcoiris, y del grupo de mujeres Afrocubanas. . . . Pertenezco a la Articulación Regional Afrodescendiente, organización que tiene un capítulo cubano. Soy colaboradora de Global Voices y recientemente me incorporé a colaborar con el TOQUE. Cada cuarto sábado del mes hago un programa de radio, *Y tenemos sabor,* en la emisora Radio Flora de la ciudad de Hannover, Alemania. (2006)

> I was born in Havana in 1973, a day after the events in the Palacio de la Moneda, Chile. . . .
> I worked as an editor for the website *Cubaliteraria,* the site for Cuban literature for almost ten years; at the same time, I became a journalist and webmaster.
> I've maintained this blog since June 2006. . . .
> As a black cyberfeminist I participate in the Proyecto Arcoiris and in the women's group Afrocubanas. . . . I belong to the Articulación Regional

Afrodescendiente, an organization that has a Cuban chapter. I am a participant in Global Voices, and I recently joined TOQUE. Every fourth Saturday of the month I do a radio program, *Y tenemos sabor*, on the Radio Flora station out of Hannover, Germany.

Therefore, we can read *Negracubana* as part of a recent intellectual and artistic output in Cuba that, as Odette Casamayor-Cisneros has pointed out, has "shifted from sketching out an identity to recreating the experience of being black in the Americas" (131). With Álvarez Ramírez, this experience grows even more complex when we consider her educational and professional background (journalist, webmaster, psychologist, and feminist), as well as the time she has spent living in Germany. Throughout her blog, she has explained that studies and love are the most important reasons for immigrating to Germany. As we will see, her relationship with this foreign land is both problematic and invigorating. But most importantly, by having started and sustained her blog in Cuba (2006–13) and having continued to develop it in Germany (since 2013), Álvarez Ramírez's network operates within and beyond the island, the constraints of Cuban identity, and the limits of political debate regarding the Cuban government. Its operation, creation, and effects become an intellectual contribution to Cuban Studies at a time when the island continues to juggle a socialist state and a neoliberal economy.

Álvarez Ramírez shares a leftist perspective, but she is critical of the restrictions that the revolutionary state has imposed on the development of other kinds of associations and affiliations, different and/or dissident from official institutions. The blogger constantly pushes her community to go beyond the binary of pro/antigovernment. Therefore, both her political stance and the focus of her debate distances her work from that of others who have exhibited an open and belligerent opposition to the Cuban government, such as Yoani Sánchez's *Generación Y* and Orlando Luis Pardo Lazo's *Lunes de Post-Revolución*. Álvarez Ramírez's intellectual enactment of her body politics has kept her blog more open to a diverse range of debates and has made her interventions even more radical than those exclusively devoted to dissenting from anything and everything with origins in the Cuban government.

THE PROMISE OF REVOLUTIONARY LOVE AND THE BLACK WOMAN'S BODY

Returning to the texts by Castro and Guevara I mentioned earlier, the key questions for their analysis will be: what is the sacrifice that is needed for happiness to arrive? Who are the subjects that will lead the path to the fulfillment of the promise? That is, who is the revolutionary subject, as imagined by the foundational discourses of the 1959 revolution? What is the specific role of the black woman's body in the revolutionary narrative?

Revolutionary love must go beyond everyday love and even reject any possibility of dwelling in it, as Guevara reminds us: "Nuestros revolucionarios de vanguardia . . . no pueden descender con su pequeña dosis de cariño cotidiano hacia los lugares donde el hombre común lo ejercita" (325) [Our avant-garde revolutionaries . . . cannot descend to the places where common men practice small ordinary affections]. The division between low and high forms of love leads us to a conceptualization of knowledge that distinguishes between experience (everyday life) and ideology. In this sense, ordinary affection is not true love, true knowledge, or truly revolutionary. The *revolucionarios de vanguardia*, as Guevara calls them, are the figures who possess a clear vision of the project; they know how to fulfill the promise of happiness. While Guevara sees no possible materiality that could embody the high ideal of revolutionary love, Castro uses rhetorical resources that involve the disembodiment of the black woman's body—which is to say, this body is stripped of her history and other possible associations—to convey that ideal. Toward the end of "Palabras a los intelectuales," Castro tells the audience an anecdote in which he and other revolutionaries met an old black woman a few days before the event at the Biblioteca Nacional. According to his story, she was

> una anciana de 106 años que había acabado de aprender a leer y a escribir, y . . . había sido esclava, y nosotros queríamos saber cómo un esclavo vio el mundo cuando era esclavo. . . . Creo que puede escribir una cosa tan interesante que ninguno de nosotros la podemos escribir. Y es posible que en un año se alfabetice y además escriba un libro a los 106 años—¡esas son las cosas de las revoluciones!—y se vuelva escritora y tengamos que traerla aquí a la próxima reunión, . . . admitirla como uno de los valores de la nacionalidad del siglo XIX. . . . ¿Quién puede escribir mejor que ella lo que vivió el esclavo? ¿Y quién puede escribir mejor que ustedes el presente?

> a 106-year-old woman who had just learned to read and write, and . . . she had been a slave, and we wanted to know how a slave saw the world when he was a slave. . . . I think she can write something so interesting that none of us can write. And it's possible that she'll learn to read in a year, and, to top it off, write a book at 106 years old—This is the stuff of revolutions!—and become a writer, and we'll have to bring her here to the next meeting, . . . admit her as one of the values of nineteenth-century nationality. . . . Who better than

she can write about what slaves experienced? And who better than all of you can write the present?

In the stenographic version, applause and laughter are indicated whenever they were heard, and both were recorded right after "es posible que . . . se vuelva escritora y tengamos que traerla aquí a la próxima reunión." Even if her old age (106 years) is the evident reason for the surprise and laughter, her gender, race, and slave history make Castro's assertion miraculous, too: to include an ex-slave black woman among the group of Cuban intellectuals and artists. Furthermore, this black woman's body is only valuable for having been once an illiterate slave. Through his reductive anecdote about this body, Castro constructs a narrative that establishes the 1959 revolution as the culmination of the struggles for the nineteenth-century Emancipation and Independence Wars. In this way, the black woman's name, her many experiences, her stories, and her relationship to and practice of ordinary affection must be sacrificed for this national (revolutionary) narrative, which demands a higher kind of love.

It is very interesting to note that Castro's anecdote can be linked to the nationalist discourse that dominated Cuba between 1898 and 1959, a period that has been conveniently erased from the narrative of the Cuban Revolution. During the 1920s and 1930s, the Cuban intellectual elite imagined and promoted a *mulato* nation: the perfect fusion, and therefore reconciliation, between Hispanic and African heritages (Rivera Pérez, 226–27). Nevertheless, even if the nationalization of African heritage in Cuba contrasted with developments in other Hispanic Caribbean islands where Hispanism was almost the sole source of nationalism during these same decades, the valorization of black culture did not translate into social equality between whites and blacks. Rather, this kind of nationalism became, at some points, a process by which an active disembodiment of black and *mulata* women also sought to fetishize them and sell them as pleasurable commodities associated with the island.[2]

---

2. The fetishization (product of a disembodiment/embodiment process) of black and *mulata* women dates back at least to the fifteenth century and has long since been tied to the imperial gaze of "discovering" supposedly new (exotic) lands (McClintock, 22). As many scholars have concluded, this colonial gaze has been culturally engraved across geographies and has persisted in the sexualized representation of black women's bodies throughout history and until today (hooks; Kuhn; Fleetwood; and Cobb). Even as the end of the nineteenth century brought emancipation (1886) and independence (1901) to Cuba, the tourist industry was probably the most tangible demonstration of how the fetishization of tropical land and women of color was essential to maintaining colonial relationships, controlling economic development, and perpetuating a national hierarchy based on class, race, and gender oppression (Pritchard and Morgan; Schwartz).

The difference between the early twentieth-century nationalistic rhetoric and the narrative that emerged after 1959 is that the revolution's official discourse affirmed the end of racial and all other forms of socioeconomic inequality in Cuba (Sawyer; Casamayor-Cisneros), insisting on erasing all kinds of difference in the furtherance of only one dominant category: revolutionaries. Even though Castro eventually addressed the subject of racism in Cuba in interviews and speeches focused on other topics, none of his texts exclusively engaged with this problem and its consequences (Martínez). Moreover, official revolutionary rhetoric still considers it an act of treason to the revolution to talk in an international forum about prejudices such as racism in Cuba.[3] In this sense, Casamayor-Cisneros's analysis of black subjectivities and the Cuban Revolution could be extended to consider the place assigned to black intellectuals within a wider network of thought: "The black subject will be integrated only when he is capable of . . . leaving behind the 'atavisms' attributed to his race and culture, and devoting himself completely to nationalist, revolutionary, and finally Marxist ideologies" (106). It seems that the black intellectual can speak only if she refrains from underlining, analyzing, and speaking about/through the politics that have marked her body.

The revolutionary discourse also contended that the new order ended gender inequality. In 1960, the official Federación de Mujeres Cubanas (FMC) was born; since then, membership has been mandatory for all women over the age of fourteen. As Mabel Cuesta has analyzed, the FMC's main purpose was to build the perfect *compañera* for the *hombre nuevo*—that is, a Cuban woman who would no longer be associated with the figures of the prostitute, the housewife, or the illiterate (13–14). Until 2007, the FMC logo reinforced this association, depicting a *guerrillera* with a baby in arms. What is more, as Cuesta also points out, the creation of the FMC and the compulsory participation of women in its ranks eliminated all previously existing women's organizations in Cuba—as well as the chance to create new ones that would be independent from the state (13–14). Thus, it effectively erased an entire history

---

3. In a case that has some parallels with the Padilla affair (1971), the publication of Roberto Zurbano's piece (2013) in *The New York Times* generated a backlash on the island that led up to Zurbano's firing from his position as editor-in-chief at Casa de las Américas, the government's biggest publishing house. Even if Zurbano did not end up in prison like Heberto Padilla, he was ostracized by the official intellectual community, and his article was subjected to extensive criticism in intellectual publications. In addition, while Padilla received worldwide support from the international intellectual community, Zurbano's odyssey was mainly covered by Cuban intellectuals and the network of black intellectuals in the Americas who publish in *AfroCubaWeb*. *Negracubana* is among the blogs that have covered the Zurbano affair, publishing many of Zurbano's writings. For more on this topic, see the *Afro-Hispanic Review*'s dossier, *El caso Zurbano*.

of women's struggles and their work to combat the patriarchy. Once again, women had to be stripped of their stories in order to embody the nation's revolutionary ideal.

Within the Cuban sociocultural hierarchy, therefore, black women confront everyday life battles because of their race and gender. More than five decades after the revolution, as Cuban sociologist Mayra Espina points out, socioeconomic success and failure in contemporary Cuba are gendered and colored: the profile of the winner, or the true revolutionary, is a young, middle- to upper-class, white man, preferably with an education in computer science (63). The revolution's delayed promise of happiness never came; but constant reward has been granted to white male bodies, while black female bodies are the ones enduring the sacrifice.

This racial and socioeconomic reality is also reflected in Internet access and use across the island. By 2015, the official report "Estrategia Nacional" informed that only twenty-five percent of the Cuban people had access to the Internet, and most of that twenty-five percent gained access through their workplaces or the cybercafes overseen by ETECSA (Empresa de Telecomunicaciones de Cuba), where they have to pay two CUC (Cuban convertible pesos), or ten percent of a salary in Cuba, for just one hour of Internet access (4). Within this panorama, a few technology specialists enjoy the high-status privileges of global connectivity and free information access, and "they are young, skilled, and 'on the inside' of strategic awareness" (Venegas, 4), a profile that coincides with that of the Cuban winner in Espina's description. Therefore, black women are the most likely to be excluded from web navigation, participation, and networking.

While the situation is improving, as more Wi-Fi spots are opening in public spaces across the island (Pérez), a heated debate continues on the status of the Internet in Cuba—a debate centered on how information access will be controlled and channeled, as well as on how democracy and expression will be enacted outside hierarchical bounds. In Claudio Peláez Sordo's documentary film *BlogBang Cuba* (2014), which examines the achievements and shortcomings of the Cuban blogosphere, Milena Recio, a social communication scholar at the Universidad de La Habana, states that blogging in Cuba responds to "un atragantamiento que había que sacar" [a blockage that needed to be removed]. Regardless of each blog's political stance (pro- or antigovernment), people wanted to speak and be heard. Furthermore, Recio argues that these new possibilities for and implementations of global democracy have not exclusively centered on the exhausted pro/antigovernment debate. I coincide with Recio in that one of the most interesting forms of online activism at work in Cuba is the one questioning structural racism on the island and in the Americas.

For blogger Francisco Rodríguez, featured in the documentary and author of *Paquito, el de Cuba,* another important form, placing Cuba at the center of the global blogosphere, focuses on advocacy for LGBTQ rights.[4] Álvarez Ramírez's *Negracubana* resides precisely at the intersection of race, gender, and sexuality politics, and her cyberfeminism has been formulating another kind of revolutionary love that works against the revolution's delayed promise of happiness for black women.

THE BLACK WOMAN'S BODY AND THE INHABITANCE OF THE INTERSECTION IN CUBA AND ABROAD

To read Álvarez Ramírez's blogging requires that we read her intellectual discourse in connection to the authors she refers us to, as well as to the ones who are silently built into her critique. Very much like Fanon and Lorde, her everyday-life experiences as a black woman in Cuba and Germany become the focal point of her analysis and her propositions. At other times, her expressed intertextuality with Cuban figures, such as Piñera and Morejón, serves to advance ideas that already inhabit poem lines and that may be elusive otherwise. The analysis of both writing strategies reveals the complex operation of systemic racism and sexism, and how these systems shift according to specific contextual characteristics. This kind of reading also reveals the varying tactics used to live in the intersection of gender, race, and sexuality.

For example, some of Álvarez Ramírez's blog entries discuss her seventeen-month experience in Germany, and, much like Fanon in Paris in the 1950s, she says that she has become conscious of her body as she meets the European white gaze. For Fanon, under the white gaze, the black body becomes a negation of the white body, therefore construing blackness as a handicap. Under the white gaze, then, the black bodies gradually change their relationship with space and time, because they become conscious of their skin's inadequacy (91). Riding the Parisian Metro, Fanon realizes that nobody wants to sit beside him. The white gaze's fear turns into disgust for the black body: "Instead of one seat, they left me two or three. . . . I approached the Other . . . and the Other, evasive, hostile, but not opaque, transparent and

---

4. To understand the significance of LGBTQ activism in Cuba, it is key to know a history of systematic persecution against nonheteronormative sexualities. In the 1970s, the Cuban Revolution established the Unidades Militares de Ayuda a la Producción (UMAPs), work camps that were supposed to habilitate "problematic" individuals (political dissidents, prostitutes, and homosexuals) and prepare them for reintegration into society. See Lillian Guerra's article for a complete analysis of this history.

absent, vanished. Nausea" (92). Disgust and fear are alerts that warn against possible contagion; there should be no proximity to the black body. The physical imprint of disgust intensifies the sensation of alienation of the self from his/her own body.

In "Pequeños detalles," when reflecting on her time in Germany, Álvarez Ramírez seems to echo Fanon's particular sense of alienation. While riding the Hanover Stadtbahn, she needs to remind herself constantly that she cannot dance to the music she is listening to, because it is "cívicamente incorrecto" [civically incorrect] to move her body as she did in Cuba, "[Comenzaba] moviendo la cabeza, hasta que mis caderas y mis pies respond[ía]n" [I began by moving my head, until my hips and feet caught on]. Even when she contains herself and simply nods her head to the rhythm of the music, "la gente me mira como si estuviera en el medio de un ataque de epilepsia" [people look at me as if I were having an epileptic seizure]. In their interaction, music and the body create an intimate knowledge based on emotions and memories—but, in the context of the German train, the manifestation of this knowledge through the black female body is read as a disease or a handicap. The perception of the black female body as a handicap is also extended to the geography of the Caribbean, a region that seems to belong to "el planeta Marte" [Mars], because it cannot be part of the America they have imagined, that is, the United States. Her body, geography, and language become a point of discussion on board the train: "En una oportunidad, una señora alemana me preguntó . . . que por qué yo hablaba castellano si en España no había negros" [Once, a German woman asked me . . . why I spoke Spanish if there were no blacks in Spain]. This confusion, as Álvarez Ramírez identifies it, ultimately leaves the text open ended: she declines to comment any further, concluding, "Huelgan los comentarios" [No comments are necessary]. Even if, like Fanon, Álvarez Ramírez understands that the white gaze is framing her body through racist structures, she also recognizes—unlike him—that she has experienced this structuring before, in the Caribbean context. After all, as we saw in Castro's anecdote, the only way the black woman's body can become part of the revolution is through a process of disembodiment/embodiment that will seek to inspire true revolutionaries, that is, white males. This is why additional comments are unnecessary for the blogger: the racist framing of her black woman's body is all too familiar.

In other entries, she further reflects on this familiar feeling and on how the Cuban Revolution failed to address the systematic racism and sexism she has experienced since girlhood. By talking about the intersectionality of race and gender, she complicates Fanon's analysis, too, which is centered on the black man's body and loses perspective when talking about gender and the

process of *mulataje* in the Caribbean.[5] Álvarez Ramírez, who has acknowledged the FMC as a fundamental experience in her feminist formation, has
been critical of the government's continued emphasis on traditional gender
roles. In one of the anecdotes that open many of her blog entries, she remembers an FMC conference in which Castro distributed pressure cookers among
the women in attendance—a gesture that denoted the sinuous relationship
between patriarchy and the revolution. Yet, in "Disidencias," she is even more
critical of the silence and paralysis that this relationship has imposed on the
FMC: "Ninguna de nosotras se paró a explicarle [a Castro] que . . . no necesitábamos cazuelas, necesitábamos menos patriarcado y más tiempo para nosotras mismas" [None of us paused to explain to Castro that . . . we didn't need
pots, we needed less patriarchy and more time for ourselves]. For Álvarez
Ramírez, then, this relationship is what keeps the FMC from actively including other women and their experiences, which in turn has produced a pre-
dominantly conservative manifestation of feminism, one still engaged in a
binary debate on gender roles (without acknowledging the complex intersectionality between gender, race, sexuality, and other body politics).

It is in this complication of the revolution's vision of what true revolutionaries must do for Cuba and in her navigating an intersectionality that
Fanon missed that I see a dialogue between Álvarez Ramírez's and Lorde's
ideas. While Fanon explored a first encounter with the white gaze as an adult,
Lorde's anecdotes showed what it means to be shaped by racism since girlhood and as a black woman. As an adult, Fanon was able to put the painful
moment on the Paris Metro into words, even if it meant acknowledging a loss
of the self in being configured by racism. What happens, then, when the self
cannot make sense of the experience, when she is only left with a sensation of
having done something wrong? Lorde establishes that, when we are not able
to name or recognize pain, it becomes suffering, which in turn becomes anger,
an emotion that has kept black women alive, but which also pits them against
each other (171–72). While Fanon's text ended in a scene where suffering and
anger engulfed the subject, "Not responsible for my acts, at the crossroads
between Nothingness and Infinity, I began to weep" (Fanon, 119), Lorde proposes that black women need to see "eye to eye" with and within themselves
in order to break through these emotions. For Lorde, mothering is the way to
see eye to eye, and this mothering must be an act of love both for the self and
for the others we see in the mirror of suffering: "I affirm my own worth by
committing myself to my own survival, in my own self and in the self of other

---

5. I am referring here to *Black Skin, White Masks*'s second chapter, "The Woman of Color
and the White Man," where Fanon develops a critical reading of Mayotte Capécia's *Je suis
martiniquaise*.

Black women, . . . being able to recognize my successes, and to be tender with myself, even when I fail" (173). It is by seeing eye to eye that black women can "establish authority over our own definition" (173) and grow a (re)new(ed) self.

Álvarez Ramírez's blogging also dwells in this sense of love as the collective political force proposed by Lorde and elaborates on ideas that address the specificity of the black woman in Cuba. Her life in Germany and online networking, which has been key for her enhanced knowledge of black women's experiences in other geographies, help her to establish a comparison between what is left to do in Cuba and what is happening in the rest of the world. In particular, however, her readings of Cuban literature and, as we have seen, her sociohistorical analyses that always start with a personal anecdote inform her political position regarding the revolution's achievements and failures in terms of body politics. I believe that her intertextuality with Piñera and Morejón, for example, positions her blogging as a skilled intellectual discourse that knows how to enter and exit the labyrinth of the pro/antirevolution debate.

In "¿Y las lesbianas feministas . . . ?", Álvarez Ramírez questions how traditional feminism in Cuba has alienated lesbian feminists. In a beautiful moment of intertextuality with Piñera's poem *La isla en peso* (1943), she declares:

En nuestra isla, que además de estar rodeada de agua, vive la maldita circunstancia del machismo y el sexismo por todas partes, existen ideas en el imaginario popular que cuestionan la condición de mujer de las lesbianas, . . . convirtiéndolas en un ser raro, negativamente masculinizado, estéril.

On our island, which, besides being surrounded by water, is afflicted by the damned circumstances of *machismo* and sexism everywhere, ideas exist in the popular imaginary that question whether lesbians are even women, . . . turning them into strange beings, negatively masculinized, sterile.

Álvarez Ramírez's appropriation of probably the most memorable lines in *La isla en peso* should not come as a surprise: "La maldita circunstancia del agua por todas partes / me obliga a sentarme en la mesa del café" (37) [The damned circumstance of water on all sides / forces me to sit on the coffee table]. Piñera, an author whose poetry was systematically chastised and silenced by critics and institutions in Cuba (T. Anderson, 35–36), wrote a poem that denounced colonialism, imperialism, racism, capitalist productivity, and cultural stasis. In the poem, subjects on the island feel the entrapment of a daily routine that has a history of slavery and forced labor while they also need to keep remembering/tracing/cutting the edges of "la isla más bella del mundo" [the most beautiful island in the world], as it has been taught to them to repeat ad nauseam (43). Resorting to a language full of "grotesque images . . . and copious vulgarisms" for its time (T. Anderson, 34), *La isla en peso* explores the paradoxes of an imperfect culture (Jambrina). As the poem advances through the hours of the day, the night becomes a rebellious time, where bodies copulate as they please, eroticism becomes a political force (Rojas, 258), and, instead of science, sex becomes the site that promises freedom (Vitier, 407).[6] The eternal cycle between the four moments of the day—which alternate between dawn, noon, dusk, and night—locates the poetic voice in a present time that remembers, lives, and foresees. If at times the poem "exposes a bloody past of conquest and a cursed future that will arise from the present circumstance" (Quiroga, 279), it also does not let us reside in the possibility of damnation or salvation. After all, the cycle goes on and so do the paradoxes of an impure and imperfect island.

Furthermore, by resorting to Piñera's poem, Álvarez Ramírez is grounding her writing within a tradition of queer literature and, most importantly, of queer intellectuals that have been ostracized in Cuba due to their sexualities and their writings' topics. It is in this vein that we should interpret the fact that both Piñera's poem and Álvarez Ramírez's blog entry contain the line, "la eterna miseria que es el acto de recordar" (Piñera, 37). At dawn, in *La isla en peso,* remembering in the present means misery, because it evokes past pleasurable moments for which laborious (queer) bodies will have to wait yet another day. Álvarez Ramírez, however, situates that misery in the opposite experience: a pleasurable (queer) present in Germany brings back past frustrations and anger. This chiasmus between the two authors' texts points toward their emotional overlap: a profound knowledge of the Cuban paradox, that within the *maldita circunstancia* of entrapment (by cultural homogenization, patriarchy, racism, homophobia, etc.) lies the potentiality of unforeseen emergencies, anchored on intersectionality, like the beast of pleasure described in Piñera's poem.

Álvarez Ramírez's blog entries describe pleasant memories of Cuba, too, and these are related to everyday-life experiences with family and friends. One of these memories comes to her through Morejón's "Mujer negra," a poem that moves the blogger to tears, because, as she said in the entry "Ese poema," "no habla de nosotras como víctimas, sino como guerreras, cimarronas, rebeldes" [it doesn't speak of us as victims, but as warriors, runaway slaves, rebels]. Morejón has been called by some the "New Woman" (Jackson, 104), in reference to (and to complement) Guevara's *hombre nuevo.* This vision of the author as an Afro-Cuban woman who is also a true revolutionary does not

---

6. Vitier's statement intends to be critical of Piñera's poem; but I find it to be a compliment.

take into consideration, however, the twelve-year period during which she could not publish a single poem, because her poetry was targeted as non grata (Cordones-Cook, 50).⁷

"Mujer negra," probably Morejón's best-known poem, comes through the poetic voice of a black woman who becomes the leading figure of Cuban history in three key moments: the kidnapping in Africa and the Atlantic passage into slavery in the Americas, the nationalist movement and War of Independence, and the revolution. Even though the poem seems to be a repetition of the official history as taught by the government, the literary discourse proposes a kind of narrative that focuses on what has been left out of the official one: the black woman experience (Sanmartín, 444). In this sense, if the old black woman in Castro's anecdote is nameless and without stories, Morejón's poem ignites a new kind of revolution, one centered on the body and its history. It is then not surprising that feminist Álvarez Ramírez relates Morejón's historical account to her intimate love for herself, her mother, her grandmother, and a whole genealogy of black women:

Me reconozco en él [el poema]; también a mi madre que se partió el lomo educando a cuatro hijas y un hijo y a mi abuela, quien al ser la única hembra de ocho hermanos no pudo llevar el apellido de su padre. Todas y cada una de las mujeres de mi familia hemos sido como la mujer negra del poema de Nancy.

I recognize myself in it [the poem]; I also recognize my mother, who broke her back raising four daughters and a son, and my grandmother, who, as the only girl among eight siblings, couldn't carry on her father's name. Each and every woman in my family has been like the black woman of Nancy's poem.

Here, in the combination between a national history (re)inscribed through/in black women's bodies and the intimacy of an "I" who establishes an affective "we" with black women (even with "Nancy"), we witness what Lorde called "mothering," seeing "eye to eye" with and within themselves. Compassion and empowerment emerge from the intertextuality that Álvarez Ramírez establishes with Morejón, as does a genealogy of stories that provides a tradition of self-knowledge. Names, stories, and relationships point to a net-

---

7. That period coincided with a time when there was a tense relationship between the revolution's white hierarchy and national and international black intellectuals, who were frustrated with the empty wording of antiracist pronouncements from the government (Cordones-Cook, 44–60).

work that feels, works, and produces beyond a historical hiatus like the Cuban Revolution. And black women's bodies only embody themselves.

FROM MOTHERING TO POLYAMORY: A CYBERFEMINIST PROPOSITION FOR/FROM THE BLACK WOMAN'S BODY

While the founding discourses of the Cuban Revolution establish love for *la patria* or *la revolución* as a high ideal, Álvarez Ramírez views love as a revolution in itself. More specifically, in "Amar más allá," she proposes polyamory as the philosophy and practice that will renew the fight against the patriarchy. Polyamory, which offers no promises of happiness, invests instead in enjoying the present and in what the blogger ventures to define as "amar multitudinariamente" [loving multitudinously]. Love is a revolution unto itself, in that it constantly changes as everyday life generates new experiences. Love is, then, a present and communal emotion. It can also be virtual, which is why Álvarez Ramírez's blog is titled "más allá de los límites de tu cuerpo" [beyond the limits of your body]: because love is "la posibilidad de amar sin límites, sin condiciones y aún sin la presencia de la persona amada. . . . El vínculo trasciende al deseo sexual" [the possibility of loving without limits, without conditions, and even without the beloved's presence. . . . The bond transcends sexual desire]. Thus, we can also see this stance as a cyberfeminist proposition; it, too, concerns this virtual community gathered around *Negracubana,* grounded in an intimacy that does not require physical bodies—even if at its very center resides the empowered black woman's body.

Nevertheless, how can such a love revolution—centered on the black woman's body—be effected through digital networking? What are the implications of this digital disembodiment? Although the phenomena of disembodiments are always at play in any kind of representation (as we can see in Castro's anecdote), virtual reality has complicated and multiplied the instances of effects like phantasmagoria, simulation, and prosopopoeia. Precisely, Álvarez Ramírez has embraced cyberfeminism as the philosophy and politics that inform her blogging, because this kind of feminism focuses on the challenges and possibilities posed by the conjunction between the body and the Internet, a connection that radicalizes the performance of body politics (race, gender, and sexuality, for example). In "¿Ciberfeminismo en Cuba?," a presentation at the LASA Congress (2013), she directed her audience to Haraway's ideas and the Australian collective VNS Matrix's practice.

In her "A Cyborg Manifesto," Haraway proposed the image of the cyborg in order to contemplate a kind of futuristic context that by 1991 was almost a tangible present. A cyborg is defined as a "hybrid of machine and organism, a creature of social reality as well as a creature of fiction [that] . . . has no origin story . . . [and] is resolutely committed to partiality, irony, intimacy, and perversity" (149–51). In her text, Haraway draws from women-of-color feminisms, such as Lorde's, to better articulate the functionality and effects of the cyborg. By resignifying Lorde's powerful title *Sister Outsider,* Haraway thinks of the politics of the cyborg as indebted to the notion of an "outsider identity," whose writing "is about the power to survive" (175). Therefore, "A Cyborg Manifesto" is not proposing a disembodied utopia; on the contrary, the image of the cyborg radicalizes the effects of gender embodiment as a fixed male/female binary. The cyborg also reminds us of the multiple body politics that crisscross women's bodies.

Haraway's ideas have been fundamental for feminist activists working and networking on the Internet. VNS Matrix, for example, has rethought her theoretical concept of the cyborg and deployed it through digital art. Written in a collective voice, their "Cyberfeminist Manifesto for the 21st Century" (1991) stresses the centrality of the vagina, which will mediate their art and politics, and transform them into a source of "jouissance, madness, poetry" that will operate as a virus. In the manifesto, words like *rupturing, sabotaging, infiltrating, disrupting, disseminating,* and *corrupting* evoke the ambition of a hacker who seeks to alter a structure or a system, but who also follows a political conviction—in this case, feminism (VNS Matrix). The communal, artistic, and political nature of VNS Matrix best describes, too, Álvarez Ramírez's own practice of cyberfeminism.

In her presentation at LASA, the blogger deployed her critique of structural racism to impart an Afro-Cuban perspective to the premises of cyberfeminism. According to this blogger, concrete cyberfeminist efforts are those destined to create safe online networks where women can openly discuss any issue without being threatened. In examining the specificities of Cuban cyberfeminism, Álvarez Ramírez explained that Cuban websites have displayed ideas and practices that, whether consciously or not, have shared cyberfeminist goals: discussions on women's professional advancement in the workplace, debates about sexual health and reproductive rights, exchanges and analyses of women's everyday experiences, and reflections on feminist philosophies. For Álvarez Ramírez in "¿Ciberfeminismo en Cuba?", all of these online interventions have increased the number of "voces con criterios alternativos que han dinamitado los paradigmas tradicionales del poder, en una isla donde cada día es un reto conectarse al Internet" [voices with alternative criteria that have dynamited the traditional paradigms of power, on an island where every passing day presents a challenge to connect to the Internet]. For Álvarez

Ramírez, queer black feminists have been the most eager contributors to the construction of such networks, as well as the effort's primary beneficiaries.

In this sense, as we can see in the entry "Krudas Cubensi," *Negracubana*'s main contribution to cyberfeminism is to form a black feminist community—and, especially, to network with all those who share "la vivencia de ser mujeres que 'gustan de papayas,' la libertad física y de pensamiento, el amor [y] la emigración" [the experience of being women who "like papaya," physical and intellectual liberty, love, and emigration]. Thus Álvarez Ramírez establishes an alliance with the Krudas Cubensi, a Cuban hip-hop trio of black feminists who emigrated to the United States and who self-identified as fat, poor, and lesbian. Their songs and visual aesthetics work against Guevara's ideal of the revolutionary; instead, their proposal argues for a "third revolution" in Cuba, a feminist one (Rivera-Velázquez, 99–100). Much like Álvarez Ramírez's feminist proposal, the Krudas' "emancipatory discourse" establishes a dialogue with black feminists across the Americas in order to push forward a social agenda that values black lesbians' experiences (Saunders, 250–51). In her blog entry, then, *Negracubana* uses the Krudas' communal *vivencia* as a starting point that can bring her readers and listeners into contact with the Afro-cyberfeminist critique. Similar to Lorde, Álvarez Ramírez's revolutionary proposition will center on loving the black woman's body, and, yet, this cyberfeminist will rely on digital networking to provide an additional layer of complexity to Lorde's notion of mothering. For the blogger, the fluidity of polyamory will place black women in charge of their sexual pleasure and their own representations, something that will also function against the revolution's discourse on love and sacrifice.

In *Negracubana*, this empowered embodiment and its love revolution are achieved through self-knowledge and the enjoyment of "our" sexualities. In "Tengo orgasmos," she addresses masturbation and describes herself as a "happy feminist": an accomplished and independent woman who enjoys life. She credits this empowerment to the capacity of pleasuring "ourselves": "no necesit[a]mos ni de un Dios ni un macho que nos indique . . . cómo alcanzar nuestros orgasmos, esos que solo nosotras sabemos de qué van" [we don't need a God or a man to tell us . . . how to reach our orgasms, the ones only we know how to give ourselves]. In Álvarez Ramírez's blogging, activism against structural racism starts by mothering "ourselves," and self-knowledge must include self-pleasure in order to create a solidarity-driven network capable of envisioning new projects.

It is within this focus on new projects that we can understand *Negracubana*'s constant call for revamping prostitution, especially in Cuba. While the neoliberal logic of tourism disembodies black and *mulata* women to represent them as sexual products, Álvarez Ramírez devotes multiple blog entries to examining pornography and prostitution as industries that can be retaken by feminist thought and practices. In "Carita," she starts by redefining the words *puta* [slut] and *jinetera* [prostitute], which "hablan de mujeres que hacen de sus cuerpos lo que ellas quieren" [speak of women who make what they want of their bodies]. She insists that the Cuban state should protect sex workers, instead of judging them with a moral hypocrisy that condemns them and their work, while still promoting Cuba as a sex tourism destination.

Intimacy plays, once again, a key role in Álvarez Ramírez's interest in this topic. In "Jinetera," an interview with an unidentified Cuban sex worker, she dedicates the blog to her dear friend Nanny, who was a psychiatrist and sex worker during the Special Period on the island. With this dedication, Álvarez Ramírez reinforces her friendship, signals her feminist stance on the topic, and practices a mothering of black women's sexualities. I would like to focus not on the interview per se but on the comments section in "Jinetera," where a debate arises between those who consider prostitution a sign of social injustice and those who see it fundamentally as a matter of women's power over their own bodies and sexualities. Among the commenters, two sex workers offer their testimonies, stressing that they chose this profession for multiple reasons—reasons that encompass both economic necessity and personal empowerment. One of them distinguishes between sex workers who answer to a man (or have a pimp) and those who oversee their own business. She declares: "Muchas putas lo somos porque nos gusta. Independientemente de la solvencia, educación e instrucción que tengamos, abrazamos la profesión . . . porque llena nuestras expectativas, nos gusta esa vida conociendo personas y lugares" [Many of us are prostitutes because we like it. Besides whatever financial security, education, or instruction we might have, we embrace the profession . . . because it meets our expectations, we like this life of getting to know people and places]. Álvarez Ramírez selects this comment and publishes it as another blog entry, "Testimonio: 'muchas putas lo somos porque nos gusta,'" where the discussion continues. This publication shows an instance of how the cyberfeminist creates a net among women from different backgrounds and constitutes her community of readers and interlocutors. Sharing intimate memories, testimonies, and debates, Álvarez Ramírez encourages this burgeoning community to discuss some of the thorniest topics in the Cuban society, such as prostitution. Furthermore, Álvarez Ramírez successfully alters the most predictable discourses on prostitution (as a moral or social disease) by offering texts that talk about black and *mulata* women's empowerment through taking control of their own sexualities.

All of these instances in Álvarez Ramírez's blogging show that, while the polyamory philosophy operates against patriarchy and any promise of happiness, cyberfeminism radicalizes its reach and effect by putting intersectionality at the center of the discussion of sex and love. Maybe *Negracubana*'s most significant contribution to the Cuban context is broadening online networking in such a way that debates regarding the revolution and its unfulfilled promises for once, at a global scale, come to be centered on the Afro-Cuban woman's body. At the same time, she brings another layer of complexity to cyberfeminism as she uses it to open up the *maldita circunstancia* of the Cuban context by highlighting the empowered *guerreras* that, like in Morejón's poem, become agents in the processes of embodiment/disembodiment.

EPILOGUE

Intimacies of a "We," Commonalities, and Intellectual Discourses

MANY HAVE SAID that the Ciudad Juárez poet, journalist, and activist Susana Chávez Castillo was the first one to say "ni una mujer menos, ni una muerta más" [not one woman less, not one more female death] in a 1995 poem. Chávez Castillo was murdered in 2011, and in 2015 part of her verse came back as #NiUnaMenos, a hashtag included in Argentinean journalist Marcela Ojeda's tweet: "Actrices, políticas, artistas, empresarias, referentes sociales . . . mujeres, todas, bah . . . no vamos a levantar la voz? NOS ESTÁN MATANDO" (qtd. in Annunziata et al., 46) [Actresses, politicians, artists, entrepreneurs, social referents . . . all women, c'mon . . . aren't we going to raise our voice? WE ARE BEING KILLED]. Thanks to Ojeda's colleagues, Florencia Etcheves, Ingrid Beck, Hinde Pomeraniec, and Soledad Vallejos, the tweet went viral, and, very soon, #NiUnaMenos served as the phrase coined by a movement that sprouted against femicides, gender violence in general, and patriarchy across the Americas, in social media and in the streets.

I opened this book with an analysis of Vientós Gastón's reaction to Boorstin's words about Puerto Rican intellectuals and their relationship with state politics. Back in the 1950s, her anger intended to move her readership to stick together against his discourse, which was advocating for an institutionalization of intellectuals, that is, a retreat from the public sphere and a reclusion in universities. Boorstin's exhortation never succeeded in Puerto Rico, nor in any other context in Latin America, or even in the United States. As my study of Goldman (chapter 2) shows, there is also a tradition of intellectual interventions in the U.S. public sphere, usually to connect national and international phenomena. More recently, *PMLA* published a dossier entitled *The Semipublic Intellectual: Academia, Criticism, and the Internet Age* (March 2015) as part of its periodic section "The Changing Profession." In their introduction, Lili Loofbourow and Phillip Maciak argue that, during the last decade, a new "semipublic" intellectual has emerged in the United States, an "academic hungry for new audiences and broader forms of intellectual exchange" that have "intellectual as well as political reasons" for "hybrid platforms and the ambiguous middle ground they offer" (440–41). Meanwhile, in the same dossier, Michael Bérubé points out that, since the 1980s, academics have been trying to revolutionize the crafts and outlets of academic writing in hopes of dispensing with the image of the university as an ivory tower and "promoting the ideal of the scholar-activist" (448). I would dare to say that, although there have always been U.S. intellectuals, like Goldman, wanting to take the public sphere to call for an audience interested in the relationship of the United States with the world, this urge has gained more adepts after the economic crisis (or "big recession") of 2008, when a vast majority in the United States finally experienced the effects of the neoliberal space of catastrophe that has been battering the rest of the continent since the 1970s. It can be said that a rumor became loud enough for U.S. academia to take public action.

Precisely, I want to reflect briefly on some verses from Chávez Castillo's "Ocaso" that tell us about such rumors that propel "us" to speak up:

> por un rumor indefinido.
> Surges despuntando tu lengua . . .
> (Susana Chávez Castillo, "Ocaso")

> because of an indefinite rumor.
> You emerge sprouting your tongue . . .

The poetic voice speaks of a "you" that has emerged "despuntando tu lengua"; and this is why the poem can be written. Furthermore, the "you" speaks because there has been an indefinite rumor that has moved it to emerge, to sprout the tongue. Voices and discourses that transit indistinctively between the "I," the "you," and an extended, indefinite, collectivity encompass what I see happening in Monsiváis's, Goldman's, Lemebel's, Ramos's, and Álvarez Ramírez's intellectual discourses. This is why the question should have never been, "what is the role of an intellectual?" Because, to answer that question, we would have needed a concrete origin of the discourse and the action. Neither should the question have been, "how do intellectuals mediate between this (lettered city, elite culture, the nation) and that (real city, popular culture, the people/masses)?" Rather, as Chávez Castillo's verses suggest, the questions should be, "how do intellectuals insert their speech into an ongoing rumor? Why? To whom—*not about whom*—do they speak? What are the effects of their speech in relation to the rumor, to the ongoing conversation?"

The answers to these questions always vary, as I have demonstrated in the readings of the five cases I have studied, but, in the contemporary context, they point us toward a key idea. Within the space of catastrophe of neoliberalism, which has radically impacted the relationships between bodies and space, these intellectual discourses search for intimacy in public debates. Intimacy is based, in these cases, on what "we" have in common: "our" vision for the materiality of everyday life, the function of the state, and the forms of representation. Even when this intimacy is conformed through digital media, "posting something, clicking on a hyperlink, or sending an email continue the old model of citizenship as an event of circulating opinion, now folded into the ongoing demand to respond to the next new intensified pressure, just like the last one, and the next" (Berlant, 261). And, even in transcontinental imaginations, or other forms that go beyond the national, the question returns to what "we" have in common here and now, to how "I" connect to "you" in the ephemeral present, trying to pursue something (an emergence) into the future. Within the particular cluster of identities that each of "us" may have, the connection is material, ideological, and emotional. And thus, the intellectual locus of enunciation needs to be inquired in all three.

WORKS CITED

"4 Win Prizes for Coverage of the Americas." *The New York Times,* 26 Oct. 1995, http://www.nytimes.com/1995/10/26/world/4-win-prizes-for-coverage-of-the-americas.html. Accessed 15 Aug. 2015.

"2014 American Immigration Crisis." *Wikipedia,* 4 Sept. 2015, https://en.wikipedia.org/wiki/2014_American_immigration_crisis. Accessed 15 Nov. 2015.

Achugar, Hugo. "Territorios y memorias *versus* lógica del mercado: A propósito de cartografías y shopping malls." *Planetas sin boca: Escritos efímeros sobre arte, cultura y literatura,* Ediciones Trilce, 2004, pp. 217–28.

Agamben, Giorgio. *Remnants of Auschwitz: The Witness and the Archive.* Zone Books, 1999.

"Agrupación de Familiares de Detenidos Desaparecidos." *Facebook,* https://www.facebook.com/AGRUPACION-DE-FAMILIARES-DE-DETENIDOS-DESAPARECIDOS-121832001180496/. Accessed 17 May 2017.

Aguilar Rivera, José Antonio. "La tribuna del sentimiento." *Nexos,* vol. 23, no. 281, May 2001, pp. 9–13.

Aguilar Zínser, Adolfo, et al. *Aún tiembla. Sociedad política y cambio social: El terremoto del 19 de septiembre de 1985.* Grijalbo, 1986.

Ahmed, Sara. *The Cultural Politics of Emotion.* Routledge, 2015.

———. *The Promise of Happiness.* Duke UP, 2010.

Allen, Nick, and Phillip Sherwell. "America's Border Inundated with Almost 50,000 Child Migrants." *The Telegraph,* 22 June 2014, http://www.telegraph.co.uk/news/worldnews/northamerica/usa/10916593/Americas-border-inundated-with-almost-50000-child-migrants.html. Accessed 15 Aug. 2015.

Álvarez Curbelo, Silvia. "La bandera en la colina: Luis Muñoz Marín en los tiempos de la guerra de Corea." *Luis Muñoz Marín: Perfiles de su gobernación, 1948–1964,* edited by Fernando Picó, Fundación Luis Muñoz Marín, 2003, pp. 1–20.

———. "Coartadas para la agresión: Emigración, guerra y populismo." *Polifonía salvaje: Ensayos de cultura y política en la posmodernidad,* edited by Carlos Gil and Irma Rivera Nieves, Editorial Postdata, 1995, pp. 91–107.

———. "The Color of War: Puerto Rican Soldiers and Discrimination during World War II." Rivas-Rodríguez and Zamora, pp. 110–24.

Álvarez Ramírez, Sandra. "Amar más allá de los límites de tu cuerpo." *Negra cubana tenía que ser,* 28 Jan. 2015, https://negracubanateniaqueser.com/2015/01/28/amar-mas-alla-de-los-limites-de-tu-cuerpo/. Accessed 25 June 2015.

———. "Carita de pasaporte." *Negra cubana tenía que ser,* 29 Oct. 2014, https://negracubanateniaqueser.com/2014/10/29/carita-de-pasaporte-video/. Accessed 25 June 2015.

———. "¿Ciberfeminismo en Cuba?" *Negra cubana tenía que ser,* 13 May 2013, https://negracubanateniaqueser.com/2013/05/13/ciberfeminismo-en-cuba-mi-ponencia-para-lasa-2013/. Accessed 25 June 2015.

———. "Disidencias: El socialismo no es suficiente." *Negra cubana tenía que ser,* 8 Mar. 2014, https://negracubanateniaqueser.com/2014/03/08/disidencias-el-socialismo-no-es-suficiente/. Accessed 25 June 2015.

———. "Ese poema de Nancy me puede hacer llorar." *Negra cubana tenía que ser,* 11 Feb. 2014, https://negracubanateniaqueser.com/2014/02/11/ese-poema-de-nancy-me-puede-hacer-llorar/. Accessed 25 June 2015.

———. "Jinetera." *Negra cubana tenía que ser,* 6 Apr. 2014, https://negracubanateniaqueser.com/2014/04/06/jinetera/. Accessed 25 June 2015.

———. "Krudas Cubensi: Rap desde las trompas de Falopio." *Pikara Magazine,* 24 May 2013, http://www.pikaramagazine.com/2013/05/krudas-cubensi-rap-desde-las-trompas-de-falopio/. Accessed 25 June 2015.

———. "Pequeños detalles que me recuerdan que vivo en Alemania y no en Cuba." *Negra cubana tenía que ser,* 14 Aug. 2014, https://negracubanateniaqueser.com/2015/03/15/pequenos-detalles-que-me-recuerdan-que-vivo-en-alemania-y-no-en-cuba-2/. Accessed 25 June 2015.

———. "¿Quién es Negracubana?" *Negra cubana tenía que ser,* 2006, https://negracubanateniaqueser.com/quien-es-negracubana/. Accessed 25 June 2015.

———. "Tengo orgasmos, soy feminista y vivo happy." *Negra cubana tenía que ser,* 6 Sept. 2014, https://negracubanateniaqueser.com/2014/09/06/tengo-orgasmos-soy-feminista-y-vivo-happy-video/. Accessed 25 June 2015.

———. "Testimonio: 'muchas putas lo somos porque nos gusta.'" *Negra cubana tenía que ser,* 7 Apr. 2014, https://negracubanateniaqueser.com/2014/04/25/testimonio-muchas-putas-lo-somos-porque-nos-gusta/. Accessed 25 June 2015.

———. "Volver a empezar una relación." *Hablemos de sexo y amor,* 25 May 2015, https://hablemos-desexo.com/historia/volver-empezar-una-relacion. Accessed 25 June 2015.

———. "¿Y las lesbianas feministas cubanas dónde están?" *Negra cubana tenía que ser,* 4 July 2014, https://negracubanateniaqueser.com/2014/07/04/y-las-lesbianas-feministas-cubanas-donde-estan/. Accessed 25 June 2015.

Anderson, Benedict. *Imagined Communities: Reflections on the Origin and Spread of Nationalism.* Verso, 1991.

Anderson, Mark D. *Disaster Writing: The Cultural Politics of Catastrophe in Latin America.* U of Virginia P, 2011.

Anderson, Thomas F. *Everything in Its Place: The Life and Works of Virgilio Piñera.* Bucknell UP, 2005.

Annunziata, Rocío, et al. "Argentina." *Activismo político en tiempos de internet,* compiled by Bernardo Sorj and Sergio Fausto, Plataforma Democrática, 2016, pp. 37–112.

Arellano, Jerónimo. *Magical Realism and the History of the Emotions in Latin America.* Bucknell UP, 2015.

Arias, Arturo. "Centroamericanidades: Imaginative Reformulation and New Configurations of Central Americanness." *Studies in 20th and 21st Century Literature,* vol. 37, no. 2, 2013, pp. 11–26.

———. "La psique interior de los guatemaltecos, las cuestiones del biculturalismo." *Mesoamérica,* vol. 18, no. 34, 1997, pp. 633–36.

Arias, Arturo, and Claudia Milian. "U.S. Central Americans: Representations, Agency and Communities." *Latino Studies,* vol. 11, no. 2, June 2013, pp. 131–49.

Aricó, José M. *La cola del diablo: Itinerario de Gramsci en América Latina.* Siglo Veintiuno Editores, 2014.

Avelar, Idelber. *The Untimely Present: Postdictatorial Latin American Fiction and the Task of Mourning.* Duke UP, 1999.

Avilés-Santiago, Manuel G. *Puerto Rican Soldiers and Second-Class Citizenship: Representations in Media.* Palgrave Macmillan, 2014.

Barradas, Efraín. "Para travestirte mejor: Pedro Lemebel y las lecturas políticas desde los márgenes." *Iberoamericana,* vol. 9, no. 33, 2009, pp. 69–82.

Barreto, Amílcar A. *Vieques, the Navy, and Puerto Rican Politics.* UP of Florida, 2002.

Barthes, Ronald. *A Lover's Discourse: Fragments.* Hill and Wang, 1978.

Bartra, Roger. *La jaula de la melancolía: Identidad y metamorfosis del mexicano.* De Bolsillo, 1987.

Basulto, David. "Monumento Mujeres en la Memoria." *Plataforma Arquitectura,* 28 Dec. 2006, http://www.plataformaarquitectura.cl/2006/12/28/monumento-mujeres-en-la-memoria-oficinadearquitectura/. Accessed 15 May 2017.

Beasley-Murray, Jon. *Posthegemony: Political Theory and Latin America.* U of Minnesota P, 2010.

Beech, Nick. "Ground Exploration: Producing Everyday Life at the South Bank, 1948–1951." *Urban Revolution Now: Henri Lefebvre in Social Research and Architecture,* edited by Łukasz Staneck et al., Routledge, 2014, pp. 191–206.

Benjamin, Walter. "The Storyteller." *Illuminations: Essays and Reflections,* Schocken Books, 1985, pp. 83–110.

———. "Theses on the Philosophy of History." *Illuminations: Essays and Reflections,* Schocken Books, 1985, pp. 253–64.

Berlant, Lauren. *Cruel Optimism.* Duke UP, 2011.

Bérubé, Michael. "Profession, Revise Thyself—Again." *PMLA,* vol. 130, no. 2, Mar. 2015, pp. 446–52.

Bhabha, Homi K. *The Location of Culture,* Routledge, 2004.

Blanco, Fernando A. "Comunicación, política y memoria en la escritura de Pedro Lemebel." Blanco, pp. 27–71.

———, editor. *Reinas de otro cielo: Modernidad y Autoritarismo en la obra de Pedro Lemebel*. LOM Ediciones, 2004.

Blanco, Fernando A., and Juan Gelpí. "El desliz que desafía otros recorridos: Entrevista con Pedro Lemebel." *Nómada: Creación, Teoría, Crítica*, no. 3, 1997, pp. 93–98.

BlogBang Cuba. Directed by Claudio Peláez Sordo, 2014.

Boorstin, Daniel J. "Self-Discovery in Puerto Rico." *The Yale Review*, vol. 45, no. 2, 1956, pp. 229–45.

Bortignon, Martina. "El mito de la Transición democrática en Chile: El témpano de hielo de la Expo-Sevilla 1992 y las crónicas radiales de Pedro Lemebel." *Badebec*, vol. 2, no. 4, Mar. 2013, pp. 61–82.

Bosque Pérez, Ramón, and José Javier Colón Morera. *Las carpetas: Persecusión política y derechos civiles en Puerto Rico*. Centro para la Investigación y Promoción de los Derechos Civiles, 1997.

Bosteels, Bruno. "Gramsci at the Margins." *Bruno Bosteels at Academia.edu*, 2–3 May 2013, www.cornell.academia.edu/BrunoBosteels. Accessed 19 Aug. 2016.

Boyer, M. Christine. *The City of Collective Memory: Its Historical Imagery and Architectural Entertainments*. MIT Press, 1994.

Boym, Svetlana. *The Future of Nostalgia*. Basic Books, 2001.

Brewster, Claire. *Responding to Crisis in Contemporary Mexico: The Political Writings of Paz, Fuentes, Monsiváis, and Poniatowska*. U of Arizona P, 2005.

Burnett, Christina Duffy, and Burke Marshall. "Between the Foreign and the Domestic: The Doctrine of Territorial Incorporation, Invented and Reinvented." *Foreign in a Domestic Sense: Puerto Rico, American Expansion, and the Constitution*, edited by Burnett and Marshall, Duke UP, 2001, pp. 1–36.

Caminero-Santangelo, Marta. "Central Americans in the City: Goldman, Tobar, and the Question of Panethnicity." *Lit: Literature Interpretation Theory*, vol. 20, no. 3, 2009, pp. 173–95.

Camp, Roderic A. *Mexico's Mandarins: Crafting a Power Elite for the Twenty-First Century*. U of California P, 2002.

Camp, Roderic A., et al. *Los intelectuales y el poder en México: Memorias de la VI Conferencia de Historiadores Mexicanos y Estadounidenses*. El Colegio de México / UCLA Latin American Center Publications, 1991.

Capécia, Mayotte. *Je suis martiniquaise*. Corrêa, 1948.

Cárcamo-Huechante, Luis E. "Las perlas de los 'mercados persas': Estética y economía de la crónica urbana en Pedro Lemebel." *Desdén al infortunio: Sujeto, comunicación y público en la narrativa de Pedro Lemebel*, edited by Blanco and Pobleto, Editerial Cuarto Propio, 2010, pp. 157–79.

Casamayor-Cisneros, Odette. "Confrontation and Occurrence: Ethical-Esthetic Expressions of Blackness in Post-Soviet Cuba." *Latin American and Caribbean Ethnic Studies*, vol. 4, no. 2, 2009, pp. 103–35.

Castro, Fidel. "Palabras a los intelectuales." ["Discurso pronunciado por el Comandante Fidel Castro Ruz, Primer Ministro del Gobierno Revolucionario y Secretario del PURSC, como conclusión de las reuniones con los intelectuales cubanos, efectuadas en la Biblioteca Nacional el 16, 23 y 30 de junio de 1961"]. *Discursos de Fidel Castro Ruz*, http://www.cuba.cu/gobierno/discursos/1961/esp/f300661e.html. Accessed 29 June 2015.

Cavarero, Adriana. *For More than One Voice: Toward a Philosophy of Vocal Expression*. Stanford UP, 2005.

———. *Relating Narratives: Storytelling and Selfhood*. Routledge, 2000.

Chávez Castillo, Susana. "Ocaso." *Primera tormenta. Poemas de Susana Chávez*, 19 Aug. 2005, http://primeratormenta.blogspot.com. Accessed 29 May 2017.

Chomsky, Noam. *Turning the Tide: U.S. Intervention in Central America and the Struggle for Peace.* Haymarket Books, 2015.

Clough, Patricia Ticineto, and Jean Halley. *The Affective Turn: Theorizing the Social.* Duke UP, 2007.

Cobb, Jasmine N. *Picture Freedom: Remaking Black Visuality in the Early Nineteenth Century.* New York UP, 2015.

Colón Morera, José Javier. "Puerto Rico: The Puzzle of Human Rights and Self-Determination." *Puerto Rico under Colonial Rule: Political Persecution and the Quest for Human Rights,* edited by Ramón Bosque-Pérez and Colón Morera, SUNY Press, 2006, pp. 83–102.

Comisión Nacional de Reconstrucción. *México está de pie.* Instalación de la Coordinación de Vivienda, 1985.

"Comprehensive Immigration Reform. Congress Must Act Comprehensively on Immigration Reform." *Organizing for Action,* 2014, https://www.barackobama.com/immigration-reform/. Accessed 15 Nov. 2016.

Conn, Robert T. *The Politics of Philology: Alfonso Reyes and the Invention of the Latin American Literary Tradition.* Bucknell UP, 2002.

Contreras, Félix. *La música cubana: Una cuestión personal.* Ediciones Unión, 1999.

Cordones-Cook, Juanamaría. *Soltando amarras y memorias: Mundo y poesía de Nancy Morejón.* Editorial Cuarto Propio, 2009.

Corona, Ignacio, and Beth E. Jörgensen, editors. *The Contemporary Mexican Chronicle: Theoretical Perspectives on the Liminal Genre.* SUNY Press, 2002.

———. "Introduction." Corona and Jörgensen, pp. 1–24.

Costa, Flavia. "La rabia es la tinta de mi escritura." *Revista Ñ,* 14 Aug. 2004, http://edant.clarin.com/suplementos/cultura/2004/08/14/u-813177.htm. Accessed 15 May 2017.

Cuesta, Mabel. *Cuba post-soviética: Un cuerpo narrado en clave de mujer.* Editorial Cuarto Propio, 2012.

De Ferrari, Guillermina. *Community and Culture in Post-Soviet Cuba.* Routledge, 2014.

Delgado Cintrón, Carmelo. "David Ortiz Angleró: Sus polifacéticas aportaciones." *Diálogo UPR,* 20 July 2014, http://dialogoupr.com/david-ortiz-anglero-sus-polifaceticas-aportaciones-3/. Accessed 2 May 2017.

Del Sarto, Ana. "La fugacidad de lo permanente (o la permanencia de lo fugitivo): El ingenio de Carlos Monsiváis." *Revista de Crítica Literaria Latinoamericana,* vol. 32, no. 63–64, 2006, pp. 187–205.

"Demographic Highlights." *Harper's Magazine,* 2014, http://harpers.org/wp-content/uploads/2016/03/2016-Media-Kit.pdf, p. 6. Accessed 15 Nov. 2016.

Denis, Nelson A. *War Against All Puerto Ricans: Revolution and Terror in America's Colony.* Nation Books, 2015.

Derrida, Jacques. *The Politics of Friendship.* Verso, 1997.

"Diálogo entre estudiantes y el autor de la novela *Antes de la guerra.*" *Universia Puerto Rico.* 22 Apr. 2005, http://noticias.universia.pr/vida-universitaria/noticia/2005/04/22/142300/dialogo-estudiantes-autor-novela-antes-guerra.html. Accessed 9 May 2017.

"*Diálogo UPR.*" *Wikipedia,* 17 Jan. 2017, https://es.wikipedia.org/wiki/Diálogo_UPR. Accessed 2 May 2017.

Díaz Ayala, Cristóbal. *Música cubana: Del areyto a la nueva trova.* Ediciones Universal, 1993.

Díaz Quiñones, Arcadio. *El arte de bregar: Ensayos.* Ediciones Callejón, 2000.

———. *La memoria rota.* Ediciones Huracán, 1993.

Domínguez Ruvalcaba, Héctor. "Carlos Monsiváis: Poética y política de la disidencia sexual." *Taller de letras,* no. 50, 2012, pp. 197–206.

———. "La Yegua de Troya: Pedro Lemebel, los medios y la performance." Blanco, pp. 117–50.

Dove, Patrick. *The Catastrophe of Modernity: Tragedy and the Nation in Latin American Literature,* Bucknell UP, 2004.

Draper, Susana. *Afterlives of Confinement: Spatial Transitions in Postdictatorship Latin America.* U of Pittsburgh P, 2012.

Egan, Linda. *Carlos Monsiváis: Culture and Chronicle in Contemporary Mexico.* U of Arizona P, 2001.

———. "¿Quién matará los dragones del desánimo? Los héroes de Carlos Monsiváis, paladín de categoría." *Taller de Letras,* no. 50, 2012, pp. 239–55.

El caso Zurbano. Dossier in *Afro-Hispanic Review,* vol. 33, no. 1, Spring 2014, pp. 13–228.

Eltit, Diamela. *Emergencias: Escritos sobre literatura, arte y política.* Planeta / Ariel, 2000.

Espina, Mayra, et al. "El Período especial veinte años después." *Temas,* no. 65, Jan.–Mar. 2011, pp. 59–75.

Estrada, Oswaldo. "'¿Me estás oyendo, inútil?' Carlos Monsiváis y la música del Apocalipstick mexicano." *Textos Híbridos,* vol. 1, no. 1, 2011, pp. 30–42.

"Estrategia Nacional para el Desarrollo de la Infraestructura de Conectividad de Banda Ancha en Cuba." *Resumen Ejecutivo del Ministerio de Comunicaciones de la República de Cuba,* June 2015.

Faber, Sebastiaan. "El estilo como ideología: De la *Rebelión* de Ortega a *Los rituales* de Monsiváis." Moraña and Sánchez Prado, 2007, pp. 76–103.

Fanon, Frantz. *Black Skin, White Masks.* Grove Press, 2008.

Fiol-Matta, Licia. *A Queer Mother for the Nation: The State and Gabriela Mistral.* U of Minnesota P, 2002.

Fischer, Carl. *Queering the Chilean Way: Cultures of Exceptionalism and Sexual Dissidence, 1965–2015.* Palgrave Macmillan, 2016.

Fleetwood, Nicole R. *Troubling Vision: Performance, Visuality, and Blackness.* U of Chicago P, 2011.

Florescano, Enrique. *Etnia, estado y nación. Ensayo sobre las identidades colectivas en México.* Aguilar, 1998.

Fornet, Jorge. "Un escritor que se expone." *Revista de Casa de las Américas,* no. 246, Jan.–Mar. 2007, pp. 67–68.

Fortuño, Luis G. "Mensaje sobre la situación del Estado." Capitolio de San Juan, Puerto Rico, *Government Development Bank for Puerto Rico,* 22 Feb. 2012, http://www.bgfpr.com/spa/investors_resources/documents/EstadodeSituacion-02.22.2012.pdf. Accessed 8 May 2017.

Foucault, Michel. *Madness and Civilization: A History of Insanity in the Age of Reason.* Vintage Books, 1988.

Franco, Jean. *The Decline and Fall of the Lettered City: Latin America in the Cold War.* Harvard UP, 2002.

———. "Residuales y emergentes: Carlos Monsiváis y Raymond Williams." Moraña and Sánchez Prado, 2007, pp. 193–203.

Freud, Sigmund. *Jokes and Their Relation to the Unconscious*. Norton and Company, 1960.

———. "Mourning and Melancholia." *Collected Papers*, vol. 6, edited by Philip Rieff, Collier Books, 1963, pp. 164–79.

Fuentes, Carlos. *Cristóbal Nonato*. Narrativa Mondadori, 1992.

Gallo, Rubén. "Modernist Ruins: The Case Study of Tlatelolco." *Telling Ruins in Latin America*, edited by Michael J. Lazzara and Vicky Unruh, Palgrave Macmillan, 2009, pp. 107–18.

Gandhi, Leela. *Affective Communities: Anticolonial Thought, Fin-de Siècle Radicalism, and the Politics of Friendship*. Duke UP, 2006.

García Muñiz, Humberto, and Gloria Vega Rodríguez. *La ayuda militar como negocio: Estados Unidos y el Caribe*. Ediciones Callejón, 2002.

Gelpí, Juan G. *Literatura y paternalismo en Puerto Rico*. Editorial UPR, 2005.

———. "Walking in the Modern City: Subjectivity and Cultural Contacts in the Urban *Crónicas* of Salvador Novo and Carlos Monsiváis." Corona and Jörgensen, pp. 201–20.

Gilbert, Sandra M., and Susan Gubar. *The Madwoman in the Attic: The Woman Writer and the Nineteenth-Century Literary Imagination*. Yale UP, 2000.

Goldman, Francisco. *The Art of Political Murder: Who Killed the Bishop?* Grove Press, 2008.

———. "The Children's Hour: Sandinista Kids Fight Contras and Boredom." *Harper's Magazine*, vol. 269, no. 1613, 1984, pp. 69–74.

———. "From President to Prison: Otto Pérez Molina and a Day for Hope in Guatemala." *The New Yorker*, 4 Sept. 2015, http://www.newyorker.com/news/news-desk/from-president-to-prison-otto-perez-molina-and-a-day-for-hope-in-guatemala. Accessed 15 Oct. 2015.

———. "In a Terrorized Country." *The New York Times*, 17 Apr. 1995, p. A17.

———. "In Guatemala, All Is Forgotten." *The New York Times*, 23 Dec. 1996, p. A15.

———. "Lost in Another Honduras: Of Bordellos and Bad Scenes." *Harper's Magazine*, vol. 273, no. 1637, 1986, pp. 49–57.

———. "*Moro Like Me*." *Half and Half: Writers on Growing Up Biracial and Bicultural*, edited by Claudine Chiawei O'Hearn, Pantheon Books, 1998, pp. 49–70.

———. "Murder Comes for the Bishop." *The New Yorker*, vol. 75, no. 3, 15 Mar. 1999, pp. 60–77.

———. "Sad Tales of *la libertad de prensa*: Reading the Newspapers of Central America." *Harper's Magazine*, vol. 277, no. 1659, 1988, pp. 56–62.

———. "What Price Panama? A Visit to a Barrio Destroyed by U.S. Forces." *Harper's Magazine*, vol. 281, no. 1684, 1990, pp. 71–78.

González, Aníbal. *La crónica modernista hispanooamericana*. José Porrúa Turanzas, 1983.

González, José Luis. "Una caja de plomo que no se podía abrir." *Antología personal de José Luis González*, Editorial UPR, 1998, pp. 19–26.

Gordon, Ian. "70,000 Kids Will Show Up Alone at Our Border This Year. What Happens to Them?" *Mother Jones*, July–Aug. 2014, http://www.motherjones.com/politics/2014/06/child-migrants-surge-unaccompanied-central-america. Accessed 15 Sept. 2015.

Gramsci, Antonio. "The Intellectuals." *An Anthology of Western Marxism: From Lukács and Gramsci to Socialist-Feminism*, edited by Roger S. Gottlieb, Oxford UP, 1989, pp. 113–19.

Grandin, Greg. *Empire's Workshop: Latin America, the United States, and the Rise of the New Imperialism*. Metropolitan Books, 2006.

Gregg, Melissa, and Gregory J. Seigworth. *The Affect Theory Reader*. Duke UP, 2010.

Guerra, Lillian. "Gender Policing, Homosexuality, and the New Patriarchy of the Cuban Revolution, 1965–70." *Social History*, vol. 35, no. 3, Aug. 2010, pp. 268–89.

Guevara, Ernesto. "El hombre nuevo." *Ideas en torno de Latinoamérica*, vol. 1, edited by Leopoldo Zea, Universidad Nacional Autónoma de México, 1986, pp. 313–27.

Gutiérrez Mouat, Ricardo. "Monsiváis y la crónica de la violencia." Moraña and Sánchez Prado, 2007, pp. 235–41.

Haraway, Donna J. "A Cyborg Manifesto: Science, Technology and Socialist-Feminism in the Late Twentieth Century." *Simians, Cyborgs, and Women: The Reinvention of Nature*, Free Association Books, 1991, pp. 127–48.

Harris, Dan, et al. "In El Salvador, the Murder Capital of the World, Gang Violence Becomes a Way of Life." *ABC News*, 17 May 2016, http://abcnews.go.com/International/el-salvador-murder-capital-world-gang-violence-life/story?id=39177963. Accessed 15 Dec. 2016.

Harvey, David. *A Brief History of Neoliberalism*. Oxford UP, 2005.

Herman, Susan N. *Taking Liberties: The War on Terror and the Erosion of American Democracy*. Oxford UP, 2011.

hooks, bell. *Black Looks: Race and Representation*. South End, 1992.

Huyssen, Andreas. *Present Pasts: Urban Palimpsests and the Politics of Memory*. Stanford UP, 2003.

Irizarry, Guillermo B. "Subjetividades precarias y resarcimiento literario en *The Long Night of White Chickens* de Francisco Goldman." *Istmo: Revista Virtual de Estudios Literarios y Culturales Centroamericanos*, no. 27–28, 2013, pp. 1–23.

Islam, Roumeen. "Overview: From Media Markets to Policy." *Information and Public Choice: From Media Markets to Policy Making*, edited by Islam, The World Bank, 2008, pp. 1–15.

Jackson, Richard. "Nancy Morejón, the 'New Woman' in Cuba, and the First Generation of Black Writers of the Revolution." *Singular Like a Bird: The Art of Nancy Morejón*, edited by Miriam DeCosta-Willis, Howard UP, 1999, pp. 103–13.

Jambrina, Jesús E. "Del 'yo' al 'nosotros' en *La isla en peso*, de Virgilio Piñera." *La Habana Elegante*, no. 46, Fall–Winter 2009, http://www.habanaelegante.com/Fall_Winter_2009/Invitation_Jambrina.html. Accessed 15 Aug. 2017.

James, Daniel. *El Salvador: A Case History of U.S. Media Influence upon Public Attitudes toward Central America*. The Washington Institute for Values in Public Policy, 1986.

Jarvis, Christina S. *The Male Body at War: American Masculinity during World War II*. Northern Illinois UP, 2004.

Jörgensen, Beth E. "Making History: Subcomandante Marcos in the Mexican Chronicle." *South Central Review*, vol. 21, no. 3, Fall 2004, pp. 85–106.

———. "Matters of Fact: The Contemporary Mexican Chronicle and/as Nonfiction Narrative." Corona and Jörgensen, pp. 71–94.

Kerlikowske, Gil. "Our Comprehensive Response at the Border, by the Numbers." *The White House Blog*, 15 Sept. 2014, https://obamawhitehouse.archives.gov/blog/2014/09/15/our-comprehensive-response-border-numbers. Accessed 23 Feb. 2018.

Klahn, Norma. "Monsiváis entre la nación y la migra(na)ción." Moraña and Sánchez Prado, 2007, pp. 176–90.

Kollipara, Puneet. "Wonkbook: What to Do about America's Child-Migrant Crisis." *The Washington Post*, 23 June 2014, https://www.washingtonpost.com/news/wonk/wp/2014/06/23/wonkbook-what-to-do-about-americas-child-migrant-crisis/?utm_term=.af70b7072935. Accessed 15 Aug. 2015.

Krauze, Enrique. *México: Siglo XX. El sexenio de Miguel de La Madrid.* Editorial Clío, 1999.

Kuhn, Annette. *The Power of the Image: Essays on Representation and Sexuality.* Routledge, 1994.

Lefebvre, Henri. *The Production of Space.* Wiley-Blackwell, 1991.

———. *State, Space, World: Selected Essays.* Edited by Neil Brenner and Stuart Elden, U of Minnesota P, 2009.

Lewis, Holly. *The Politics of Everybody: Feminism, Queer Theory, and Marxism at the Intersection.* Zed Books, 2016.

Lemebel, Pedro. *De perlas y cicatrices.* LOM Ediciones, 1996.

———. *La esquina es mi corazón.* Seix Barral, 2004.

———. *Loco afán: crónicas de sidario.* LOM Ediciones, 1996.

Lojo, Martín. "Mi escritura es un género bastardo." *La Nación,* 13 Mar. 2010, http://www.lanacion.com.ar/1241380-mi-escritura-es-un-genero-bastardo. Accessed 15 May 2017.

Lomnitz-Adler, Claudio. *Exits from the Labyrinth: Culture and Ideology in the Mexican National Space.* U of California P, 1992.

Loofbourow, Lili, and Phillip Maciak. "Introduction: The Time of the Semipublic Intellectual." *PMLA,* vol. 130, no. 2, 2015, pp. 439–45.

Lorde, Audre. *Sister Outsider.* The Crossing Press, 1984.

Lynch, Claire. "Trans-Genre Confusion: What Does Autobiography Think It Is?" *Life Writing: Essays on Autobiography, Biography and Literature,* edited by Richard Bradford, Palgrave Macmillan, 2010, pp. 209–18.

Mahieux, Viviane. "Carlos Monsiváis y el Bicentenario que nunca fue." *Revista de Crítica Literaria Latinoamericana,* vol. 36, no. 72, 2010, pp. 489–92.

Manning, Robert. "*Harper's Magazine*: A Survivor!" *Nieman Reports,* 15 Sept. 2000, http://niemanreports.org/articles/harpers-magazine-a-survivor. Accessed 15 Aug. 2015.

Martin, Brian Joseph. *Napoleonic Friendship: Military Fraternity, Intimacy, and Sexuality in Nineteenth-Century France.* U of New Hampshire P, 2011.

Martínez, Iván C. *The Open Wound: The Scourge of Racism in Cuba from Colonialism to Communism.* Arawak, 2007.

Martínez-Ramírez, Héctor M. "Pentecostal Expansion and Political Activism in Puerto Rico." *Caribbean Studies,* vol. 33, no. 1, Jan.–June 2005, pp. 113–47.

Masiello, Francine. *The Art of Transition: Latin American Culture and Neoliberal Crisis.* Duke UP, 2001.

———. *Between Civilization and Barbarism: Women, Nation, and Literary Culture in Modern Argentina.* U of Nebraska P, 1992.

Massumi, Brian. *Parables for the Virtual: Movement, Affect, Sensation.* Duke UP, 2002.

Mateo del Pino, Ángeles. "Descorriéndole un telón al corazón. Pedro Lemebel: *De perlas y cicatrices.*" *Revista Chilena de Literatura,* no. 64, Apr. 2004, pp. 131–43.

Maurer, Noel, and Carlos Yu. *The Big Ditch: How America Took, Built, Ran, and Ultimately Gave Away the Panama Canal.* Princeton UP, 2011.

McCaffrey, Katherine T. *Military Power and Popular Protest: The U.S. Navy in Vieques, Puerto Rico.* Rutgers UP, 2002.

McClintock, Anne. *Imperial Leather: Race, Gender and Sexuality in the Colonial Contest.* Routledge, 1995.

Mignolo, Walter D. *The Idea of Latin America.* Wiley-Blackwell, 2005.

———. *Local Histories/Global Designs: Coloniality, Subaltern Knowledges, and Border Thinking.* Princeton UP, 2012.

Monsiváis, Carlos. "De la Santa Doctrina al Espíritu Público. (Sobre las funciones de la crónica en México)." *Nueva Revista de Filología Hispánica,* vol. 35, no. 2, 1987, pp. 753–71.

———. *Días de guardar.* Era, 1971.

———. *Entrada libre: Crónicas de la sociedad que se organiza.* Era, 2001.

———. "Lemebel: 'Yo no concebía cómo se escribía en tu mundo raro,' del barroco desclosetado." *Nuevo Texto Crítico,* vol. 22, no. 42–43, 2009, pp. 27–37.

———. *"No sin nosotros": Los días del terremoto, 1985–2005.* Era, 2006.

———. *Que se abra esa puerta: Crónicas y ensayos sobre la diversidad sexual.* Editorial Paidós, 2010.

———. *El 68: La tradición de la resistencia.* Era, 2008.

Monsiváis, Carlos, et al. *EZLN: Documentos y comunicados,* vol. 1–6, Era, 1994.

Moraña, Mabel. "El culturalismo de Carlos Monsiváis: Ideología y carnavalización en tiempos globales." Moraña and Sánchez Prado, 2007, pp. 21–59.

———. "Postscríptum: El afecto en la caja de herramientas." Moraña and Sánchez Prado, 2012, pp. 313–37.

Moraña, Mabel, and Ignacio Sánchez Prado, editors. *El arte de la ironía: Carlos Monsiváis ante la crítica.* Universidad Nacional Autónoma de México, 2007.

———, editors. *El lenguaje de las emociones: Afecto y cultura en América Latina.* Iberoamericana Vervuert, 2012.

———. "Prólogo." Moraña and Sánchez Prado, 2007, pp. 9–20.

Morejón, Nancy. "Mujer negra." *Mujer negra,* http://faculty.cord.edu/gargurev/morejon.htm. Accessed 15 Sept. 2015.

Moreno, María Eugenia, and Clemente Ruiz Durán. "Desafíos de la expropiación." Aguilar Zínser et al., pp. 155–86.

Mosse, George L. *Nationalism and Sexuality: Respectability and Abnormal Sexuality in Modern Europe.* Howard Fertig, 1997.

Moulian, Tomás. *Chile actual: Anatomía de un mito.* LOM-Arcis, 1997.

Nachon, Andi. "La rabia." *Página 12,* 19 Oct. 2003, https://www.pagina12.com.ar/diario/suplementos/libros/10-778-2003-10-23.html. Accessed 20 Feb. 2018.

Nail, Thomas. "Child Refugees: The New Barbarians." *Pacific Standard,* 19 Aug. 2014, https://psmag.com/child-refugees-the-new-barbarians-666b8b7e5efb#.n4sxcrifh. Accessed 15 Aug. 2015.

———. *The Figure of the Migrant.* Stanford UP, 2015.

Nancy, Jean-Luc. *After Fukushima: The Equivalence of Catastrophes.* Fordham UP, 2015.

———. *Being Singular Plural.* Stanford UP, 2000.

Navy Recruiting Command. "Buddy Program." *Navy Recruiting Manual,* vol. 4, May 2011, http://navybmr.com/study%20material/CNRCINST%201130.8J%20(VOLUME-IV).pdf. Accessed 5 May 2017.

Negrón-Muntaner, Frances. *Boricua Pop: Puerto Ricans and the Latinization of American Culture.* New York UP, 2004.

Ngai, Sianne. *Ugly Feelings.* Harvard UP, 2005.

Nissen, Axel. *The Romantic Friendship Reader: Love Stories Between Men in Victorian America.* Northeastern UP, 2003.

Nora, Pierre. *Realms of Memory: Rethinking the French Past.* Columbia UP, 1996–98.

O'Gorman, Edmundo. *La invención de América.* Fondo de Cultura Económica, 1958.

Ojeda, L. Cecilia. "*De perlas y cicatrices: Crónicas radiales* by Pedro Lemebel." *Chasqui,* vol. 30, no. 2, 2001, pp. 157–59.

Olea, Raquel. "Las estrategias escriturales de Pedro Lemebel." *Critica.cl,* 16 Nov. 1998, http://critica.cl/literatura-chilena/las-estrategias-escriturales-de-pedro-lemebel-comentario-sobre-el-libro-de-perlas-y-cicatrices. Accessed 15 May 2017.

Ong, Walter J. *Orality and Literacy: The Technologizing of the Word.* Methuen, 1982.

Órgano Teórico del Comité Ejecutivo Nacional del Partido Revolucionario Institucional. *Línea: Los intelectuales y la política.* Partido Revolucionario Institutional, 1976.

Ortega, Josefina. "Ese sentimiento que se llama . . . filin." *La Jiribilla,* vol. 95, no. 3, 2003, http://epoca2.lajiribilla.cu/2003/n095_03/memoria.html. Accessed 27 Nov. 2017.

Pacheco, Cristina. *Zona de desastre.* Ediciones Océano, 1986.

Paralitici, José "Ché." *No quiero mi cuero pa' tambor: La voz no silenciada y la sentencia Impuesta. 100 años de encarcelamientos por la independencia de Puerto Rico.* Ediciones Puerto, 2006.

Pastén, J. Agustín. "Paseo crítico por una crónica testimonial: De *La esquina es mi corazón* a *Adiós mariquita linda* de Pedro Lemebel." *A Contracorriente: A Journal on Social History and Literature in Latin America,* vol. 4, no. 2, 2007, pp. 103–42.

"Pedro Lemebel—*Cancionero*: Crónicas en Radio Tierra." *YouTube,* uploaded by Virgo, 14 Mar. 2016, https://www.youtube.com/watch?v=waRqOmQI8Co. Accessed 20 Nov. 2017.

Pérez, Carlos Alberto. "Abrirán salas de wi-fi en 35 puntos del territorio cubano, anuncia ETECSA," *CubaDebate,* 18 June 2015, http://www.cubadebate.cu/noticias/2015/06/18/abriran-salas-de-wi-fi-en-35-puntos-del-territorio-cubano-anuncia-etecsa/#.WWEqNMa-ImI. Accessed 29 June 2015.

Pew Research Center. "Demographics and Political Views of News Audiences." *Pew Research Center: U.S. Politics and Policy,* 27 Sept. 2012, http://www.people-press.org/2012/09/27/section-4-demographics-and-political-views-of-news-audiences. Accessed 15 Aug. 2015.

"Photos: Inside a Detention Center for Migrant Children." *Aljazeera America,* 19 June 2014, http://america.aljazeera.com/multimedia/photo-gallery/2014/6/photos-inside-a-detentioncenter-formigrantchildren.html. Accessed 15 Aug. 2015.

Pierluisi, Pedro, in TV interview with Yolanda Vélez Arcelay. *Las Noticias,* Univisión, 27 July 2011.

Piñera, Virgilio. *La isla en peso.* Tusquets Editores, 2000.

Piñero Cádiz, Gerardo M. *Puerto Rico, el Gibraltar del Caribe: Intereses estratégicos estadounidenses y la base aeronaval Roosevelt Roads.* Isla Negra Editores, 2008.

Poblete, Juan. "De la loca a la superestrella: Crónicas y trayectoria escritural en Pedro Lemebel." *INTI: Revista de Literatura Hispánica,* no. 69–70, 2009, pp. 289–304.

———. "Globalización, mediación cultural y literatura nacional." *América Latina en la "literatura mundial,"* edited by Ignacio M. Sánchez Prado, U of Pittsburgh P, 2006, pp. 271–306.

Poniatowska, Elena. *Nada, nadie: Las voces del temblor.* Era, 1988.

Potter, Sara. "There Goes My Hero: Heroic Figures, Utopic Discourse, and Cultural Identity in Carlos Monsiváis's *Aires de familia.*" *Textos Híbridos,* vol. 1, no. 2, 2011, pp. 16–30.

Pratt, Mary Louise. *Imperial Eyes: Travel Writing and Transculturation.* Routledge, 1992.

"Preguntas frecuentes." *El Periódico,* http://elperiodico.com.gt/single_redaccion/. Accessed 15 Nov. 2016.

Pritchard, Annette, and Nigel J. Morgan. "Privileging the Male Gaze: Gendered Tourism Landscapes," *Annals of Tourism Research,* vol. 27, no. 4, 2000, pp. 884–905.

Proyecto Desaparecidos: Chile. http://www.desaparecidos.org/chile/. Accessed 17 May 2017.

"Quiénes somos." *Diálogo UPR,* 2017, http://dialogoupr.com/quienes/. Accessed 2 May 2017.

"Quiénes somos." *Letras Libres,* http://www.letraslibres.com/equipo. Accessed 2 May 2017.

Quiroga, José. "Virgilio Piñera: On the Weight of the Insular Flesh." *Hispanisms and Homosexualities,* edited by Sylvia Molloy and Robert McKee Irwin, Duke UP, 1998, pp. 269–85.

Rama, Ángel. *La ciudad letrada.* Ediciones del Norte, 2002.

Ramos, Josean. "Alerta ante la Ley Patriótica." *Diálogo,* Mar. 2002, pp. 4–5.

———. *Antes de la guerra.* Editorial Cultural, 2005.

———. "De espaldas al mar." *Diálogo,* Sept. 2002, pp. 6–9.

———. "Encuentros y desencuentros entre dos poderosas instituciones." *Diálogo,* Aug. 2000, pp. 8–9.

———. "La guerra en el cancionero boricua." *Diálogo,* May–June 2006, pp. 24–25, and Aug.–Sept. 2006, p. 20.

———. "Iglesia y Estado . . . entre la espada y la cruz." *Diálogo,* Aug. 2000, pp. 6–7.

———. "Memorias de un recluta." *Diálogo,* Jan. 2003, pp. 18–20, and Feb. 2003, pp. 26–27.

———. *Palabras de mujer: Una época reflejada en la vida de Felisa Rincón.* Editorial Universidad de América, 1988.

———. *Vengo a decirle adiós a los muchachos.* Sociedad de Autores Libres, 1989.

Ramos, Julio. *Desencuentros de la modernidad en América Latina: Literatura y política en el siglo XIX.* Fondo de Cultura Económica, 1989.

Ramos-Zayas, Ana Y. 2012. *Street Therapists: Race, Affect, and Neoliberal Personhood in Latino Newark.* U of Chicago P, 2012.

Reber, Dierdra. *Coming to Our Senses: Affect and an Order of Things for Global Culture.* Columbia UP, 2016.

Reuters. "Refugee Crisis Grows in Central America as Women 'Run for Their Lives.'" *The Guardian,* 28 Oct. 2015, https://www.theguardian.com/world/2015/oct/28/refugee-crisis-grows-in-latin-america-women-children. Accessed 15 Nov. 2015.

Rhys, Jean. *Wide Sargasso Sea.* W. W. Norton, 1982.

Richard, Nelly. *Fracturas de la memoria: Arte y pensamiento crítico.* Siglo Veintiuno Editores, 2007.

———. *Masculine/Feminine: Practices of Difference(s).* Duke UP, 2004.

———, editor. *Políticas y estéticas de la memoria.* Editorial Cuarto Propio, 2000.

———. *Residuos y metáforas: ensayos de crítica cultural sobre el Chile de la Transición.* Editorial Cuarto Propio, 1998.

Rico Galindo, Rosario, et al. *Historia de México II.* Santillana, 2013.

Risager, Bjarke Skærlund. "Neoliberalism Is a Political Project." *Jacobin*, 23 July 2016, https://www.jacobinmag.com/2016/07/david-harvey-neoliberalism-capitalism-labor-crisis-resistance/. Accessed 15 Aug. 2016.

Rivas-Rodríguez, Maggie, and Emilio Zamora, editors. *Beyond the Latino World War II Hero: The Social and Political Legacy of a Generation.* U of Texas P, 2009.

———. "Introduction." Rivas-Rodríguez and Zamora, pp. 1–10.

Rivera Pérez, Aymée. "El imaginario femenino negro en Cuba." *Afrocubanas: Historia, pensamiento y prácticas culturales,* edited by Daisy Rubiera Castillo and Inés María Martiatu Terry, Editorial de Ciencias Sociales, 2011, pp. 225–50.

Rivera-Velázquez, Celiany. "Brincando bordes, cuestionando el poder: Cuban Las Krudas' Migration Experience and Their Rearticulation of Sacred Kinships and Hip Hop Feminism." *Letras Femeninas,* vol. 34, no. 1, 2008, pp. 97–123.

Robinson, Linda S. *Intervention or Neglect: The United States and Central America Beyond the 1980s.* Council on Foreign Relations Press, 1991.

Rodríguez, Ana Patricia. "Diasporic Reparations: Repairing the Social Imaginaries of Central America in the Twenty-First Century." *Studies in 20th and 21st Century Literature,* vol. 37, no. 2, 2013, pp. 27–43.

———. "Genealogías transnacionales centroamericanas: De Máximo Soto Hall a Francisco Goldman." *Revista Iberoamericana,* vol. 79, no. 242, Jan.–Mar. 2013, pp. 243–56.

Rodríguez, Ileana. "Criminal States/Necrophiliac Governments: Bishop Gerardi's *Enemy of the State* and Targeted for Elimination." *Hispanic Issues on Line,* vol. 14, 2014, pp. 91–103.

Rodríguez, Juan Carlos. "Del 'trauma de la literatura' al 'relato del trauma': (Con)figuraciones de la vergüenza en los relatos sobre la presencia militar norteamericana en Puerto Rico." *Revista Iberoamericana,* vol. 75, no. 229, Oct.–Dec. 2009, pp. 1139–74.

Rodríguez Beruff, Jorge. *Política militar y dominación: Puerto Rico en el contexto latinoamericano.* Ediciones Huracán, 1988.

Rodríguez Beruff, Jorge, and Humberto García Muñiz. *Fronteras en conflicto: Guerra contra las drogas, militarización y democracia en el Caribe, Puerto Rico y Vieques.* Red Caribeña de Geopolítica, Seguridad Regional y Relaciones Internacionales afiliada al Proyecto Atlantea, 1999.

Rojas, Rafael. "Newton huye avergonzado." *Virgilio Piñera: La memoria del cuerpo,* edited by Rita Molinero, Editorial Plaza Mayor, 2002, pp. 249–59.

Rosenthal, Lecia. *Mourning Modernism: Literature, Catastrophe, and the Politics of Consolation.* Fordham UP, 2011.

Rossi, Aldo. *The Architecture of the City.* MIT Press, 1988.

Rotker, Susana. *La invención de la crónica.* Ediciones Letra Buena, 1992.

Rowland, Christopher, editor. "Introduction: The Theology of Liberation." *The Cambridge Companion to Liberation Theology,* Cambridge UP, 2006, pp. 1–16.

Ruisánchez, José Ramón. "Carlos Monsiváis, historiador." Moraña and Sánchez Prado, 2007, pp. 242–55.

Salazar, Jezreel. *La ciudad como texto: La crónica urbana de Carlos Monsiváis.* Universidad Autónoma de Nuevo León, 2006.

Sánchez Prado, Ignacio. "Carlos Monsiváis: crónica, nación y liberalismo." Moraña and Sánchez Prado, 2007, pp. 300–36.

———. "De ironía, desubicación, cultura popular y sentimiento nacional: Carlos Monsiváis en el cambio de siglo." *Revista de Literatura Mexicana Contemporánea,* vol. 9, no. 20, July–Sept. 2003, pp. 15–23.

———. *Naciones intelectuales: Las fundaciones de la modernidad literaria mexicana (1917–1959).* Purdue UP, 2009.

———. "Presentación." Moraña and Sánchez Prado, 2012, pp. 11–16.

Sanmartín, Paula. "'Una poesía trascendida en historia': Las poéticas de la (re)escritura de la historia en la obra de Nancy Morejón." *Revista Iberoamericana,* vol. 77, no. 235, Apr.–June 2011, pp. 441–59.

Santiago, Carlos. *El rostro oculto de la desobediencia civil. Testimonios desde la cárcel.* Sociedad de Autores Libres, 2003.

Saunders, Tanya L. *Cuban Underground Hip Hop: Black Thoughts, Black Revolution, Black Modernity.* U of Texas P, 2015.

Sawyer, Mark Q. *Racial Politics in Post-Revolutionary Cuba.* Cambridge UP, 2006.

Scarry, Elaine. *The Body in Pain: The Making and Unmaking of the World.* Oxford UP, 1985.

Schwartz, Rosalie. *Pleasure Island: Tourism and Temptation in Cuba.* U of Nebraska P, 1997.

Scott, Peter Dale, and Jonathan Marshall. *Cocaine Politics: Drugs, Armies, and the CIA in Central America.* U of California P, 1991.

Sedgwick, Eve K. *Between Men: English Literature and Male Homosocial Desire.* Columbia UP, 1985.

The Semipublic Intellectual: Academia, Criticism, and the Internet Age. Dossier in *PMLA,* vol. 130, no. 2, pp. 439–87.

Sierra, Marta. "'Tu voz existe': Percepción mediática, cultural nacional y transiciones democráticas en Pedro Lemebel." Blanco and Poblete, pp. 101–34.

Sifuentes-Jáuregui, Ben. *The Avowal of Difference: Queer Latino American Narratives,* SUNY Press, 2014.

———. *Transvestism, Masculinity, and Latin American Literature: Genders Share Flesh.* Palgrave Macmillan, 2002.

Silva Gotay, Samuel. *Catolicismo y política en Puerto Rico: Bajo España y Estados Unidos, siglos xix y xx.* Editorial Universidad de Puerto Rico, 2005.

———. *Protestantismo y política en Puerto Rico, 1898–1930.* Editorial de la Universidad de Puerto Rico, 1997.

Silva Gruesz, Kirsten. "Utopía Latina: *The Ordinary Seaman* in Extraordinary Times." *Modern Fiction Studies,* vol. 49, no. 1, pp. 54–83.

Simendinger, Alexis. "Obama Turns to Congress to Stem Migrant Children Surge." *Real Clear Politics,* 8 July 2014, http://www.realclearpolitics.com/articles/2014/07/08/obama_turns_to_congress_to_stem_migrant_children_surge_123237.html. Accessed 15 Aug. 2015.

Sørensen, Majken Jul. *Humour in Political Activism: Creative Nonviolent Resistance.* Palgrave Macmillan, 2016.

"S.2328—PROMESA." 114th Congress (2015–2016), *Congress.gov,* 30 June 2016, https://www.congress.gov/bill/114th-congress/senate-bill/2328. Accessed 15 May 2017.

Sutherland, Juan Pablo. *Nación marica: Prácticas culturales y crítica activista.* Ripio Ediciones, 2009.

Taylor, Diana. *The Archive and the Repertoire: Performing Cultural Memory in the Americas.* Duke UP, 2003.

Templeton, Michael. "Becoming Transnational and Becoming Machinery in Francisco Goldman's *The Ordinary Seamen*." *Symplokē*, vol. 14, no. 1–2, 2006, pp. 271–88.

Tobia, P. J. "No Country for Lost Kids." *PBS Newshour*, 20 June 2014, http://www.pbs.org/newshour/updates/country-lost-kids. Accessed 15 Aug. 2015.

Tyler, Mary. "The Crack in the Façade: Social Aftershocks of Mexico's 1985 Earthquake." *Social and Political Change in Literature and Film*, edited by Richard L. Chapple, U of Florida P, 1994, pp. 83–92.

U.S. Customs and Border Protection (U.S. CBP). "La carta." *Dangers Awareness Campaign. Defense Video and Imagery Distribution System*, 2 July 2014, https://www.dvidshub.net/video/347905/la-carta-honduras-60-second-psa. Accessed 15 Aug. 2015.

———. "Sombras." *Dangers Awareness Campaign. Defense Video and Imagery Distribution System*, 2 July 2014, https://www.dvidshub.net/video/347893/sombras-el-salvador-30-second-psa. Accessed 15 Aug. 2015.

Venegas, Cristina. *Digital Dilemmas: The State, the Individual, and Digital Media in Cuba*. Rutgers UP, 2010.

Vientós Gastón, Nilita. "Comentario a un ensayo sobre Puerto Rico." *Índice Cultural*, vol. 1, Editorial de la Universidad de Puerto Rico, 1962–71, pp. 191–94.

Vieques: Una batalla inconclusa. Directed by Juan C. Dávila, Frutos Fílmicos, 2015.

Vigil, Ariana. "*The Divine Husband* and the Creation of a Transamericana Subject." *Latino Studies*, vol. 11, no. 2, 2013, pp. 190–207.

Vitier, Cintio. *Lo cubano en la poesía*. Instituto del Libro, 1970.

VNS Matrix. "Cyberfeminist Manifesto for the 21st Century," *Sterneck*, http://www.sterneck.net/cyber/vns-matrix/index.php. Accessed 15 July 2015.

Volpi, Jorge. *La imaginación y el poder: Una historia intelectual de 1968*. Era, 1998.

Weeks, Jeffrey. "The Friendship Ethic." *Same Sex Intimacies: Families of Choice and Other Life Experiments*, edited by Weeks, Routledge, 2001, pp. 51–76.

Williams, Raymond. *Marxism and Literature*. Oxford UP, 1977.

Winter, James P., and Chaim H. Eyal. "Agenda-Setting for the Civil Rights Issue." *Public Opinion Quarterly*, vol. 45, no. 3, 1981, pp. 376–83.

Yanes Gómez, Gabriela. "El entramado de *Una Larga Noche*: 'Guatemala no existe.'" *Mesoamérica*, vol. 18, no. 34, 1997, pp. 637–50.

Zimmerman, Marc. "'Woody Allen visita Guatemala' o una reivindicación frustrada: Consideraciones sobre la novela de Francisco Goldman." *Mesoamérica*, vol. 18, no. 34, 1997, pp. 651–65.

Zumthor, Paul. *Oral Poetry: An Introduction*. U of Minnesota P, 1990.

Zurbano, Roberto. "For Blacks in Cuba, the Revolution Hasn't Begun." *The New York Times*, 23 Mar. 2013.

INDEX

academia, 1–2, 13, 46, 138, 140–41, 144–48,
  154, 167, 171, 190
acción épica (epic action), 45–47
Achugar, Hugo, 94, 97
affect, 1–4; brotherly love and, 136, 142–44;
  civil society and, 47; cruel optimism
  and, 19, 25, 32, 37, 51–53; emotion and,
  15; feminism and, 107–8; friendship
  and, 161; militarism and, 144, 164–66;
  Monsiváis and, 23, 30–31, 47, 51–53,
  58–59; structures of feeling, 24, 28–31, 37,
  44–45, 54–55, 57. *See also* emotion
affect theory, 12–16
affection, 174–75
affective communities, 18–20, 23, 164–66
affective learners, 75
affective locus of enunciation, 19–20, 31, 53.
  See also locus of enunciation
affective turn, 12–16
affective "we," 3, 58, 100, 183
Afghanistan, 137, 140
Afro-Cuban cyberfeminism, 21, 169–88
Agamben, Giorgio, 41, 158
Agrait, Fernando, 144
Aguilar Rivera, José, 53

Ahmed, Sara, 3, 13–16, 31, 62, 110, 158
Allende, Salvador, 94, 105
Álvarez Curbelo, Silvia, 134–35, 138, 166
Álvarez Ramírez, Sandra, 3, 8, 11–12, 18,
  20–21, 169–88, 190; "Amar más allá de
  los límites de tu cuerpo," 184; "Carita de
  pasaporte," 187; "¿Ciberfeminismo en
  Cuba?," 184–86; "Disidencias: El socialismo no es suficiente," 180; "Ese poema
  de Nancy me puede hacer llorar," 182–
  84; "Jinetera," 187; "Krudas Cubensi,"
  186; *Negracubana tenia que ser* (blog),
  20–21, 170–88; "Pequeños detalles,"
  179; polyamory and, 170–71, 184–88;
  "Tengo orgasmos, soy feminista y vivo
  happy," 186; "Testimonio: 'muchas putas
  lo somos porque nos gusta,'" 187; "¿Y
  las lesbianas feministas cubanas dónde
  están?" 181–82
American Red Cross, 61–62
American University, 137
Anderson, Benedict, 142, 166
Anderson, Mark D., 6, 43
anger, 80–81, 99; Gastón's reaction to
  Boorstin, 2, 189; *la loca* and 102–31; love
  and, 103–10; melancholy and, 103–10;

209

GLOBAL LATIN/O AMERICAS

FREDERICK LUIS ALDAMA AND LOURDES TORRES, SERIES EDITORS

This series focuses on the Latino experience in its totality as set within a global dimension. The series will showcase the variety and vitality of the presence and significant influence of Latinos in the shaping of the culture, history, politics and policies, and language of the Americas—and beyond. We welcome scholarship regarding the arts, literature, philosophy, popular culture, history, politics, law, history, and language studies, among others. Books in the series will draw from scholars from around the world.

Affective Intellectuals and the Space of Catastrophe in the Americas
JUDITH SIERRA-RIVERA

Spanish Perspectives on Chicano Literature: Literary and Cultural Essays
EDITED BY JESÚS ROSALES AND VANESSA FONSECA

Sponsored Migration: The State and Puerto Rican Postwar Migration to the United States
EDGARDO MELÉNDEZ

La Verdad: An International Dialogue on Hip Hop Latinidades
EDITED BY MELISSA CASTILLO-GARSOW AND JASON NICHOLS

CPSIA information can be obtained
at www.ICGtesting.com
Printed in the USA
FFHW022008091118
49357565-53644FF